Accurate English

A COMPLETE COURSE IN PRONUNCIATION

Rebecca M. Dauer

University of Massachusetts
at Amherst

PRENTICE HALL REGENTS

Library of Congress Cataloging-in-Publication Data

Dauer, Rebecca M.
  Accurate English : a complete course in pronunciation / Rebecca M.
Dauer.
    p.   cm.
  Includes index.
  ISBN 0-13-007253-2
  1. English language--Pronunciation. 2. English language-
-Textbooks for foreign speakers.   I. Title.
PE1137.D36   1993
428.3'4--dc20   92-33049
                                                          CIP

Editorial/Production Supervision
   and Interior Design: *Ros Herion Freese*
Acquisitions Editor: *Nancy Leonhardt*
Copyeditor: *Jennifer Carey*
Cover Design: *Marianne Frasco*
Cover Photo: *Reginald Wickham*
Prepress Buyer: *Ray Keating*
Manufacturing Buyer: *Lori Bulwin*
Scheduler: *Leslie Coward*

© 1993 by Rebecca M. Dauer

Published by Prentice Hall Regents
Prentice-Hall, Inc.

Printed in the United States of America
20 19 18 17 16 15 14 13

ISBN 0-13-007253-2

Contents

Preface

Accurate English is a textbook and reference guide to the pronunciation of English in North America as it is spoken by educated native speakers in fluent speech. The vowels, consonants, rhythm, and intonation of American English are taught using the principles of articulatory phonetics. Students are led to discover these principles through experimenting with their own vocal tracts, using kinesthetic, visual, and auditory feedback. Theory is reinforced by numerous practice exercises working up from phrases to dialogues, reading passages, and oral presentations. In addition, spelling patterns for ordinary words, academic words, and exceptions, as well as rules for stress placement, are included. The goal of this book is to enable students to improve their pronunciation of English so that they can be understood effortlessly by native speakers in both formal and informal situations. The focus on English as it is actually spoken, including reductions, simplifications, and regional variations, also helps to improve listening comprehension.

Simple imitation is not sufficient for many adults to overcome the speech patterns of their native language. A student's cognitive abilities also need to be involved. Through understanding the sound system of English and developing self-awareness, students are given the means to improve their accent. The teacher is a helper in this process, by providing a model, appropriate feedback, and an environment that promotes self-discovery. Change, however, comes from within the individual. It takes motivation, practice, and time. Hopefully, the knowledge and methods students gain from this book will enable them to continue to improve their English in the future.

This book is designed primarily for adults who are non-native speakers of English, including undergraduates, graduates, college-bound students, professionals, and English as a Second Language (ESL) teachers—in short, anyone who wants to achieve a near-native accent. It is appropriate for those who are already living in the United States or Canada, who plan to come, or who need to communicate extensively with Americans or Canadians abroad. Language teachers, teacher trainers, and speech therapists will also find this text to be a useful reference for understanding present-day English as it is actually spoken. The level of the book is intermediate through advanced (TOEFL 475 and above). It assumes no previous knowledge of phonetics. Terminology is reduced to a minimum; all technical terms and words that might not be familiar to intermediate students are clearly defined. The International Phonetic Alphabet is used as a teaching aid, but the goal is for learners to be able to read standard orthography. The book can be used as the main text in a semester-long pronunciation course, as a supplemental text in a listening–speaking, teacher-training, or speech communication course, as a teacher resource book, or by students engaged in independent study with a tutor.

Accurate English was written with flexibility in mind. It is divided into introductory material and four main areas—vowels, stress and rhythm, consonants, and intonation. These areas are to some extent independent, and the suggested order does not need to be followed, except that stress should precede intonation. Important points are recycled and included in review chapters. Chapters are broken down into short sections that can be covered in a 50-minute period or less. A variety of oral and written tasks are included in each lesson to ensure the active participation of the learner. Sections and exercises marked "Advanced" or labeled for particular language groups can be skipped. Thus, teachers can focus on what their students need most. Alternatively, teachers may decide to wait until questions on those points arise in class and then go over them. In Chaps. 4 and 15, which cover the vowels and consonants in detail, only those sounds that present difficulties need to be covered.

Overcoming the habits of one's native language, in pronunciation as well as in other areas of language learning, is not easy. It requires understanding, intensive practice, and the desire to change. Students may achieve a certain level of communicative competence in everyday situations but still not be well understood by native speakers in an intellectual discussion. Understanding might require a great deal of strain on the part of listeners. Even if they are understood, non-native speakers with a heavy accent may not gain respect and may find it difficult to advance in their careers. Both fluency *and* accuracy are necessary.

Overview and Suggested Plan

INTRODUCTION AND DIAGNOSTIC SPEECH SAMPLE (Chapter 1)

In the first week of class, each student should be tape-recorded (or videotaped) reading the diagnostic passage and giving a short speech in front of the class. Students working with a private tutor might also want to record the vowels and consonants in sentences (Secs. 3.3 and 12.3) and a reading for stress (Sec. 11.1, Ex. A or B). The teacher can then ask class members what problems they noticed in each other's speech and why some people were more difficult to understand than others. Using the self-analysis questions (Sec. 1.3) and examples (write *frustrating* on the board and ask how it's pronounced), the teacher may try to elicit a basic analysis of the different levels of speech (sounds, syllables, grammar, etc.). The teacher listens to each tape later, fills out the analysis (Sec. 1.5), and goes over it with the student. If the student records the diagnostic speech sample again at the end of the course, a comparison of the two recordings will show how much improvement has been made.

PHONETIC ALPHABET AND VOWELS (Chapters 2–5)

The phonetic alphabet (Sec. 2.2) should be introduced (at least briefly) to point out the difference between spelling and pronunciation and to encourage students to use their dictionaries. Chapter 3, "Vowel Overview," follows logically because the vowel symbols tend to be the most difficult to learn and clearly demonstrate the difference between phonetic symbols and orthographic letters. Students should be encouraged to use their mirrors and do the **TO DO** experiments in order to understand how vowels are made and can be modified. This also "loosens them up." Chapter 4 gives intensive practice with vowels and their spelling, focusing on /ɪ, ə, ʊ, ɚ/, which tend to be difficult for most students. In a shorter course, the teacher might want to do just the **PRACTICE** exercises in class and assign the spelling rules for students to review on their own. It is often the orthography, not a physical limitation, that is the source of students' pronunciation problems. Chapter 5 briefly reviews the phonetic alphabet and vowels with dialogues for additional practice of difficult vowel contrasts.

STRESS AND RHYTHM (Chapters 6–11)

The chapters on stress and rhythm follow those on vowels because vowel reduction is easier to explain after /ɪ/ and /ə/ have been covered. Chapter 6, "Stress," is very important. The teacher can try to elicit the rules for stress placement by putting some examples on the board, and the tables can be assigned for homework or lab. Most advanced students already have implicit knowledge of where stress usually falls, but they tend to over-generalize initial stress and resist shifting stress. The exercises for marking stress (Sec. 6.4) can be assigned for homework or done in groups, but at least some of them should be gone over orally in class. Some students can pronounce a word with correct stress but they may put the stress mark in the wrong place; others have the opposite problem. Chapter 7 is labeled "advanced" and can be skipped if time is limited or if the vocabulary might present problems. The specific noun–verb word pairs in Sec. 7.1 (*a contract* versus *to contract*) are not so important in themselves, but they do help students understand vowel reduction. Chapter 8, "Rhythm," is very important. Most students are unaware that they must reduce function words and link words together. Chapter 9 (advanced) involves breaking rules and may be omitted in a class comprised of students who get upset or confused by exceptions to rules. These exceptions do come up, however, when marking stress in real texts. Section 9.1 is also good for students who have a tendency to stress function words.

After introducing compound nouns (Chap. 10) and reviewing rhythm (Chap. 11), the teacher may choose to jump ahead to intonation (Chap. 16) before going on to consonants. This order is preferred if students are having more difficulty with intonation than with consonants. Alternatively, Chap. 10 can be saved and done later with Chap. 16 if the teacher would like to go on to consonants more quickly. Again, the difference between the compound and non-compound expressions in Sec. 10.3 (*blackboard* versus *black board*) is not so important in itself; the section may be skipped with lower-level students, but it does help to point out the importance of sentence stress. It is also challenging and fun.

CONSONANTS (Chapters 12–15)

Chapter 12 gives an overview of how consonants are made. Going over the general principles in Sec. 12.1 first, especially voicing, encourages students to think analytically. The **TO DO** sections are fun to do together in class. Most students can be led to produce the consonants correctly at least once, even if they cannot integrate the new sounds into all words at this point. This gives them confidence that they *can* do it and enables them to master the individual sounds (Chap. 15) more quickly. Chapter 13, "Differences Between Voiced and Voiceless Consonants," is important. Although some students have little difficulty with aspiration, nearly all need work on vowel length. Some teachers may choose to go over North American English /t/ (Sec. 13.4) for listening comprehension only. The pronunciation of <ed> and <s> endings (Chap. 14) is also very important and can be done at any time, although it is easier to explain after the differences between voiced and voiceless consonants have been understood. Chapter 15 gives intensive practice with consonants that cause the most problems. Individual sections can be done in any order. In a short course, the teacher might go over just a few contrasts in class, such as /θ–ð/ or /l–r/, and skip the spelling exercises. The fast speech rules in Sec. 15.11 can be done at any time.

INTONATION (Chapter 16)

Sections 16.1 and 16.2 cover the two most important aspects of intonation, the location of sentence stress and basic pitch patterns. Since stress and intonation are closely related, this chapter can be done right after covering stress and before consonants. However, when intonation is done at the end, it allows some review of stress and rhythm. This book covers the essentials of intonation but does not attempt to address all the finer points. The subject is complex, and it is often difficult for teachers to analyze and explain intonation patterns. Intonation is closely connected to a speaker's intentions and discourse structure so that there is more than one "correct" way to say the same sentence. Once students develop the ability to hear basic intonation patterns, they can begin listening to native speakers and trying to imitate them.

Types of Exercises

TO DO

These sections should be done in class together with the teacher in an atmosphere of play and self-discovery. It takes some time to develop awareness of one's own vocal organs. Silent practice and visual feedback, as well as feedback from the teacher and other students, can help bring to consciousness what one is doing and how one can change. If listening and repeating alone were enough, no one would need a pronunciation class.

PRACTICE

The minimal pair sentences ("That's a high **hill**. That's a high **heel**.") can be taught in various ways; the same order does not always have to be used.

1. Review how the sounds are made and the main differences between them. Practice silently and aloud, alternating between the two sounds to feel and hear the difference. Using a mirror, students can also see the difference and compare their own lip positions to those in the illustrations.

2. Students repeat each *sentence* after the teacher. The teacher can call on individuals to read sentence pairs aloud and then ask the class if they sound the same or different and, if the same, whether they hear two number 1s or two number 2s. Some students actually can hear their classmates quite well even if they can't make the distinction consistently themselves. The teacher will give his or her opinion, offer suggestions for improvement, and try to lead the class to perceive the difference. At a more advanced level, students can be asked if there is any other mistake, even when the two sentences sound different. If a contrast is particularly difficult, the teacher can begin with just the two words in boldface, saying either two of the same words or two different words and asking if they are the same or different, and then have students repeat just the words in pairs, as above, before going on to sentences.

3. The teacher reads only one sentence randomly selected from each pair and asks the class to indicate which they heard by putting up one or two fingers. This can be done again later with students writing down *1* or *2* on paper. One student volunteers to write on the board; then the answers are checked all together by individual students reading back the sentences that they heard. Class members keep their own score and try to "beat the board."

4. The class breaks into pairs, preferably from different language backgrounds, and practices the sentences. One student reads first both sentences trying to make them different, then just one of each pair while the other listens and judges as the teacher circulates around the class. An alternative grouping is by ability: those for whom the contrast is easier can go on to practice dialogues or other exercises. If more than one contrast is introduced in class, students can select the ones they need to practice.

EXERCISES

These exercises can be done in class together, for homework, or in groups. Homework exercises that are difficult may be checked orally or from answers written on the board. Reading passages in which students need to identify certain sounds (such as how <ed> is pronounced) are effective done in groups (after marking, they read aloud). Dialogues are good practiced in pairs or threes (one listens and criticizes) or recorded in the lab. Students should be encouraged to tape-record themselves reading aloud the dialogues and reading passages as much as possible. The class may choose to meet once a week in the lab so that the teacher can monitor each student more closely. Tables, spelling rules, and lists of consonants and vowels can be assigned for homework—be sure they say all examples *aloud*. The tables, lists of consonants and vowels, dialogues, and reading passages are on cassette and can be practiced in the lab or at home.

ORAL PRESENTATIONS

Suggested topics for four short oral presentations are included in the exercises on pp. 99, 161, 188, and 238. It is recommended that students give speeches at regular intervals during the course to give them the opportunity to integrate what they have learned into their speaking. These speeches can be given at any time to fit in with the course schedule. Students should be given about a week to prepare. By assigning an outline to turn in, the teacher can recommend changes. Other free-speaking activities such as role plays may also be used. The advantage of a speech is that it can be practiced in advance, everyone gets a chance to speak, and it can be easily tape-recorded for feedback or evaluation. Students in the class can also fill out simple, anonymous evaluation forms to be given to the speaker. If at all possible, at least one speech should be videotaped and played back to students.

How to Use Audio Tapes

Cassette tape recordings accompany the text and can be used in several ways. The symbol [▭] appears before exercises that are on the tape.

Repetition of words and sentences aloud in the blank spaces on the tape. This should be done first without, and then with, looking at the text. It is important to be guided by the sound and not the writing system, and to notice the differences between them. The student should always try to imitate the overall rhythm, pausing, linking, relative syllable length, and intonation when repeating. Both *fluency* (saying everything smoothly without stopping) and *accuracy* (saying all vowels and consonants correctly without dropping any) need to be worked on. In a language lab setting, students can record their voices and play back the tape to compare their voices to the model. Playback should be done without looking at the text. It is extremely important for students to repeat whole phrases and sentences *aloud* at a normal volume and not just listen to the tapes. The speech muscles must be exercised.

Reading before the model. The student can read each phrase aloud in the pause before the voice on the tape and then listen to hear if he or she was correct.

Shadowing (advanced). In order to build speed and fluency, the student may try to talk at the same time as the voice on the tape. As soon as the model begins, he or she starts reading aloud and tries to keep up with the tape, without going ahead or falling behind. Mispronunciations, omissions, and errors in pausing occur where the student is having problems.

Recording without the model. After listening and practicing with the tape, students should then record themselves on a blank tape reading aloud sentences (with pauses between them), dialogues, or reading passages. The student, alone or together with a teacher or tutor, plays the tape back, pausing after each sentence and listening carefully to figure out what sounds right and what still needs to be worked on. In order to concentrate on the auditory signal, it is best to play back without looking at the text. The idea is for students to develop their ability to think analytically about their speech and to become aware of how they sound in comparison to how they would like to sound. They should re-record the passage as many times as necessary. A teacher or tutor can offer corrections and additional practice for problem areas. At lower levels, students can record both sentences of a minimal pair ("That's a high **heel**. That's a high **hill**."), play them back, and listen to see if the sentences sound the same or different and, if they are not different, which one needs to be improved. Advanced students should record texts from their areas of interest or talk for two minutes on a topic they are interested in. In this way, new problems can be discovered while old problems are reviewed.

—R.M.D.

CHAPTER 1

Introduction

PREREADING QUESTIONS

What is spoken language? What does a foreign accent consist of?

1.1 The Speech Process

SPOKEN LANGUAGE

Speech is a process that involves several stages, beginning with the speaker's ideas and ending with the understanding of those ideas by the listener:

1. The *speaker thinks*, decides what he or she is going to say, and puts the ideas into words and sentences of a particular language. The speaker's brain then transforms the words and sentences into nerve impulses that it sends to the muscles in the speech organs.

2. The *speaker's speech organs move*. The lungs push air up through the larynx and into the mouth and nose. The air is shaped by the tongue and lips and comes out of the speaker's mouth as sound waves.

3. The *sound travels through the air*. Sometimes, the sound is changed into electrical signals, as in a telephone or tape recorder, and then is changed back into sound waves by an electronic speaker.

4. The *listener hears* the sounds when the sound waves hit his or her ear. The ear changes the sound waves into nerve impulses and sends them to the brain.

5. The *listener understands* the message. The listener's brain identifies specific speech sounds, interprets them as words and sentences of a particular language, and figures out their meaning.

At any point in this process, there could be a problem that results in the message intended by the speaker not being understood by the listener. Perhaps the speaker doesn't know the right words or grammar to put his or her idea into language (step 1); perhaps he or she can't produce a particular sound (step 2); perhaps there is too much background noise or a bad telephone connection (step 3); perhaps the listener is "hard of hearing" (can't hear very well) (step 4); perhaps the listener identifies some speech sounds incorrectly or figures out a different meaning from the one intended by the speaker (step 5). Effective oral communication depends on accuracy in all of these stages.

Speech is not only a mental activity but also a muscular activity. When learning a sport such as tennis, you need to learn how to make your muscles do what you want them to do, and you need to practice to get those muscles to perform regularly. Children at a young age often seem to learn speech, just as they learn sports, without much effort or instruction. Most adults, however, want and need instruction. By *observing* the speech organs carefully, *feeling* what is happening, and *listening critically* to the sounds that you produce, you can become conscious of what you are doing and what you should be doing to improve your own speech. In this book, the TO DO and PRACTICE sections give you an opportunity to get this kind of feedback. Observing, feeling, and listening to your voice or a tape recording of it are windows that allow you direct access to some of the steps of the speech process. These sections are very important, although you may at first find it embarrassing to look at your mouth in a mirror. They will allow you to "tune in" to yourself and work on your own to improve your speech. Acquiring good pronunciation of another language is not mysterious: knowledge, hard work, practice, and the desire to change is as important in pronunciation as it is in any other field. Although teachers and other native speakers can tell you whether or not you've been successful in pronouncing a particular word or sentence, only you can produce change in yourself.

WRITTEN LANGUAGE

The sound waves that come out of the mouth when someone is speaking are continuous and constantly changing. There are no spaces between words as there are in writing. Speech flows like a river; sounds gradually change from one to another and stop only when there is a pause. Languages have different writing systems or orthographies that analyze the continuous flow of speech and break it down into a limited number of visual symbols. English uses only twenty-six letters, plus punctuation marks and spaces, to represent the entire language. The same letter is often used in more than one way. Some important aspects of the spoken language, such as stress, are not represented at all. This book introduces a phonetic writing system with more symbols to represent the spoken language more closely. However, any writing system is still an analysis. Sounds blend together with preceding and following sounds and are pronounced differently depending on the neighboring sounds, the overall stress pattern, and the rate of speech.

It is important to become aware of the differences between spoken and written language. You may mispronounce a word, not because you can't say it correctly, but because it has an unusual spelling pattern or because it looks like a word in your own language where the letters represent different sounds. Many spelling rules are given in this book to help you learn the correct correspondence between sounds and letters. As you do the practice sections and exercises, concentrate on the sound first (close your eyes if necessary) and then look at the spelling. Try to develop the ability to remember words as sound patterns, using the phonetic alphabet as an aid. Don't expect every word to sound the way it is traditionally spelled. Don't listen for pauses or breaks between every word. You will be surprised at how much better you will be able to speak and understand English.

1.2 Language Variation

All speakers of the same language do not speak exactly alike, and the same speaker may speak differently in different situations. Language varies or changes in regular ways according to the speaker's style and the geographic area that he or she comes from.

STYLISTIC VARIATION

The style of speaking includes differences between formal and informal speech, slow and fast speech, careful and casual speech, "correct" (or standard) and "incorrect" or (non-standard) speech. A native speaker can speak in different styles depending on the situation. The language used in a lecture or at a job interview is not the same as in a casual conversation with family or friends. A college professor does not usually speak the same way as a truck driver. What is acceptable in one style may be considered an error in another style. The style of speech that this book is based on is that used by educated speakers, in connected speech, at a normal rate of speed.

The way people pronounce a single word by itself (in isolation) is not the same as when they say that word in a sentence; however, most native speakers are not aware of this fact. The changes that native speakers make when speaking fluently follow certain rules that they are not conscious of but that non-native speakers can easily learn. If they don't learn how to make these changes, they may use the fast speech rules of their own language or try to speak too slowly and carefully. Thus, rules for connected speech, such as pronouncing *months* as /məns/[1] instead of /mənθs/, will be given in this book, and their usage will be discussed. Some fast speech rules will be included that some people might consider "incorrect" or "sloppy", such as pronouncing *did you* as /dɪdʒə/. Knowledge of these rules can help non-native speakers understand spoken English better, even if they choose not to use them. Since we usually speak in whole phrases and sentences, not in isolated words surrounded by pauses, most exercises in this book will present sounds in short sentences.

GEOGRAPHIC VARIATION

People from different parts of the country speak with accents that show which region they come from. An accent includes minor differences in vocabulary, grammar, and especially pronunciation. Of course, everyone believes that the accent from his or her part of the country is the best and most beautiful. The accent that this book is based on is that of college-educated speakers from the Northeast of the United States, excluding urban New York City and Boston. This accent is typically used on national television and radio news programs. Therefore, it is comprehensible throughout the United States and corresponds to the pronunciation in current American English dictionaries. Nevertheless, important regional differences in pronunciation will be pointed out. These differences mostly concern the pronunciation of the letters <r>,[1] <a>, and <o>. Although non-native speakers are generally expected to use a standard accent, becoming aware of regional variation can help their listening comprehension and analytic ability.

The pronunciation of Canadian English is very similar to American English especially as it is spoken in the Mid-West. Standard British English has the same basic consonant

---

[1]Those students who are unfamiliar with the // and < > symbols may turn to p. 13 for an explanation of their usage.

system, rhythm, and general intonation patterns as North American English. The main difference is how the letters <t> and <r> are pronounced in words like *winter, forty, letter, barrel,* and *very.* The vowel system of British English differs greatly from that of most varieties of North American English. It is more complex, primarily due to dropping syllable final <r>; and the letters <a> and <o> are pronounced differently in many words.

Language also changes over time; we do not speak the same way as our grandparents. These historical changes are sometimes responsible for stylistic and geographic variation. An older pronunciation might be used in a more formal style, or older pronunciations may be preserved in rural areas or remote towns. More importantly for readers of this book, older pronunciations are preserved in the spelling system of English.

1.3 Self-Analysis

At the beginning of this course, you should tape-record yourself reading Parts I and II of the Diagnostic Speech Sample (Sec. 1.4) (or a few paragraphs from your field of interest) and speaking freely for two to three minutes. Then listen very carefully and try to analyze your errors. Ideally, you should have a teacher or native speaker listen to your tape and fill out the Analysis of Problems (Sec. 1.5). However, you can get a general idea on your own by stopping the tape whenever you hear a mistake or something that sounds unclear. Be objective. Pretend that the voice on the tape belongs to someone else. Try to figure out which areas you need to work on. Once you have identified your problem areas, use the table of contents or the index to find the chapters in this book that you need to study.

Think about the answers to the following questions to help you analyze your problems speaking English.

Sounds:

Which vowels do you have difficulty with? (Do you make a difference between the vowels in *seat* and *sit, good* and *food, cap, cup,* and *cop*?)
Which consonants do you have difficulty with? (Do you make a difference between *sheep* and *cheap, save* and *safe, sad* and *sat, pride* and *bride*?)
Do you know the correspondence between sounds and letters of the alphabet? (How is <h> pronounced in *high, ghost, laugh,* and *drought*? How is <ea> pronounced in *wheat, spread, great,* and *read*?)
Do you omit some sounds that you shouldn't, or add sounds that don't belong? (Does *think* sound like *thing*? Do you say *speak* or *espeak*? Do you pronounce all <s> and <ed> endings?)

Syllables:

Do you pronounce all words with the correct number of syllables? (How many syllables are in *watched, lives, splendid, appropriate,* and *studying*?)
Do you pronounce consonants at the ends of words or do you omit some of them? (Do you say all the consonants in *next, first, world, girls,* and *found*?)
Can you pronounce some sounds perfectly in one position in a syllable but not in another? (Can you make a difference between *lake* and *rake* but not between *cloud* and *crowd* or *little* and *litter?* Are *Sue* and *zoo* different but not *ice* and *eyes, racer* and *razor*?)
Do you make syllables that end in voiced consonants long enough? (Which is longer—*hid* or *heat, bag* or *back, ten* or *tent*?)

Stress and Rhythm:

Do you stress the correct syllable in a word? (Which syllable is stressed in *locate, occur, develop, engineer,* and *laboratory*?)

Do you make a large difference between stressed and unstressed syllables, or do they all sound about the same?

Do you know which one-syllable words are not normally stressed? (Which of the following are stressed: *I, can, can't, read, the, book*?)

Do you reduce the vowels in unstressed syllables and function words? (How do you pronounce <to> in *today, I want to go,* and *I really want to*? Do you make a difference in the vowel sounds of *a record* and *to record*?)

Do you link words smoothly together within a phrase or is your speech very choppy?

Do you pause in the right places?

Do you speak at a regular rate, or do you speak too quickly (rush) or too slowly (hesitate)?

Intonation:

Do you group phrases together into smooth overall intonation patterns with one main rise or fall, or are you constantly going up and down on almost every word?

Does your voice rise on important words, or does it rise and fall unconnected to your meaning?

Does your voice rise and fall enough so your meaning is clear, or does it remain flat and monotonous for long periods?

Do you make a difference between compound words (*the White House*) and ordinary phrases (*a white house*)?

Should you rise or fall on questions beginning with *How, When, Do,* and *Are*?

Should you rise or fall in choice questions ("Would you like tea or coffee?") and in direct address ("Good morning, Dr. Smith.")?

Do you speak loudly and clearly, or do you mumble, whisper, or let the ends of sentences trail off (die)?

This book should help you to improve all of the above. Other language problems that can affect your accent and may make you hard to understand include the following.

Grammar:

Do you use past tense endings and plural endings?

Do you know when to use the singular and when to use the plural of nouns (*two machines* but *some machinery*)?

Do you make subject and verb agree (*I go, he goes; the girl is, the girls are*)?

Do you use correct verb tenses, articles, and prepositions?

Sentence Structure:

Are your sentences clear and direct, or do you link everything together with "and . . . and . . . and" and never end your sentences?

Do you use subordination to relate ideas when you are talking (*who, which, although,* and *before*), or is every sentence extremely short and simple?

Vocabulary:

Do you use precise words to express your meaning or vague words like *thing, they,* and *like*?

Do you repeat the same ordinary words over and over again?

Do you use idiomatic expressions or are you always translating and using words that resemble words in your native language?

Content:

> Do you speak in a logical, well-organized way that is easy for your listener
> to follow?
> Do you know precisely what you want to say or do you get confused?

Self-confidence:

> Are you comfortable speaking English aloud, or do you feel nervous or fright-
> ened in some situations?
> Are you always afraid of making mistakes and being misunderstood?
> Do you know when people misunderstand you and how to repeat yourself in a
> way that they will understand?
> How do you look when you talk? Do you smile and look directly at people?

1.4 Diagnostic Speech Sample

My name is _____. I come from _____. My native language is _____.

Part I (Formal Reading)

Learning to speak a foreign language fluently and without an accent isn't easy. In most educational systems, students spend many years studying grammatical rules, but they don't get much of a chance to speak. Arriving in a new country can be a frustrating experience. Although they may be able to read and write very well, they often find that they can't understand what people say to them. English is especially difficult because the pronunciation of words is not clearly shown by how they're written. But the major problem is being able to listen, think, and respond in another language at a natural speed. This takes time and practice.

Part II (Informal Dialogue)

A: Hi, Bob. Gee, I haven't seen you in a while. How are you doing?

B: Not so good. Unfortunately, I've had a bad cold for the last three or four days, and I feel a little tired. How about you? What have you been up to recently?

A: Well, I just came back from a weekend at the shore. Do you know Liz? She invited me out to her family's place on Martha's Vineyard.

B: Is her house on the beach or in town?

A: It's a few minutes away from a big beach on the south coast. We usually walked out there in the morning, brought sandwiches and soft drinks with us, and stayed all day.

B: I've heard enough! Would you take me along some time?

A: With pleasure.

Part III (Free Speech)

Give a short, two-minute speech about one of the following topics. Tell a story about what happened to you. Two minutes is a very short time, so only describe the most important details.

1. An embarrassing or humorous situation that you had with the English language or culture.
2. An interesting or unusual experience that you had over vacation.
3. Your first day in this country, at this university, or at your job.
4. Your problems speaking English and why you're taking this course.
5. Define a technical term or describe a process related to your professional field.

PHONETIC TRANSCRIPTION[1]

/maɪ 'neɪm ɪz _____ | aɪ 'kəm frəm _____ | maɪ 'neɪtɪv 'læŋgwɪdʒ ɪz _____ /

Part I

/'lɝnɪŋ tə 'spik ə 'fɑrɪn 'læŋgwɪdʒ 'fluəntli| ən wɪ'θaʊt ən 'æksent| 'ɪzənt 'izi| ɪn 'moʊst ɛdʒə 'keɪʃənəl 'sɪstəmz| 'studənts ˌspɛnd 'mɛni 'yiɚz 'stədiɪŋ grə'mætɪkəl 'rulz| bət ðeɪ 'doʊnt ˌgɛt 'mətʃ əv ə 'tʃæns tə 'spik| ə'raɪvɪŋ ɪn ə 'nu 'kəntri| kən bi ə 'frəstreɪtɪŋ ɪk'spɪriəns| ɔ'ðoʊ ðeɪ 'meɪ bi 'eɪbəl tə 'rid ən 'raɪt vɛri 'wɛl| ðeɪ 'ɔfən 'faɪnd ðət ðeɪ 'kænt əndɚ'stænd wət 'pipəl 'seɪ tə ðəm| 'ɪŋglɪʃ ɪz ə'spɛʃəli 'dɪfɪkəlt| bɪkəz ðə prənənsi'eɪʃən əv 'wɝdz| ɪz 'nɑt 'kliɚli 'ʃoʊn baɪ 'haʊ ðɛɚ 'rɪtən| bət ðə 'meɪdʒɚ 'prabləm| ɪz 'biɪŋ 'eɪbəl tə 'lɪsən| 'θɪŋk| ən rɪ'spand ɪn ə 'nəðɚ 'læŋgwɪdʒ| ət ə 'nætʃɚəl 'spid| 'ðɪs 'teɪks 'taɪm ən 'præktɪs/

Part II

A: /'haɪ 'bab| 'dʒi| aɪ 'hævənt 'sin yu ɪn ə 'waɪl| 'haʊ ɚ yu 'duɪŋ/

B: /'nɑt soʊ 'gʊd| ən 'fɝtʃənɪtli | aɪv 'hæd ə 'bæd 'koʊld fɚ ðə 'læst 'θri ɚ 'fɔɚ 'deɪz| ən aɪ 'fil ə 'lɪtəl 'taɪɚd| 'haʊ əbaʊt 'yu| 'wət əv yu bɪn 'əp tu 'rɪsɪntli/

A: /'wɛl| aɪ 'dʒəst ˌkeɪm 'bæk frəm ə 'wikɛnd ət ðə 'ʃɔɚ| dʊ yʊ 'noʊ 'lɪz| ʃi ɪn 'vaɪtɪd mi 'aʊt tʊ ɚ 'fæmliz 'pleɪs ɔn 'mɑɚθəz 'vɪnyɚd/

B: /ɪz ɚ 'haʊs ɔn ðə 'bitʃ ɚ ɪn 'taʊn/

A: /ɪts ə 'fyu 'mɪnɪts ə'weɪ frəm ə 'bɪg 'bitʃ ɔn ðə 'saʊθ 'koʊst| wi 'yuʒəli 'wɔkt aʊt 'ðɛɚ ɪn ðə 'mɑɚnɪŋ| 'brɔt 'sænwɪtʃɪz ən 'sɔft drɪŋks wɪθ əs| ən 'steɪd ɔl 'deɪ/

B: /aɪv 'hɝd ə 'nəf| wʊd yʊ 'teɪk 'mi ə'lɔŋ 'səm 'taɪm/

A: /wɪθ 'plɛʒɚ/

---

[1] Syllables in **boldface type** receive sentence stress.

1.5 Analysis of Problems

Native Language _____   Name _____

Country _____   Date _____

Vowels (Incorrect Pronunciation)

1. /i/ → _____   11. /u/ → _____
2. /ɪ/ → _____   12. /ɚ/ → _____
3. /eɪ/ → _____   13. /aɪ/ → _____
4. /ɛ/ → _____   14. /aʊ/→ _____
5. /æ/ → _____   15. /ɔɪ/ → _____
6. /ɑ/ → _____   Vowels before <l>   _____
7. /ə/ → _____   Vowels before <r>   _____
8. /ɔ/ → _____   Spelling and
9. /oʊ/→ _____   pronunciation of _____
10. /ʊ/ → _____

Consonants (Incorrect Pronunciation or Omission)

Voiceless			Voiced		
Initial or medial	**Final**		**Initial or medial**	**Final**	
/p/→ _____	_____	/b/ → _____	_____		
/t/ → _____	_____	/d/ → _____	_____		
/k/→ _____	_____	/g/ → _____	_____		
/f/ → _____	_____	/v/ → _____	_____		
/h/→ _____	_____	/w/→ _____	_____		
/θ/→ _____	_____	/ð/ → _____	_____		
/s/ → _____	_____	/z/ → _____	_____		
/ʃ/ → _____	_____	/ʒ/ → _____	_____		
/tʃ/→ _____	_____	/dʒ/→ _____	_____		
			/y/ → _____		

Nasals			/l/ *and* /r/	
/m/ → _____	_____	/l/→ _____		
/n/ → _____	_____	in /Cl/→ _____		
/ŋ/ → _____	_____	/r/→ _____	_____	
		in /Cr/→ _____		

\<ed\> ending is omitted or mispronounced _____

\<s\> ending is omitted or mispronounced _____

Initial voiceless stops are not aspirated _____
Final voiced consonants are often voiceless _____
Final consonants are often omitted _____

Many problems with consonant groups _____

Spelling and pronunciation of _____

Other problems with consonants _____

Stress Placement

Stress on the wrong syllable of a word _____
Stress on the wrong syllable of a compound noun _____
Stress on the wrong word of a two-word verb _____
Function words are stressed _____

Vowel Reduction

Unstressed vowels are not reduced _____
Function words are not reduced _____
   /h/ is not reduced in function words _____
   can't = can _____

Rhythm, Length, and Timing

Too even—all syllables are nearly the same length _____
Stressed syllables are too short _____
Stressed vowels before voiced consonants are too short _____
Unstressed vowels are too short or omitted _____
Syllables in long words are mispronounced or omitted _____
Too fast _____
Too slow _____
Irregular rhythm (speeds up and slows down) _____

Linking and Pausing

Choppy: Words are not smoothly linked within phrases _____
   Glottal stop is inserted before vowels _____
   Glottal stop is inserted at ends of words _____
   Final consonants are released or aspirated _____
   /ə/ or /ɛ/ is inserted in consonant groups _____
Sloppy: Words are slurred or excessively run together _____
   /d/ or /t/ between vowels is excessively weakened _____
Poor phrasing and pausing _____
Not fluent in reading aloud _____
Not fluent in speaking freely _____

Other problems with rhythm _____

Intonation: Location of Sentence Stress (the major rise or fall)

Sentence stress on the wrong word _____
    Sentence stress often falls at the beginning of a sentence _____
    Sentence stress often falls on adjectives instead of nouns _____
    Sentence stress does not shift for contrast or emphasis _____
Sentence stress falls on function words (especially pronouns) _____
Too many sentence stresses (too many rises and falls) _____
No clear sentence stress (flat, narrow pitch range) _____

Intonation: Pitch Pattern—Problems with:

Fall in statements _____
    Doesn't jump up enough before falling _____
    Rises instead of jumping up before falling _____
    Doesn't fall enough on one-syllable words _____
    Doesn't fall low enough at end of sentence _____
Fall in information ("WH") questions _____
Rise in "yes–no" questions _____
Rise before a pause _____
Rise in a series _____
Rise in direct address _____
Pitch pattern in choice ("or") questions _____

Jumps up and down; doesn't fall and rise smoothly within groups _____
Monotonous when reading _____
Not loud enough _____

Other problems with intonation _____

Overall Evaluation and Additional Comments

_____

_____

_____

_____

_____

_____

_____

_____

_____

_____

_____

_____

_____

_____

_____

_____

_____

_____

CHAPTER 2

The Phonetic Alphabet

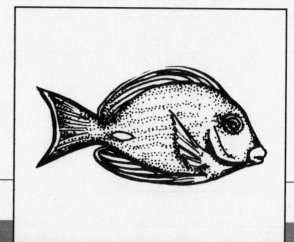

PREREADING QUESTION

G. B. Shaw once said that *fish* **could be spelled** *ghoti:* **<gh> as in** *laugh,* **<o> as in** *women,* **<ti> as in** *nation.* **Why did he say this?**

2.1 English Spelling

English was first written down over 1200 years ago. Since that time, the English language has changed a great deal. Even though many words are not pronounced the same way as they were hundreds of years ago, we still spell them the same way. The oldest words in English are words of one or two syllables, such as *sun, moon, night, man, wife, father,* and *butter,* and are similar to German. These native English words are very common, but because of their long history, they sometimes have very irregular spelling patterns. After the French-speaking Normans conquered England in 1066, many French words and French spellings entered the language and became a regular part of English (such as *money, language,* and *discover*). Many words were also taken from Latin, Greek, Spanish, and Italian (such as *architect, influenza, formula, character,* and *calculate*). These words are usually longer and are used more in academic or specialized fields (science, religion, music, medicine). Over the years, English has continued to borrow words from other languages. Sometimes new words keep the same spelling that they had in their original language, and sometimes they are spelled like native English words. This is why English spelling is so difficult—for native speakers as well as non-native speakers.

The spelling patterns given in this book fall into three main categories. The usual spelling patterns for a sound, given first, are found in the largest number of words. Less common spelling patterns, given next, apply to only a limited set of words. Finally, exceptional spelling patterns are used only in the few words listed. These words may be common native English words or words borrowed from other languages (mostly from Classical or Romance languages). The borrowed words are generally less common in everyday conversation but form an important part of the vocabulary of an educated speaker.

The goal is *not* for students to memorize how every spelling pattern is pronounced. The goal of learning spelling rules and the phonetic alphabet is for students to become familiar with the most common patterns and or exceptions that they may not be aware of, to break an often incorrect association between a letter and a sound, and to begin to trust their ears rather than their eyes when they learn new words.

2.2 The Phonetic Alphabet

English spelling or **orthography** is the traditional way that words are written in English using the 26 letters of the Latin alphabet. This system is very complex and does not represent very well how English words are spoken today. Sometimes the same sound is spelled many different ways, and sometimes different sounds are written the same way. More than one letter often represents a single sound. The Latin alphabet has only 26 letters (5 vowel and 21 consonant letters), but American English has at least 40 different sounds (15 vowels and 24 consonants). In this book, the **symbol < >** will be used to indicate letters in English spelling.

The **phonetic alphabet** is a writing system in which each letter corresponds to a different sound in the language. A word that is written in the phonetic alphabet will always be pronounced exactly the way that it is written, since the same sound is always represented by the same letter. The phonetic alphabet consists of the letters of the Latin alphabet plus a number of special letters and symbols. We will use the **symbol / /** around letters of the phonetic alphabet. Words written this way are in phonetic **transcription**.

English Spelling	Phonetic Alphabet
*The **same** sound is spelled **different** ways:*	*The **same** sound is spelled the **same** way:*
to, too, two	/tu/
one, won	/wən/
there, their, they're	/ðɛɚ/
***Different** sounds are spelled the **same** way:*	***Different** sounds are spelled **different** ways:*
to	/tu/
son	/sən/
not	/nɑt/
most	/moʊst/
cost	/kɔst/
doctor	/ˈdɑktɚ/
woman	/ˈwʊmən/
women	/ˈwɪmɪn/

Once you know how to pronounce all the letters in the phonetic alphabet, you can look up English words in a dictionary and be able to pronounce them. You will also be able to write down in phonetic transcription any English word that you hear so that you can remember the word and ask someone its meaning. The phonetic alphabet used in this book is based on the alphabet of the International Phonetic Association.[1] This is just one possible system. Other books and dictionaries use slightly different systems. It is best for a non-native speaker to consult a dictionary that uses a phonetic alphabet (such as the *Longman Dictionary of American English* or *Oxford Student's Dictionary of American English*) and that represents American, rather than British, pronunciation. Most dictionaries written for Americans, such as *Webster's*, still use only the Latin alphabet to represent pronunciation and can be very confusing. You should look up the example words in Table 2-1 in your own dictionary and write down the way the sounds are represented in it for comparison.

Table 2-1
The Phonetic Alphabet

	Sound	English Spelling	Phonetic Transcription
Consonants			
1.	/b/	be, table, job	/bi, ˈteɪbəl, dʒɑb/
2.	/d/	day, ready, glad	/deɪ, ˈrɛdi, glæd/
3.	/f/	food, after, life	/fud, ˈæftɚ, laɪf/
4.	/g/	go, begin, dog	/gou, brˈgɪn, dɔg/
5.	/h/	head, behind	/hɛd, brˈhaɪnd/
6.	/k/	keep, become, back	/kip, brˈkəm, bæk/
7.	/l/	love, hello, little	/ləv, hɛˈlou, ˈlɪtəl/
8.	/m/	make, woman, some	/meɪk, ˈwumən, səm/
9.	/n/	no, animal, sun	/nou, ˈænɪməl, sən/
10.	/p/	put, happy, cup	/put, ˈhæpi, kəp/
11.	/r/	right, marry	/raɪt, ˈmæri/
12.	/s/	see, possible, place	/si, ˈpɑsɪbəl, pleɪs/
13.	/t/	take, letter, night	/teɪk, ˈlɛtɚ, naɪt/
14.	/v/	very, never, leave	/ˈvɛri, ˈnɛvɚ, liv/
15.	/w/	word, when,[2] quick, away	/wɚd, wɛn, kwɪk, əˈweɪ/
16.	/y/	yes, use, million	/yɛs, yuz, ˈmɪlyən/
17.	/z/	zoo, easy, always	/zu, ˈizi, ˈɔweɪz/
18.	/θ/	thought, nothing, month	/θɔt, ˈnəθɪŋ, mənθ/
19.	/ð/	this, mother, breathe — *A lito ruin*	/ðɪs, ˈməðɚ, brɪð/
20.	/ʃ/	show, station, English	/ʃou, ˈsteɪʃən, ˈɪŋglɪʃ/
21.	/ʒ/	measure, television, beige	/ˈmɛʒɚ, ˈtɛləvɪʒən, beɪʒ/
22.	/tʃ/	child, picture, watch	/tʃaɪld, ˈpɪktʃɚ, watʃ/
23.	/dʒ/	jump, religion, page	/dʒəmp, rɪˈlɪdʒən, peɪdʒ/
24.	/ŋ/	singing, think, long	/ˈsɪŋɪŋ, θɪŋk, lɔŋ/

---

[1]All symbols used in this book follow the IPA except for the symbol /y/, which is represented as /j/ in the IPA.

[2] In this book, the symbol /hw/ (= [ʍ]) is not used. The difference that some speakers make between the initial sound in *where* and *wear* usually disappears in connected speech, and it does not cause problems for non-native speakers.

Table 2-1
(Continued)

Vowels[3]

1.	/i/	eat, see, read, money	/it, si, rid, ˈməni/
2.	/ɪ/	it, big, minute, wishes	/ɪt, bɪg, ˈmɪnɪt, ˈwɪʃɪz/
3.	/eɪ/	ate, say, paid	/eɪt, seɪ, peɪd/
4.	/ɛ/	ever, yes, bed	/ˈɛvɚ, yɛs, bɛd/
5.	/æ/	apple, fat, sad	/ˈæpəl, fæt, sæd/
6.	/ɑ/	odd, stop, father	/ɑd, stɑp, ˈfɑðɚ/
7.	/ə/	up, bus, the, above	/əp, bəs, ðə, ə ˈbəv/
8.	/ɔ/	off, saw, talk, gone [may = /ɑ/]	/ɔf, sɔ, tɔk, gɔn/
9.	/oʊ/	oh, boat, nose, yellow	/oʊ, boʊt, noʊz, ˈyɛloʊ/
10.	/ʊ/	good, book, should	/gʊd, bʊk, ʃʊd/
11.	/u/	you, food, boot	/yu, fud, but/
12.	/ɚ/	early, were, bird, hurt, better	/ˈɚli, wɚ, bɚd, hɚt, ˈbɛtɚ/
13.	/aɪ/	I, ride, life	/aɪ, raɪd, laɪf/
14.	/aʊ/	out, now, crowd	/aʊt, naʊ, kraʊd/
15.	/ɔɪ/	oil, boy, voice	/ɔɪl, bɔɪ, vɔɪs/

Vowels Followed by <r>

16.	/iɚ/	ear, beard, fierce	/iɚ, biɚd, fiɚs/
17.	/ɛɚ/	air, scared, scarce	/ɛɚ, skɛɚd, skɛɚs/
18.	/ɑɚ/	art, car, hard	/ɑɚt, kɑɚ, hɑɚd/
19.	/ɔɚ/	order, wore, bored, course	/ˈɔɚdɚ, wɔɚ, bɔɚd, kɔɚs/
20.	/ʊɚ/	sure, poor [may = /ɔɚ/]	/ʃʊɚ, pʊɚ/
21.	/aɪɚ/	iron, fire, tired	/ˈaɪɚn, faɪɚ, ˈtaɪɚd/
22.	/aʊɚ/	hour, flower, coward	/aʊɚ, flaʊɚ, ˈkaʊɚd/

Other Symbols

1.	'	**per**son	/ˈpɚsən/	Stress mark—shows that the *following* syllable is stressed or accented (**boldface type** indicates sentence-stressed syllables in English spelling).
		per**cent**	/pɚ ˈsɛnt/	
2.	< >	<i>	'little'	Used around letters of the English alphabet and show that the letters represent normal English spelling.
		<igh>	'tight'	
3.	/ /	/ɪ/	/ˈlɪtəl/	Used around normal phonetic transcriptions and show that each letter represents one of the 24 consonant or 15 vowel sounds.
		/aɪ/	/taɪt/	

(continued)

---

[3]/eɪ/ and /oʊ/ can be represented more simply as /e/ and /o/. The reason for not doing so is to make this system more comparable to other systems that might appear in students' dictionaries. The representations <iy, ey, ow, uw> are not used because they are based on a particular phonemic analysis and mix vowel and consonant symbols.

Table 2-1
(continued)

Other Symbols (continued)

4.	[ ]	[l̩]	[ˈlɪɾl̩]	Used around detailed phonetic transcriptions and show more precisely how certain sounds are pronounced. These differences are predictable and automatic for native speakers.
		[tʰ]	[tʰaɪtʔ]	
5.	|		ˈyɛs | hiz ˈkəmɪŋ|	Shows a pause in a phonetic transcription.
6.	‿	an‿apple	/ənæpəl/	Linking mark—shows that two words should be pronounced together, like one word.
7.	ʔ	uh oh!	[ˈəʔoʊ]	Glottal stop—sometimes replaces syllable final /t/.
		it was	[ɪʔwəz]	
8.	ɾ	butter	[ˈbəɾɚ]	Tap—sometimes replaces medial /t/ or /d/.
		ladder	[ˈlæɾɚ]	
9.	ː	leave	[liːv]	Length mark—shows that the preceding sound is lengthened (longer).
		big	[bɪːg]	
10.	ʰ	take	[tʰeɪk]	Aspiration mark—shows that the preceding consonant is aspirated.
		pay	[pʰeɪː]	
11.	̥	crash	[kr̥æʃ]	Voiceless mark—shows that a normally voiced sound is voiceless.
		please	[pl̥iːz]	
12.	̩	middle	[ˈmɪdl̩]	Syllabic consonant mark—shows that the consonant makes a syllable by itself.
		button	[ˈbəʔn̩]	
13.	.	un.for.tu.nate.ly /ən.ˈfɔɚ.tʃə.nɪt.li/		Syllable division mark—shows the boundaries between syllables.
14.	C	food	CVC	"C" means any consonant.
15.	V	me	CV	"V" means any vowel.
16.	¢	come	C¢	"/" through a letter means that it is silent (not pronounced).
17.	+	yes	+ C(C)	"+" means followed by. "+ C(C)" means followed by one or more consonants.
		left		
18.	Hello.	How are you doing?		Used below words to show their intonation. The top and bottom lines are the highest and lowest levels of one's normal pitch range. Dots indicate unstressed syllables; lines indicate stressed syllables. Their position indicates their relative pitch level.

EXERCISES FOR LEARNING THE PHONETIC ALPHABET

A. Memorize the symbols in the phonetic alphabet. Cover the words in English spelling with your hand and read aloud the words in phonetic spelling. For each consonant and vowel symbol, think of *at least one other English word that contains that sound.*

ADVANCED

B. *Discussion Questions.*

1. Compare the 24 consonant and 15 vowel sounds of English to the sounds in your own language. Which of them are the same? If your language uses the Latin alphabet, do you write them the same way? Which sounds don't exist at all in your language? If you have the same or similar sounds, are they *exactly* the same?

2. Consonants #5 /h/, 15 /w/, and 16 /y/ cannot occur at the end of an English word. Consonants #21 /ʒ/ and 24 /ŋ/ cannot begin a word. Most other English consonants can occur in the beginning, in the middle, or at the end of a word. Can all the consonants in your language occur at the beginning, in the middle, and at the end of a word? Which consonants cannot end a word? If only a few consonants occur at the end of a word in your language, you will have to be careful not to drop final consonants in English.

3. How many vowels does your language have? If your language only has five vowels, you may have to pay special attention to the difference between neighboring vowels, such as 1&2, 3&4, 5&6&7, 8&9, and 10&11.

4. Many Americans and Canadians do not distinguish between vowel #6 /ɑ/ and vowel #8 /ɔ/. They have just one vowel, which is similar to /ɑ/. Ask your teacher or a friend to say the following pairs of words: *caught, cot; Don, dawn; collar, caller; stock, stalk.* Do they say the vowels the same or differently?

C. What sounds do the following phonetic letters stand for? Give an example of a word which contains that sound.

EXAMPLE: /t/ as in *take*

1. /ʃ/	**5.** /θ/	**9.** /w/	**13.** /ɪ/
2. /ŋ/	**6.** /ʒ/	**10.** /æ/	**14.** /ʊ/
3. /ð/	**7.** /tʃ/	**11.** /ɔ/	**15.** /ə/
4. /y/	**8.** /dʒ/	**12.** /ɛ/	**16.** /ɑ/

D. Say each of the following words *aloud* and write them using normal English spelling.

EXAMPLE: /pɪk/ = pick

1. /ðæt/	**6.** /ləŋz/	**11.** /dʒədʒ/	**16.** /nɑk/
2. /kɔf/	**7.** /θɪŋ/	**12.** /pʊʃ/	**17.** /baɪz/
3. /gləv/	**8.** /kʊd/	**13.** /fɪks/	**18.** /kəp/
4. /watʃ/	**9.** /gəˈrɑʒ/	**14.** /tʃɛk/	**19.** /ʃoʊd/
5. /hɚd/	**10.** /sɔ/	**15.** /maʊθ/	**20.** /eɪdʒ/

E. Say each of the following words *aloud* and write them using normal English spelling.

1. /ˈbɚθdeɪ/	**7.** /ˈpærəgræf/	**13.** /əˈlaɪv/
2. /livz/	**8.** /ˈdɔtɚ/	**14.** /pɑpyəˈleɪʃən/
3. /əˈnəðɚ/	**9.** /ˈneɪtʃɚ/	**15.** /əndɚˈstʊd/
4. /kənˈdɪʃənz/	**10.** /ɪnˈdʒɔɪ/	**16.** /ˈdʒoʊkɪŋ/
5. /ˈplɛʒɚ/	**11.** /yəŋ/	**17.** /bæθ/
6. /ˈɛksɚˌsaɪz/	**12.** /ˈmyuzɪk/	**18.** /ˈʃaʊɚ/

F. Say each of the following short sentences *aloud* and write them using normal English spelling. (Hint: Stressed syllables often begin words.)

EXAMPLE: /ðeɪ'noʊɚ/ = they know her

1. /'ðizɚmaɪ'bʊks/
2. /aɪlbi'siŋyu/
3. /ʃizə'byutɪfəl'gɚl/
4. /ðeɪkən'spiktəðə'titʃɚ/
5. /ʃi'dʒəst'hædə'beɪbi/

6. /aɪ'θɪŋki'lʌvzmi/
7. /ðə'stɔɚəz'kloʊzd/
8. /wi'nidsəm'məni/
9. /ðæts'nɑtə'gʊd'rizən/
10. /hiz'tɔktə'baʊtɪtbɪ'fɔɚ/

G. Say the following English words *aloud* and write the phonetic symbol for the underlined sound. Check in groups or with your teacher.

EXAMPLE: shoe /ʃ/ why /aɪ/

1. father
2. cheap
3. ship
4. bought
5. map
6. clock
7. move
8. sir
9. say
10. weather
11. high
12. usually
13. thick
14. down
15. laugh
16. George

H. *Dictionary Practice 1.* Some dictionaries use different phonetic letters from the ones presented in this book.
What is the name of your dictionary? _____
What symbol does your dictionary use for the phonetic letters used in this book? Look up the following words and copy the symbol for each of the underlined letters.

EXAMPLE: /eɪ/ (ate) = _e^y_ (Longman Dictionary)

1. /i/ (eat) = _____
2. /ɪ/ (it) = _____
3. /eɪ/ (ate) = _____
4. /ɛ/ (ever) = _____
5. /æ/ (apple) = _____
6. /ɑ/ (odd) = _____
7. /ə/ unstressed (above) = _____
   /ə/ stressed (above) = _____
8. /ɔ/ (off) = _____
9. /oʊ/ (boat) = _____
10. /ʊ/ (good) = _____
11. /u/ (blue) = _____

12. /ɚ/ unstressed (murder) = _____
    /ɝ/ stressed (murder) = _____
13. /aɪ/ (I) = _____
14. /aʊ/ (out) = _____
15. /ɔɪ/ (oil) = _____
16. /y/ (yes) = _____
17. /θ/ (thought) = _____
18. /ð/ (this) = _____
19. /ʃ/ (show) = _____
20. /ʒ/ (measure) = _____
21. /tʃ/ (child) = _____
22. /dʒ/ (jump) = _____
23. /ŋ/ (sing) = _____

24. How does your dictionary indicate stress? Does it use an accent mark *before* the stressed syllable (*baby* = /'beɪbi/), *after* the stressed syllable (/beɪ'bi/), or *above* the stressed vowel (/béɪbi/)?

I. *Dictionary Practice 2.* Look up the following words in your dictionary and write down their pronunciation using phonetic symbols. OPTIONAL: Write down the pronunciation of the word a second time using the phonetic symbols from this book.

1. although
2. asthma
3. athletic
4. child
5. headache
6. journal
7. know
8. knowledge
9. muscle
10. muscular — MASQUIULAS

11. nation
12. national
13. persuasion
14. reason
15. sign
16. sing
17. southern SUDOESTE
18. tongue
19. unique
20. Xerox ZEROX

CHAPTER **3**

Vowel Overview

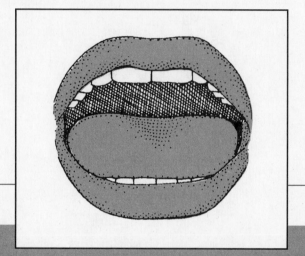

PREREADING QUESTIONS

What vowel is this? Can you explain how to make it?

3.1 Production of Vowels

TONGUE POSITION

Vowels can be **high** (close) or **low** (open). In a **high** vowel, such as /i/ in *see*, the tongue is pushed up high so that the upper surface of the tongue is very close to the roof of the mouth. In a **low** vowel, such as /æ/ in *cat*, the tongue is flattened out and the mouth is more open so that the top of the tongue is much farther away from the roof of the mouth.

TO DO

Try going back and forth between /i/ and /æ/ several times while observing your mouth *in a mirror*. Then try it again *silently* and try to *feel* it. Say /i – eɪ – ɛ – æ/ slowly and continuously. Your mouth should be opening and your tongue should be moving slowly down. Now try going back and forth between /u/ as in *too* and /ɑ/ as in *hot*. Then try /u – ʊ – ɔ – ɑ/. Concentrate on the movement of the tongue; you will probably feel that it moves less than from /i/ to /æ/.

The tongue position for /eɪ/ and /ɛ/ is midway between /i/ and /æ/, so they are called **mid** vowels. /oʊ/ and /ɔ/ are also mid vowels.

Vowels can be either **front** or **back**. In a **front** vowel, such as /i/ or /æ/, the front part of the tongue is pushed forward, and the tongue can be easily seen in a mirror. In a **back** vowel, such as /u/ or /ɑ/, the highest point of the tongue is the back, and the whole tongue moves back in the mouth.

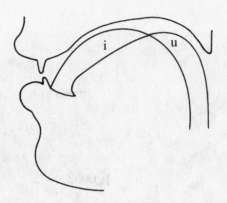

High Vowels
front /i/   back /u/

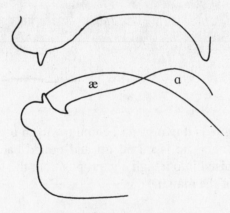

Low Vowels
front /æ/   back /ɑ/

FIGURE 3-1
Tongue positions for /i, u, æ, ɑ/

TO DO

Try going back and forth between /æ/ (or /ɛ/ as in *bed*) and /ɑ/ and *look in the mirror*. Can you see your tongue shooting forward and back? Try it *silently and feel it.* You will feel that in /æ/ the tip of the tongue touches the back of the lower teeth, but in /ɑ/ it moves away from them. Try going back and forth between /i/ and /u/ and between /eɪ/ and /oʊ/. Do it silently and try to feel the tongue moving. You will notice that the lips are also changing at the same time.

A vowel that is neither front nor back is called a **central** vowel. Some languages do not have central vowels, so they are often difficult for non-native speakers. In English the central vowels are /ɪ/, /ə/, /ʊ/ and /ɚ/ as in *sit, up, good*, and *bird*. To make a central vowel, your tongue needs to be in the middle, between high and low and between front and back.

TO DO

Try to glide *very, very slowly* between /i/ and /ɑ/. Try it a few times, both aloud and silently, in order to feel it. Then try it again and stop as soon as you start to move away from /i/: this is /ɪ/. Hold your tongue there and try a few words that use this vowel, such as *if, it, sit, did,* and *give*. You can also produce /ɪ/ by gliding the other way. Say the sound /aɪ/ as in *I* very slowly, and stop near the end; you should have a good /ɪ/.

In order to make /ʊ/, glide very, very slowly between /u/ and /ɛ/ a few times. Then stop as soon as you move off /u/ and repeat that sound a few times. Try saying a few words with /ʊ/, such as *hood, good, could, put*, and *look*.

/ə/ is a completely central vowel that is a little lower than /ɪ/ or /ʊ/. You can make it by again gliding slowly from /i/ to /ɑ/ and stopping about halfway down to /ɑ/, before your mouth opens completely. Another way to find /ə/ is to go back and forth very slowly from /ɛ/ to /ɔ/ and then try to stop halfway between them, before the lips begin to round. Then try a few words with /ə/, such as *uh* (the pause sound people use in English), *up, us, of, does, but,* and *luck*.

In most vowels, the **tip of the tongue** is **down** (right behind the teeth in the front vowels). However, in the vowel /ɚ/, the tongue tip is raised **up** and pulled back. The whole tongue is bunched up, and the back is raised into a high central position; the tongue tip lifts up a little, but it *never touches* the roof of the mouth.

TO DO

Open your mouth a little and move the tongue tip up and down a few times, first touching behind the lower teeth and then touching behind the upper teeth. Try to feel the tongue tip. Slide the tongue tip as far back as you can from the upper teeth while touching the roof of the mouth. If you do this with your mouth open and look in a mirror, you will see the underside of the tongue. To make /ɚ/, start with /oʊ/ as in *oh* and then lift the tongue tip up a little, but do not touch the roof of the mouth. Do this a few times silently and aloud.

Finally, unround the lips a little while your tongue tip is raised, and you will have a vowel close to /ɚ/. If you look in a mirror, you should be able to see the underside of your tongue. Try going into /ɚ/ slowly from /ə/ while looking in a mirror. Since /ɚ/ is more rounded than /ə/, you will have to round the lips a little (by pushing in the sides of the mouth) while you raise the tongue tip. Now try some syllables like /gɚ/ and /kɚ/ and then some words like *her, hurt, were, sir,* and *bird*.

LIP POSITION

The lips can be **rounded** or **unrounded (spread)**. In a **rounded** vowel, such as /u/ in *too*, the sides of both lips are pushed in. In an **unrounded** vowel, such as /i/ in *see*, the sides of the lips are pulled out, as in a smile. (Photographers tell you to say *cheese* when they take your picture.)

TO DO

Say /u – i – u – i/ slowly and continuously. Look in the mirror and watch your lips. Now go back and forth between /u/ and /i/ silently and feel your lips changing position. (Close your eyes to concentrate better on the feeling.) Do the same thing with /eɪ – oʊ/. Then slowly glide between /ɑ – ɔ – oʊ – u/ and see how the lips gradually become more and more rounded and closer together.

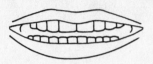 

Spread /i/   Neutral /ə/   Rounded /u/

FIGURE 3-2
Lip positions for /i, ə, u/

The front vowels /i, eɪ, ɛ, æ/ have spread lips; in the vowels /ɔ, oʊ, u, ɚ/, the lips are rounded. Lip-rounding is important in English not only in vowels but also in some consonants. In /w/, the lips are even more tightly rounded than in /u/. The lips are slightly rounded in /r, ʃ, ʒ, tʃ, dʒ/. Thus, it is a good idea to practice rounding and unrounding the lips silently, as in the exercise above, in order to become aware of the position of the lips.

If the lips are neither rounded nor spread, their position is **neutral:** the lips are relaxed, similar to when you are not talking. The lips are neutral in /ə/ and /ɑ/. The lips are neutral or very slightly spread in /ɪ/. If you have trouble with the sound /ɪ/ and make it sound too much like /i/, that is, if *sit* sounds like *seat*, then make the lips neutral (less spread) for /ɪ/. The lips are neutral or very slightly rounded in /ʊ/. If you have trouble with this sound, take away the lip-rounding.

Vowel Summary

	Tongue			Lips		
	Front	Center	Back	Spread	Neutral	Rounded
High	i	ɚ	u	i	ɪ ʊ	u
		ɪ ʊ				
	eɪ		oʊ	eɪ	ə	oʊ
Mid						
	ɛ	ə	ɔ	ɛ		ɚ
Low	æ		ɑ	æ	ɑ	ɔ

VOICING

In English, all vowels are **voiced,** that is, the vocal folds are vibrating while you make vowel sounds. Even very short vowels are voiced and are the center of a syllable. This is important for determining how many syllables a word has. *Campus* should not sound the same as *camps*. Be sure that all the vowels are voiced in words like *accident*, *activity*, *wait-ed*, *excited*, *situation*, and *sympathy*. Some speakers of Japanese, Chinese, Greek, Russian, and French tend to make the unstressed /ɪ/ in these words voiceless or to omit it.

TO DO

Put your hand over your larynx /ˈlærɪŋks/ (the part on your throat that sticks out) and say /ɑ, i, eɪ, oʊ, u/. You should feel the vibrations of your vocal folds. Now whisper those same vowels. You should not feel any vibrations. Try slowly alternating /ɑɑhhɑɑhhɑɑ/ and /iihhiihhii/ and feel the voicing go on during the vowel and off during /h/. (See Sec. 12.1 for more on voicing.)

PURE VOWELS AND DIPHTHONGS

In **pure** or simple vowels such as /ɪ, ɛ, æ, ə, ɑ, ɔ, ʊ, ɚ/, the quality of the vowel stays about the same from the beginning to the end. In **diphthongs** /ˈdɪfθɔŋz/, the quality of the vowel changes: they start out sounding like one vowel and end up sounding like another vowel. In order to show this in the phonetic alphabet, two letters are used to represent the approximate beginning and ending sounds. Diphthongs move either toward /i/ or toward /u/; but since the sound usually ends before the tongue actually reaches /i/ or /u/, the second part of a diphthong is represented as either /ɪ/ or /ʊ/. The movement is greatest in /aɪ, aʊ, ɔɪ/, as in *high*, *how*, and *boy*, and can be clearly seen in a mirror. There is a smaller movement in /eɪ/ and /oʊ/, which is especially noticeable in open syllables (when no consonant follows), as in *day* and *no*.

TO DO

Pronounce some words with /eɪ/, such as *A, hay,* and *day*, while you look at your mouth in a mirror. You should see your lips coming closer together and your mouth closing during the sound. If this is not happening, try gliding slowly from /ɛ/ to /i/, and then speed the sound up. Then pronounce some words with /oʊ/, such as *oh, hoe,* and *go*, and watch your mouth in a mirror. You should see your lips start at a neutral or slightly rounded position and then become more and more rounded. If this is not happening, try gliding slowly from /ə/ to /u/, and then speed up the sound.

The vowels /i/ and /u/ are also slightly diphthongal in English in open syllables such as *see* and *you*. In /i/ the tongue keeps pushing forward and moving toward the roof of the mouth; in /u/ the lips continue rounding more strongly.

VOWEL LENGTH

How long a vowel is in English depends on several factors. The two most important factors are the following sound and stress.

The Following Sound.   The length of a vowel changes depending on the following sound. All vowels are *shorter before voiceless consonants* /p, t, k, f, θ, s, ʃ, tʃ/ than before voiced consonants (all others) or before a pause (in open syllables).

1. Short Vowel	2. Long Vowel	3. Long Vowel
Syllables closed by a voiceless consonant	Syllables closed by a voiced consonant	Open syllable
a. suit	sued	sue
b. ice	eyes	eye
c. note	known	no
d. beat	bead	be
e. bit	bid	—
f. late	laid	lay
g. let	led	—

Many non-native speakers do not make the vowels in columns 2 and 3 long enough. This can make both the vowel and the final consonant difficult to identify. Note that /i/ in *beat* is *shorter* than /ɪ/ in *bid*, and /eɪ/ in *late* is *shorter* than /ɛ/ in *led*.

Stress.   Vowels are *shorter when they are unstressed* than when they are stressed (when followed by the same sounds). Many vowels also change in quality when they are unstressed (see Sec. 6.2).

Shorter Vowel—Unstressed	Longer Vowel—Stressed
per̲cent /pɚˈsɛnt/	person /ˈpɚsən/
all o̲f it /ˈɔləvɪt/	I lo̲ve it /aɪˈləvɪt/
vis̲it /ˈvɪzɪt/	to si̲t /təˈsɪt/

Vowel Quality.   /ɪ, ɛ, ə, ʊ/ are all relatively short vowels in English and are shorter than /i, eɪ, ɑ, u/ when they are followed by the same sound. Note that /ɪ, ɛ, ə, ʊ/ do not occur in stressed open syllables; that is, they must always be followed by a consonant when they are stressed.

Shorter Vowel	Longer Vowel
bit /bɪt/	beat /bit/
red /rɛd/	raid /reɪd/
cup /kəp/	cop /kɑp/
look /lʊk/	Luke /luk/

Position.   Syllables are longer before a pause.

Shorter Syllable	Longer Syllable
My *new* shirt is dirty.	My shirt is *new*.
Your *bag* is on the floor.	That's your *bag*.

EXERCISES

 A. *Vowel Warm-up* [to be done at the beginning of class each day]. Read down the list of words and try to make all 15 vowels sound different. Listen to each other. Which vowels sound too much alike? Read some words and have the class identify the vowel by number. (Vowels 6 and 8 sound the same in some accents.)

	Vowel	Key Words	Short	Long
1.	/i/	be	beat	heed[1]
2.	/ɪ/	sick	bit	hid
3.	/eɪ/	day	bait[2]	aid
4.	/ɛ/	get	bet	head
5.	/æ/	fat	bat	had
6.	/ɑ/	stop	pot	odd
7.	/ə/	up	but	HUD[3]
8.	/ɔ/	talk	bought	awed[4]
9.	/oʊ/	no	boat	owed
10.	/ʊ/	good	put	hood[5]
11.	/u/	new	boot	who'd
12.	/ɚ/	her	Bert	heard
13.	/aɪ/	I	bite	hide
14.	/aʊ/	now	bout[6]	how'd
15.	/ɔɪ/	boy	voice	Hoyd

B. Read the words in Sec. 3.2 (p. 28). Make sure that all the words in each group have the same vowel sound, regardless of spelling. Learn the symbols for each vowel sound.

C. Record yourself reading the sentences in Sec. 3.3 (p. 29). Which vowels are difficult for you? All the underlined vowels in the same sentence should have the same quality, but the length will vary.

---

[1]heed = pay attention to

[2]bait = food to attract an animal

[3]HUD = Housing and Urban Development, a U.S. government agency

[4]awe = to be amazed, to wonder

[5]hood = metal cover over the engine of a car; covering for the head

[6]bout = a short period of intense activity; a fight

ADVANCED

D. The following sound affects the way that a vowel sounds. This is especially true when <m, n, ng, l, r> follow a vowel in the same syllable. (There is no difference between vowels 1&2, 3&4, 8&9, and 10&11 before <r>; in some accents *poor* sounds the same as *pore*.)

	Vowel	+ Nasal	+ <l>	+ <r>
1.	/i/	dean	feel	fear
2.	/ɪ/	din[7]	fill	
3.	/eɪ/	Dane[8]	fail	fair, fare
4.	/ɛ/	den[9]	fell	
5.	/æ/	Dan	shall	
6.	/ɑ/	Don	doll	far
7.	/ə/	done	dull	
8.	/ɔ/	dawn	fall	four, pore[10]
9.	/oʊ/	tone	fold, pole	
10.	/ʊ/		full	pure, poor
11.	/u/	dune[11]	fool	
12.	/ɚ/	turn	furl[12]	fur
13.	/aɪ/	dine[13]	file	fire
14.	/aʊ/	down	foul[14]	flour, flower
15.	/ɔɪ/	coin	foil[15]	foyer,[16] employer

---

[7]din = a loud, continuous noise

[8]Dane = a person from Denmark

[9]den = home of a wild animal; room in a house for playing or relaxing

[10]pore = a small opening in the skin that allows water (sweat) to pass out

[11]dune = a long hill of sand (sand dune)

[12]furl = to roll up (to unfurl the flag)

[13]dine = to eat dinner (formal)

[14]foul = against the rules of a sport; to spoil or mess up

[15]foil = a paper-thin piece of metal (aluminum foil)

[16]foyer = entrance hall (of a hotel or theater, for example)

3.2 American English Vowel Sounds

For each sound, first common and then uncommon spelling patterns are given.

1. /i/   be, beat, bead, tree, these, happy, money, piece, receive, machine, ski, suite, people, key
2. /ɪ/   this, bit, bid, children, give, system, busy, build, examine, dishes, minute, women, Mrs., been, pretty, English
3. /eɪ/   day, bait, made, name, radio, weigh, great, they, veil, gauge
4. /ɛ/   get, bet, bed, death, heavy, says, said, again, any, many, friend, guess
5. /æ/   fat, bat, bag, have, habit, bad, man, class, laugh, half,[1] salmon
6. /ɑ/   stop, pot, God, rock, college, John, watch, father, calm, knowledge
7. /ə/   up, but, bud, study, the, of, love, another, one, country, enough, today, idea, what, does, blood
8. /ɔ/[2]   talk, bought, dog, cost, off, all, saw, cause, caught, gone, broad
9. /oʊ/   no, boat, road, those, most, phone, slow, sew, toe, although, shoulder, yolk, oh, plateau
10. /ʊ/   good, put, foot, book, would, could, should, cushion, sugar, woman
11. /u/   new, boot, food, soup, through, who, move, use, true, suit, shoe, two, neutral, beautiful
12. /ɚ/   her, hurt, bird, first, were, work, heard, turn, journal, girl, mother, doctor, dollar, future, iron
13. /aɪ/   I, bite, ride, why, time, child, high, right, died, buy, eye, aisle
14. /aʊ/   now, about, crowd, house, downtown, around
15. /ɔɪ/   boy, voice, avoid, point, oil, enjoy

---

[1]In *bad, man, class, laugh,* and *half,* /æ/ sounds more like [ɛə] or [eə] in some accents.
[2]/ɔ/ = /ɑ/ in many accents.

3.3 American English Vowel Sounds in Sentences

1. /i/ Please be seated in these three seats near the speaker.
2. /ɪ/ Mr. and Mrs. Smith have been living in this big city since Christmas.
3. /eɪ/ A famous play is going to take place on this stage in eight days.
4. /ɛ/ Her friends said she'd better not get a red wedding dress.
5. /æ/ Half of that bad class can't add or subtract very fast.
6. /ɑ/ John was shocked when his father got robbed in the parking lot.
7. /ə/ My mother would love to buy another rug, but she doesn't have enough money.
8. /ɔ/ We all thought we saw a small dog walk across Broad Street.
9. /oʊ/ Most local folks know they can take the old road home even though it's closed.
10. /ʊ/ The good cook said she wouldn't put too much sugar in the cookies.
11. /u/ Your new blue shoes look truly beautiful with that suit.
12. /ɚ/ The girl heard many birds on her way to work early Thursday morning.
13. /aɪ/ My wife doesn't have time to ride her bike five miles a day.
14. /aʊ/ A loud crowd surrounded the brown house downtown.
15. /ɔɪ/ At one point, the boys' joyful voices rose above the noise.

The girl heard many birds on her way to work early
Thursday morning.

CHAPTER 4

Vowels in Detail

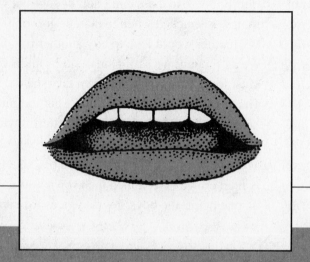

PREREADING QUESTIONS

Which sound is being made, /i/ or /ɪ/? Which vowel occurs in the verb *live*?

4.1 Vowels 1–4: /i, ɪ, eɪ, ɛ/

VOWEL #1: /i/

/i/ is usually spelled <ee>, <ea>, <e> alone, <e> + CV (followed by a consonant and vowel), or <e> + C¢ (followed by a consonant and silent <e>). In unstressed syllables at the end of a word, it is often spelled <y> or <ey>.[1]

<ee>	see, week, cheese, between	_____
<ea>	tea, repeat, each, leave	_____
<e>	we, these, equal, complete	_____
<y>	baby, happy, friendly, money	_____

---

[1]Final <y> and <ey> are pronounced /ɪ/ in some forms of British English and American English.

/i/ is sometimes spelled <ie> or less commonly <ei>. In borrowed words, /i/ may be spelled <i> + C¢; these words are often stressed on the last syllable.

<ie>	believe, piece, field, movie, chief, priest
<ei>	receive, ceiling, leisure, seize
<i>	police, machine, magazine, fatigue, suite, ski
Exceptions:	people, key

VOWEL #2: /ɪ/

/ɪ/ is one of the most common vowels in English. It is usually spelled <i> + C(C) (followed by one or more consonants). In stressed syllables of academic words, it may be spelled <y> + C(C).

<i>	sit, this, big, pick, middle _____
<y>	rhythm, syllable, system, physics _____

Some less common spelling patterns are <u>, <ui>, or <i> + <ve>.

<u>	busy, business, lettuce
<ui>	build, guilt, guitar, biscuit
<i>	to live, give, river, deliver
Exceptions:	been, pretty, English, England, women /ˈwɪmɪn/, Mrs. /ˈmɪsɪz/

PRACTICE 1

For /i/, keep pushing the body of the tongue forward and spread the lips. For /ɪ/, pull the tongue back and down toward /ə/, and make sure the lips are neutral. Silently alternate between /i/ and /ɪ/ to feel the difference.

1. /i/	*2.* /ɪ/
a. I don't want to **sleep**.	I don't want to **slip**.
b. The **peach** was excellent.	The **pitch**[2] was excellent.
c. He **beat** them again.	He **bit** them again.
d. Are they **leaving** there?	Are they **living** there?
e. They **skied** on the ice.	They **skid**[3] on the ice.
f. The son has **reason**.	The sun has **risen**.
g. That's a high **heel**.	That's a high **hill**.
h. It was a terrible **scene**.	It was a terrible **sin**.[4]
i. They always **heat** their food.	They always **hid** their food.
j. It was beyond our **reach**.	It was beyond our **ridge**.[5]
k. Do you see the **peak**?[6]	Do you see the **pig**?

---

[2]pitch = throw of the baseball (by the pitcher)
[3]skid = to slide out of control
[4]sin = a wrong thing to do, behavior against God's laws

[5]ridge = the long, narrow raised part of a mountain
[6]peak = highest point

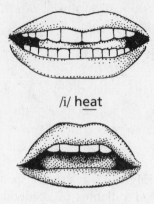

/i/ heat

/ɪ/ hit

FIGURE 4-1

In *unstressed* syllables, /ɪ/ is usually spelled <i> or <e>, but it can have many different spellings since unstressed syllables are often reduced to /ɪ/ or /ə/ (see Chap. 6).

<i>   individual, office, imagine, visiting

<e>   prepare, decided, secret, misses, begin

PRACTICE 2   ADVANCED

Like all vowels, /ɪ/ is longer when it is followed by a voiced consonant such as /b, d, g, v, z, dʒ/ than by a voiceless consonant (see Sec. 13.2). When you lengthen /ɪ/, try not to change the quality to /i/. Some Americans add /ə/ after /ɪ/: say /ɪə/ in *big, live, begin, will,* and *kid* if it helps you. Compare the length of the vowels in the following words:

Shortest ──────────────────────────▶ Longest

bit	beat	bid	bead
[bɪt]	[bit]	[bɪːd] or [bɪəd]	[biːd]

1. /ɪ/ *Short*	2. /ɪ/ *Long*
a. They always **hit** them.	They always **hid** them.
b. It's a **Bic** pen.	It's a **big** pen.
c. My sweater is **ripped**.	My sweater is **ribbed**.[7]
d. I know they're **rich**.	I know their **ridge**.

1. /i/ *Short*	2. /i/ *Long*
e. Where're the dog's **feet**?	Where's the dog's **feed**?
f. There are many **leaks**[8] now.	There are many **leagues**[9] now.
g. We need **peace**.	We need **peas**.

---

[7]rib = raised line in a knitted fabric (as on the cuffs of a sweater)

[8]leak = a small hole or crack that lets water come through

[9]league = a group of people, countries, or sports teams, with a common goal

VOWEL #3: /eɪ/

/eɪ/ is usually spelled <a> + CV or C¢, <ai>, or <ay>.

<a>	came, lady, famous, April _____
<ai>	wait, raise, contain, straight _____
<ay>	say, today, play, crayon _____

In a few words, /eɪ/ is spelled <eigh>, <ea>, <ey>, or <ei>.

<eigh>	weigh, eight, eighty, neighbor, freight
<ea>	break, great, steak
<ey>	they, obey, convey, grey (=gray)
<ei>	veil, vein, reign
Exceptions:	gauge[10] (=gage), bass (meaning low voice or tone)

VOWEL #4: /ɛ/

/ɛ/ is usually spelled <e> + C(C).

<e>	yes, pencil, left, exit, several _____

It is sometimes spelled <ea> + C.

<ea>	head, weather, death, pleasant, sweatshirt, breakfast
Exceptions:	says, said, again, against, any, many, friend, guess, guest, leopard, jeopardy

In some American accents (South, Southwest), /ɛ/ and /ɪ/ sound the same before /n/ and /m/: *pen* and *pin* both sound like /pɪn/.

PRACTICE 3

Be sure to make /eɪ/ different from /ɛ/ before voiceless consonants, where they are both short. The tongue position is lower and the mouth is more open for /ɛ/. Silently alternate between /eɪ/ and /ɛ/.

1. /eɪ/	*2.* /ɛ/
a. Did they **taste** it?	Did they **test** it?
b. The rain made her **wait**.	The rain made her **wet**.
c. She has a lot of **dates**.	She has a lot of **debts** /dɛts/.[11]
d. Where's the **paper**?	Where's the **pepper**?
e. Let me see you **later**.	Let me see your **letter**.
f. He **laid** them aside.	He **led** them aside.
g. It was a terrible **pain**.	It was a terrible **pen**.
h. I think he'll **fail**.	I think he **fell**.

---

[10]gauge = scale or meter

[11]debt = something owed to someone; money to pay back

EXERCISES FOR /i, ɪ, eɪ, ɛ/

A. Study the spelling patterns for vowels 1–4. Say all example words aloud. Circle any words with pronunciations that surprised you. In the blank spaces or on a piece of paper, write down at least two other words with the *same vowel sound* and *same major spelling pattern* as the examples.

EXAMPLE:

\<ee\>	see, week, cheese, between	*feet, agree*
\<ea\>	tea, repeat, each, leave	*season, neat*
\<e\>	we, these, equal, complete	*legal, Portuguese*

B. How is stressed \<e\> pronounced in the following words? Divide into two groups: *scene, clever, cereal, secret, federal, effort, even, seven.*

1. /i/ as in *see* ___*scene,*___

2. /ɛ/ as in *get* ___*clever,*___

C. How is \<ea\> pronounced in the following words? Divide into two groups: *mean, meant, measure, sweater, ready, to read, dead, spread, heavy, easy, leave, breath, breathe, bread, heat, instead.*

1. /i/ ___MEAN, BREATHE, to READ EASY, LEAVE, HEAT___

2. /ɛ/ ___MEANT, MEASURE, SWEATER, READY, DEAD, SPREAD, HEAVY, BREATH, BREAD, INSTEAD___

D. /i/ *and* /ɪ/. Record yourself reading the following sentences. Listen to make sure that the underlined vowels sound differently.

1. Don't sit in my seat.
2. Each arm itches.
3. These shoes don't fit my feet.
4. Those boys still steal.
5. The field was filled with wheat.
6. You should at least make a list.
7. This is his, and these are yours.
8. The little bird had a big beak.
9. We hid from the heat.
10. That leaf won't live very long.

E. /eɪ/ *and* /ɛ/. Record yourself reading the following sentences. Listen to make sure that the underlined vowels sound differently.

1. He takes his vacations in Texas.
2. You'll waste a lot of time driving out West.
3. Don't let me be late.
4. These lace curtains cost less than those.
5. I'll read your letter later.
6. What's the age of the house on the edge of the river?
7. He fell down and failed to finish the race.
8. They hope to sell everything that's on sale.

4.2 Vowels 5–8: /æ, ɑ, ə, ɔ/

VOWEL #5: /æ/   ~~LONG···~~

/æ/ is almost always spelled <a> + C(C).

    <a>   fat, add, practice, habit _____

Exceptions: laugh, aunt (but some people say /ɑnt/), draught (= draft beer), half, calf, salmon, plaid, guarantee

In many American accents, particularly in East Coast cities, /æ/ sounds more like [ɛə] or [eə] before certain consonants: the tongue position is higher and the sound is somewhat diphthongal. This occurs in some very common words such as *ham, man, can't, mad, bad, class, glass, laugh,* and *half.* For this reason, the difference between *man* and *men* or between *bad* and *bed* may not be as clear to you as the difference between *bat* and *bet.*

VOWEL #6: /ɑ/

/ɑ/ is usually spelled <o> + C(C). In some very common words, especially before <r>, it is spelled <a>.

    <o>   stop, God, rock, dollar, modern _____

    <a>   father, watch, garage, arm, start _____

Exceptions: calm, palm, knowledge, yacht, bureaucracy   *BUROCANCIA*

PRACTICE 4   SPANISH

In both /æ/ and /ɑ/, the mouth is wide open, but the tongue comes forward for /æ/ and is further back and much less visible for /ɑ/. Alternate silently and look in your mirror.

1. /æ/	*2.* /ɑ/
a. I think it's a **hat**.	I think it's **hot**.
b. **Dan**'s over there.	**Don**'s over there.
c. Do you see those **caps**?	Do you see those **cops**?
d. He's sitting on the **cat**.	He's sitting on the **cot**.[1]
e. His **sack**[2] is on the floor.	His **sock** is on the floor.
f. Is the **bag** wet?	Is the **bog**[3] wet?
g. They're **stacking**[4] up books.	They're **stocking**[5] up books.

---

[1]cot = a small, portable bed, often used in the army

[2]sack = bag

[3]bog = soft, wet ground; a marshy area

[4]stack = put on top of each other

[5]stock = to keep or accumulate a supply (for sale)

VOWEL #7: /ə/

/ə/ ("schwa") is one of the most common vowels in English. In stressed syllables, it is usually spelled <u> + C(C), but in some very common words it may be spelled <o> + C, <o> + C¢, or <ou> + C.

<u>	but, mud, uh, jump, study _____
<o>	won, love, mother, some, of _____
<ou>	young, cousin, enough, country _____

Exceptions: bl<u>oo</u>d, fl<u>oo</u>d, wh<u>a</u>t, d<u>oe</u>s

In *unstressed* syllables, /ə/ may be spelled <a>, <o>, <e>, or <u>. It can also have other spellings since many vowels in unstressed syllables are reduced to /ə/ (see Chap. 6).

<a>	about, agree, soda, America, banana, magazine
<o>	occur, today, political, photograph, common, Europe
<e>	violent, secretary, believe, problem
<u>	instrument, unhappy, success \

VOWEL #8: /ɔ/ (compare to vowel #6)

/ɔ/ is usually spelled <o> + C(C), <al> + C, <au>, or <aw>.

<o>	dog, off, on, song, cost _____
<al>	talk, always, salt, call[6] _____
<au>	pause, author, caution, laundry _____
<aw>	law, dawn, draw, awful _____

In a few common words, it is spelled <ough>, <augh>, or <a> after <w>.

<ough>	bought, brought, fought, ought, thought, cough /kɔf/
<augh>	caught, daughter, slaughter
<a>	war, warm, quarter, award, toward, reward

Exceptions: g<u>o</u>ne, br<u>oa</u>d

There is a lot of variation in North America between words pronounced with /ɔ/ and /ɑ/: some people pronounce *fog* /fɔg/ and others say /fɑg/; *wash* is /wɑʃ/ or /wɔʃ/; *orange* is /ˈɔrɪndʒ/ or /ˈɑrɪndʒ/. Increasingly, words that are listed in the dictionary as /ɔ/ are pronounced as /ɑ/. In fact, in some accents (the Midwest and most of Canada), there is no difference between /ɔ/ and /ɑ/: words with /ɔ/ are all pronounced more like /ɑ/ (with or without rounded lips). For example, *Don* and *dawn* are both /dɑn/; *stock* and *stalk* are both /stɑk/. If you are not sure about how to pronounce a word with one of the spelling patterns for vowel #6 or 8, use /ɑ/.

How words spelled with <o> and <a> are pronounced is also one of the main differences between British English and American English. The word *pot* pronounced by an American might sound like *pat* to someone from Great Britain. The word *mask* said by an Englishman might be heard as *mosque* by an American. If you're confused about this, so are we!

---

[6]<l> is silent when followed by a consonant but is pronounced when followed by a vowel: *call them* /ˈkɔðəm/, *call it* /ˈkɔlɪt/.

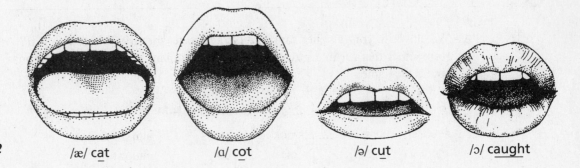

FIGURE 4-2 /æ/ c<u>a</u>t /ɑ/ c<u>o</u>t /ə/ c<u>u</u>t /ɔ/ c<u>au</u>ght

PRACTICE 5

The mouth only opens a little for /ə/ (like /ɪ/), whereas it opens a lot for /ɑ/. Try holding your teeth together when you say /ə/ so that your mouth won't open too much. Alternate between /ə/ and /ɑ/ and look in your mirror. /ə/ is also shorter than /ɑ/.

1. /ə/	*2.* /ɑ/
a. He had good **luck**.	He had a good **lock**.
b. They made a **hut**.[7]	They made it **hot**.
c. That **color** is beautiful.	That **collar** is beautiful.
d. Are the **cups** over there?	Are the **cops** over there?
e. She's standing by the **duck**.	She's standing by the **dock**.[8]
f. Is that **done**?	Is that **Don**?
g. He tried to **rub** them.	He tried to **rob** them.
h. I think they're **stuck**.[9]	I think they're in **stock**.

PRACTICE 6

The lips are rounded for /ɔ/ but not for /ə/. Check in your mirror.

1. /ə/	*2.* /ɔ/
a. They **cut** it.	They **caught** it.
b. I think it's a **gun**.	I think it's all **gone**.
c. His sister's **nutty**.[10]	His sister's **naughty**.[11]
d. When will it be **done**?	When will it be **dawn**?
e. The **bus** is coming soon.	The **boss** is coming soon.
f. We need **Chuck** right away.	We need **chalk** right away.
g. I know it was, **but** . . .	I know it was **bought**.
h. The **other** will sign it.	The **author** will sign it.

---

[7]hut = a small house, often made of wood
[8]dock = place where boats come in and stay
[9]stuck = can't be moved (past tense of "stick")

[10]nutty = crazy ("nut" is slang for a crazy person)
[11]naughty = bad, disobedient

EXERCISES FOR /æ, ɑ, ə, ɔ/

A. Watch while your teacher says one of the words silently. Which one is it? Remember that for many Americans and Canadians, the words in columns 3 and 4 sound the same.

	1. /æ/	2. /ə/	3. /ɑ/ ←	4. /ɔ/
a.	stack	stuck	stock	stalk
b.	cat	cut	cot	caught
c.	Dan	done	Don	dawn
d.	—	color	collar	caller
e.	cap	cup	cop	—
f.	hat	hut	hot	—
g.	calf	cuff[12]	—	cough
h.	lack	luck	lock	—

B. Study the spelling patterns for vowels 5–8. Say all example words aloud. Circle any words with pronunciations that surprised you. In the blank spaces or on a piece of paper, write down at least two other words with the *same vowel sound* and *same major spelling pattern* as the examples. Check your dictionary if necessary for <o>.

C. How is <a> pronounced in the following words? Divide into two groups: *later, matter, made, mad, back, bake, tobacco, act, ache, place, plastic.*

    1. /æ/ as in *fat* ___MATTER___

    2. /eɪ/ as in *day* ___LATER___

ADVANCED

D. How is <o> pronounced in the following words? Divide into two groups: *glove, lost, cover, color, tongue, wrong, long, done, gone, come, month, cross, other, often, of, off, on, one.*

    1. /ə/ as in *up* ___GLOVE, COVER, COLOR, TONGUE, DONE, COME, OTHER, OF, ONE, MONTH___

    2. /ɔ/ as in *talk* ___OFF, LOST, ON, WRONG, LONG, GONE, CROSS___ ___OFTEN, OFF___

SPANISH

E. In English, <au> is pronounced /ɔ/ as in *talk*, not /aʊ/ as in *loud*. /ɔ/ is a pure vowel; make sure that the quality stays the same throughout the vowel. Read the following sentences aloud.

    1. The audience applauded loudly.

    2. Laura's become a famous author.

    3. Our faucet leaked all autumn.

    4. His daughter was exhausted from doing the laundry.

    5. She paused automatically to taste the sauce.

    6. The awful sausage caused them to laugh.

---

[12]cuff = the end of pants or sleeves, which is often folded back

F. Record yourself reading the following sentences. Listen to make sure that the underlined vowels sound differently. If you have trouble with /ɔ/, you may pronounce it like /ɑ/ (but *not* like /oʊ/). If the spelling confuses you, write in the phonetic symbol for each italicized vowel.

1. It was very h*o*t in that h*u*t.
2. Good l*u*ck opening that l*o*ck.
3. Those n*u*ts are n*o*t very good.
4. D*o*n is all d*o*ne now.
5. A d*u*ck is swimming under the d*o*ck.
6. What c*o*lor is your c*o*llar?   *COIIAR ____ LONG*
7. The g*u*n is g*o*ne!
8. The b*o*ss never takes the b*u*s.
9. He'll be d*o*ne by d*a*wn.
10. Chuck threw away the ch*a*lk.
11. Don't c*ou*gh into the c*u*ff of your shirt.
12. Their d*o*g d*u*g a big hole in our lawn.
13. The c*o*p was wearing a black c*a*p.
14. Everything in st*o*ck was st*a*cked on the shelves.
15. She t*a*pped the t*o*p of the jar.   *✓ STAKED*
16. The s*u*n was so h*o*t that I had to wear a h*a*t.
17. They picked a b*a*g of cranberries in the b*o*g.
18. We caught the c*a*t sleeping on the c*o*t.

4.3 Vowels 9–11: /oʊ, ʊ, u/

VOWEL #9: /oʊ/

/oʊ/ is usually spelled <o> alone, <o> + Cȼ, <oa> + C, or <ow>.

<o>	no, close, open, cold	_____
<oa>	road, boat, toast	_____
<ow>	show, own, below	_____

Unusual spelling patterns are <ough>, <ou> + <l>, and <oe>.

<ough>	although, though, dough
<ou>	soul, shoulder, boulder, poultry
<oe>	toe, Joe, doe, foe
Exceptions:	sew, oh, folk, yolk, mauve, plateau, bureau /ˈbyʊroʊ/.

BʒoʊRoʊ

Móʊe

PRACTICE 7 | KOREAN and POLISH |

/oʊ/ has strong lip rounding that increases toward the end: think of moving toward /u/. The mouth is more open and the lips are only slightly rounded for /ɔ/ and not rounded for /ɑ/. Be sure to make /oʊ/ different from /ɔ/ and /ɑ/ even when it is followed by a consonant.

1. /oʊ/	*2. /ɔ/ or /ɑ/*
a. Do you know the **coast**?	Do you know the **cost**?
b. They **boat** a lot on Sunday.	They **bought** a lot on Sunday.
c. He's got a nice **loan**.	He's got a nice **lawn**.
d. Give me the **bowl**.	Give me the **ball**.
e. We sometimes **woke** early.	We sometimes **walk** early.
f. Did you see her **close** it?	Did you see her **closet**?
g. They **won't** fish.	They **want** fish.
h. That's not **Polish**.	That's not **polish**.[1]

VOWEL #10: /ʊ/

/ʊ/ is only found in a relatively small number of words. It is spelled <u> + C(C) or <oo> + C.

<u>   put, push, full, sugar, butcher _____

<oo>   good, foot, book, cookie, wool _____

It is spelled <oul> in three very common words (<l> is *silent*).

<oul>   could /kʊd/, would /wʊd/, should /ʃʊd/

Exceptions: woman /ˈwʊmən/, bosom /ˈbʊzəm/.

/u/ and /ʊ/ have the same major spelling patterns, but /ʊ/ occurs in far fewer words. Therefore, if you learn which words are pronounced with /ʊ/, you can assume that all the others are pronounced with /u/.

/ʊ/ l<u>oo</u>k   /u/ L<u>u</u>ke

FIGURE 4-3

---

[1]polish = a substance that makes a surface smooth and shiny

VOWEL #11: /u/

/u/ is most often spelled <oo>, <u> + CV, or <u> + Cȼ.

<oo>   too, room, food, choose, tooth _____

<u>   student, June, computer, flu _____

In a smaller number of words, it is spelled <ou>, <ew>, <o> alone, or <o> + Cȼ.

<ou>   you, soup, through, group, acoustic

<ew>   new, threw, blew, chew, sewer

<o>   do, who, to, tomb, lose, move, prove

Some less common spelling patterns are <ue>, <ui>, and <eu>.

<ue>   blue, true, avenue, pursue, due, Tuesday

<ui>   suit, fruit, juice, bruise

<eu>   neutral, pneumonia, feud, maneuver

Exceptions: two, shoe, canoe, lieutenant, beauty /'byuti/,

The <u>, <eu>, and <ue> spelling indicates /yu/ in many words, as in *union* /'yunyən/, *use* /yuz/, *accuse* /ə'kyuz/, *music* /'myuzɪk/, *huge* /hyudʒ/, and *pupil* /'pyupəl/ (see Sec. 15.4). Compare *fuel* /fyul/ with *fool* /ful/; *hue* versus *who*, and *cue* versus *coo*.

PRACTICE 8

/ʊ/ is a central vowel. The tongue position is closer to /ə/ and the lips are neutral or very slightly rounded. Push the tongue high and back and round the lips strongly for /u/. Alternate silently between /ʊ/ and /u/.

[handwritten: ROUPA DE LIMPAR CHAMINÉ]

1. /ʊ/

a. The black **soot**[2] was dirty.
b. The birds **could**.
c. Do you think he's **full**?
d. They **stood** it on the stove.
e. It was a long **pull**.
f. They **should** again.
g. That **looks** wonderful.
h. My **foot**'s cold.

2. /u/

The black **suit** was dirty.
The birds **cooed**.[3]   *[handwritten: PASSARINHO RUNGINDU]*
Do you think he's a **fool**?
They **stewed**[4] it on the stove.
It was a long **pool**.
They **shoot** again.
That **Luke's** wonderful.
My **food**'s cold.

Note that Vowel #12 is covered in Sec. 4.6.

---

[2]soot = black powder produced by burning

[3]coo = low, soft sound made by birds like pigeons

[4]stew = to cook in water for a long time

EXERCISES FOR /oʊ, ʊ, u/

A. Study the spelling patterns for vowels 9–11. Say all example words aloud. Circle any words with pronunciations that surprised you. Write down at least two other words with the *same major spelling pattern* and *same vowel sound* as in the examples. Check in your dictionary if necessary.

ADVANCED

B. How is \<o\> pronounced in the following words? Divide into two groups: *soft, most, cost, lost, post, cloth, clothes, won't, gone, phone, over, offer.*

1. /oʊ/ as in *no* ___MOST, POST, CLOThES, WONt, PHONE, OVER___
2. /ɔ/ as in *talk* ___SOFt, COSt, LOSt, CloTh, GONE, OFFER___

ADVANCED

C. How is \<o\> pronounced in the following words? Divide into two groups: *close, nose, lose, whose, rose, move, prove, hope, note.*

1. /oʊ/ as in *no* ___ClOSE, NOSE, ROSE, hOPE, NOtE___
2. /u/ as in *new* ___lOSE, WhOSE, MOVE, PROVE___

ADVANCED

D. How is \<o\> pronounced in the following words? Divide into two groups: *son, bone, done, alone, won, none, zone, above, love.*

1. /oʊ/ as in *no* ___bONE, AlONE, ZONE, AbOVE___
2. /ə/ as in *up* ___SON, DONE, NONE, lOVE, WON___
   A

ADVANCED

E. How is \<oo\> pronounced in the following words? Divide into two groups: *wood, food, foot, shoot, tooth, stood, fool, wool, books, boots.*

1. /ʊ/ as in *good* ___WOOD, FOOt STOOD, WOOL BOOKS___
2. /u/ as in *new* ___FOOD, tOOth, ShOOt FOOl, BOOtS___
   UUUU

F. /ʊ/. Record yourself reading the following sentences. Make sure to pronounce all underlined vowels as /ʊ/, regardless of their spelling.

1. That wou̱ld be a goo̱d book to read.
2. The bu̱tcher is a goo̱d cook.
3. You shou̱ld pu̱t more sugar in the pu̱dding.
4. The croo̱k stoo̱d behind some bu̱shes.
5. Cou̱ld I pu̱t my foo̱t on that cu̱shion?
6. "How much woo̱d wou̱ld a woo̱dchuck chuck
   If a woo̱dchuck cou̱ld chuck woo̱d?"
7. No one understoo̱d one wo̱man in my neighborhood.
8. That's a goo̱d-loo̱king woo̱l pu̱llover.

G. /ʊ/ *and* /u/. Record yourself reading the following sentences. Listen to make sure that the underlined vowels sound differently.

1. Luke loo̱ks terrible.
2. This shoe shou̱ld fit.
3. Coo̱k it and then let it coo̱l.
4. You cou̱ld hear the birds coo̱.
5. It's foo̱lish not to have a fu̱ll tank.
6. They serve really goo̱d foo̱d.

4.4 Vowels 13–15: /aɪ, aʊ, ɔɪ/

VOWEL #13: /aɪ/

/aɪ/ is usually spelled <i> or <y>, often followed by C¢.

<i>	I, decide, silent, find, child _____
<y>	cry, reply, hydrogen, type, bye _____

It is sometimes spelled <ie> or <igh>.

<ie>	lie, die, cried, fried
<igh>	high, sigh, light, night
Exceptions:	eye, buy, guy, guide, sign /saɪn/, design, paradigm, island /ˈaɪlənd/, aisle /aɪl/, height, seismic, choir /ˈkwaɪɚ/

In some American accents and in Canada, the starting point for /aɪ/ is more like /ə/ before voiceless consonants. Thus, the quality of the diphthongs in the following word pairs sounds noticeably different. /aɪ/ is also shorter before voiceless consonants. Ask your teacher or a friend to read these word pairs. Is the vowel quality the same or different?

1. /aɪ/ Before a Voiced Consonant or Alone	*2. /aɪ/ Before a Voiceless Consonant → [əɪ] in Some Accents*
a. prize	price
b. alive	a life
c. ride	write/right
d. rider	writer
e. high	height
f. lie	light

In many southern states, /aɪ/ is not a diphthong, but sounds more like a long front [aː].

VOWEL #14: /aʊ/

/aʊ/ is usually spelled <ou> + C(C), <ou> + C¢, or <ow>.

<ou>	loud, sound, thousand, house _____
<ow>	down, how, crowd, vowel, flower _____
Exception:	drought

In Canada, the starting point for /aʊ/ is more like /ə/ before voiceless consonants, as in *house* /haʊs/ → [həʊs]. Thus, the word *about* almost sounds like *a boat*.

VOWEL #15: /ɔɪ/

/ɔɪ/ is the least common vowel in English. It is spelled <oi> or <oy>.

<oi>	join, oil, poison, voice _____
<oy>	boy, enjoy, loyal, oyster _____

In many southern states, /ɔɪ/ is not a diphthong but sounds more like a long [ɔː]. Thus the word *oil* may sound like *all*.

EXERCISES FOR /aɪ, aʊ, ɔɪ/

(handwritten margin note: FOR NEXT WEEK)

A. Study the spelling patterns for vowels 13–15. Say all example words aloud. Write down at least two other words with the *same major spelling pattern* and *same vowel sound* as in the examples.

B. How is <i> pronounced in the following words? Divide into two groups: *quit, quite, child, children, writing, written, ride, ridden, to live, alive.*

  1. /ɪ/ as in *sick* ___Quit, CHILDREN, RIDDEN, to Live___

  2. /aɪ/ as in *I* ___Quite, CHILD, RIDE, Alive___

ADVANCED

C. How is <y> pronounced in the following words? Divide into two groups: *system, style, sympathy, typical, type, cycle, bicycle, analyze, analysis, rhythm, rhyme.*

  1. /ɪ/ ___System, simpathy, bicycle, Cycle___

  2. /aɪ/ ___Style, Type, analyze,___

ADVANCED

D. How is <i> pronounced in the following words? Divide into two groups: *machine, shine, routine, title, polite, police, unique, iron, require, pint.* → *PoTE*

  1. /i/ as in *be* _____

  2. /aɪ/ as in *I* _____

ADVANCED

E. How is <ie> pronounced in the following words? Divide into two groups: *tied, field, niece, applied, die, piece, brief, skies.*

  1. /i/ _____

  2. /aɪ/ _____

ADVANCED

F. How is <ou> pronounced in the following words? Divide into two groups: *country, county, cousin, double, doubt, young, lounge, tough, touch, trout, couch, trouble, south, southern.*   *sur do estado*

  1. /aʊ/ as in *now* _____

  2. /ə/ as in *up* _____

ADVANCED

G. How is <ow> pronounced in the following words? Divide into two groups: *low, allow, pillow, below, own, town, brown, powder, bowl, owl, cow, crow, plow, flow.*

  1. /aʊ/ as in *now* _____

  2. /oʊ/ as in *no* _____

4.5 Same Spelling, Different Pronunciation ADVANCED

Sometimes, stressed vowels may be pronounced differently in different forms of a word, such as *nature* /ˈneɪtʃɚ/ and *natural* /ˈnætʃɚəl/. Table 4-1 lists some common words of this type. In general, the pronunciations /eɪ, i, aɪ, oʊ, u/ are found in the root or base word (often a final syllable ending in silent <e>). The vowels change to /æ, ɛ, ɪ, ɑ, ə/ when suffixes such as <ic>, <al>, and <ity> are added.

Table 4-1
Alternations of Vowel Quality in Stressed Syllables

/eɪ/ *day*	/æ/ *fat*	/i/ *be*	/ɛ/ *get*
grade	graduate	meter	metric
grateful	gratitude	serene	serenity
nation	national	obscene	obscenity
nature	natural	supreme	supremacy
profane	profanity	equal	equity
sane	sanity	'athlete	athletic
state	static	compete	competitive
volcano	volcanic	recede	recession
to bathe	a bath	hero	heroine
		please	pleasant
		mean	meant

/aɪ/ *I*	/ɪ/ *sick*		
mine	mineral	read (present)	read (past)
line	linear	to breathe /brið/	a breath /brɛθ/
divine	divinity		
crime	criminal	/oʊ/ *no*	/ɑ/ *stop*
sign	signal, signature	cone	conical
decide, decisive	decision	phone	phonic
precise	precision	sole	solitude, solitary
revise	revision	atrocious	atrocity
Bible	Biblical	provoke	provocative
cycle	cyclical	joke	jocular
type	typical	diagnosis	diagnostic
wild	wilderness	'microscope	microscopic
child	children	know	knowledge
		close	closet
/u/ *new*	/ə/ *up*	to clothe /kloʊð/	a cloth /klɔθ/
reduce	reduction	clothing	
produce	production, productive	clothes	
consume	consumption		
resume	resumption	/aʊ/ *now*	/ə/ *up*
numeral	number	south	southern

EXERCISES

 A. Read through Table 4-1 aloud and make a note of words that are useful to you. Write in the phonetic symbol for each underlined vowel in the following sentences. Then record yourself reading them.

1. It's natural for children to love nature.

2. There was a story about the United Nations on the national news.

3. She took a bath after sunbathing for two hours.

4. The metric system measures length in meters.

5. Many athletes get athletic scholarships to attend college.

6. Take a deep breath, and then breathe out.

7. I didn't know he had so much knowledge about computers.

8. You could make some beautiful clothes with this cloth.

9. Do I sign my own name or get someone else's signature?

10. Certain types of plants are typically grown indoors.

11. The producers thought the cost of production was too high.

12. A person who comes from the South is called a Southerner.

B. Match the following words with their definitions. Use your dictionary or do this exercise in groups.

——— 1. wound /wund/   a. not dead (Adj)

——— 2. wound /waʊnd/   b. a kind of bird, a pigeon (N)

——— 3. row /roʊ/   c. to injure; an injury (V and N)

——— 4. row /raʊ/   d. a noisy argument, a quarrel (N)

——— 5. bow /boʊ/   e. a ribbon tied in a knot (N)

——— 6. bow /baʊ/   f. bend forward at the waist (V and N); the pointed end of a ship (N)

——— 7. dove /dəv/   g. a drop of liquid from the eye (N)

——— 8. dove /doʊv/   h. a soft, heavy metal; Pb (N)

——— 9. live /lɪv/   i. to go first; first position (V and N)

——— 10. live /laɪv/   j. to understand something written (V)

——— 11. wind /wɪnd/   k. understood something written (past V)

——— 12. wind /waɪnd/   l. to turn around and around (V)

——— 13. lead /lid/   m. turned around and around (past V)

——— 14. lead /lɛd/   n. past tense of *dive* (V)

——— 15. read /rid/   o. to rip or pull apart in pieces (V)

——— 16. read /rɛd/   p. moving air (N)

——— 17. tear /tiɚ/   q. to be alive (V)

——— 18. tear /tɛɚ/   r. a neat line of things (N); to move a boat using oars (V)

4.6 Vowel 12: /ɚ/ and Vowels Followed by <r>

VOWEL #12: /ɚ/

/ɚ/ is one of the most common vowels in American English. In *stressed* syllables, it is usually spelled <er>, <ur>, <ir> alone, or <ir> + C.

<er>   her, term, person, serve, were _____

<ur>   fur, hurt, church, urban, return _____

<ir>   sir, bird, first, girl, dirty _____

It is spelled <or> in a few common words beginning with <w>, and it is sometimes spelled <ear> + C.

<or>   work, word, worry, worm, world, worse, worth, attorney

<ear>   heard, learn, earn, early, earth, search, pearl, rehearse

Exceptions: journal, journey, courage, flourish,[1] colonel /ˈkɚnəl/

In *unstressed* syllables, /ɚ/ is usually spelled <er> or <or>, but it may also be spelled <ar>, <ure>, and occasionally <ur>.

<er>   father, butter, modern, perhaps, energy

<or>   doctor, visitor, information, effort, forget

<ar>   dollar, similar, sugar, collar, coward, backward

<ure>   picture, pleasure, figure, furniture, injure

<ur>   survive, murmur

Exceptions: glamour,[2] amateur /ˈæmətʃɚ/, soldier, iron /ˈaɪɚn/

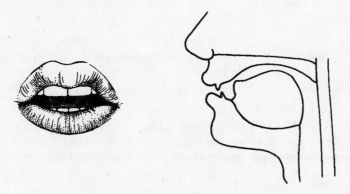

FIGURE 4-4
/ɚ/ her: Lip and tongue position

---

[1]Alternate pronunciations of *courage, flourish, worry,* and *hurry* are /ˈkɚɪdʒ/, /ˈflɚɪʃ/, /ˈwɚi/, and /ˈhɚi/.

[2]Most British <our> spellings (*flavour, colour, armour, vapour*) are spelled <or> in American English (*flavor, color, armor, vapor*).

PRACTICE 9

In /ɚ/, the back of the tongue is bunched up and pulled back, and the tip of the tongue is slightly raised but never touches the roof of the mouth. The lips are slightly rounded or pushed in at the sides.

	1. /ɚ/	*2.* /ə/
a.	A new **bird** is on that branch.	A new **bud** is on that branch.
b.	It's worth a **turn**.	It's worth a **ton**.
c.	The **hurt** is terrible.	The **hut** is terrible.
d.	I saw a beautiful **girl**.	I saw a beautiful **gull**.
e.	That's an ice**berg**.[3]	That's a nice **bug**.
f.	She made a **shirt**.	She made it **shut**.

	1. /ɚ/	*2.* /ɑ/
g.	It was a loud **shirt**.[4]	It was a loud **shot**.
h.	Her **curler** is dirty.	Her **collar** is dirty.
i.	They really **hurt**.	They're really **hot**.
j.	What a beautiful **birdie**![5]	What a beautiful **body**!
k.	Where's the **curtain**?	Where's the **cotton**?

VOWELS FOLLOWED BY <r>

When vowels are followed by <r>, their quality changes. In most accents of American English, no difference is made between /i/ and /ɪ/, /eɪ/ and /ɛ/, /oʊ/ and /ɔ/, or /u/ and /ʊ/ when <r> follows these vowels in the same syllable. For example, the word *here* may be pronounced either /hiɚ/ or /hɪɚ/: either way is acceptable. In addition, many Americans make no difference between the four back vowels /ɔ, oʊ, ʊ, u/ before <r> in conversational speech (*pore = pour = poor*).

Dictionaries write the vowel plus <r> sequences in different ways: sometimes <r> is written as a vowel and sometimes as a consonant. For non-native speakers, it is best to think of <r> here as a vowel, like /ɚ/, that blends together with the preceding vowel to form a diphthong in words like *here* /hiɚ/, *hair* /hɛɚ/, and *hire* /haɪɚ/. To make these diphthongs, make the first vowel sound and slowly move your tongue and lips to the position for /ɚ/. You will notice that the words *fire* and *fear* almost sound like two syllables /ˈfaɪ.yɚ/, /ˈfi.yɚ/, but that in *far* and *four*, the two sounds blend together more. In the word *fur*, however, the tongue does not change position during the vowel: there is just one vowel /ɚ/.

Some Americans from New York City, parts of New England (Boston), and the South, like many British English speakers, do not have an /ɚ/ sound. They "drop their r's." The sound /ɚ/ is replaced by a sound close to /ə/ in *fear, fair, fur, poor, fire, flower, employer*, which are pronounced approximately /fɪə/, /fɛə/, /fəː/, /pʊə/, /faɪə/, /flaʊə/, /ɪmˈplɔɪə/. In *far* and *for*, /ɚ/ is dropped completely (approximately /fɑː/, /fɔː/). In this accent, the following word pairs sound alike: *floor–flaw, source–sauce, fort–fought*. However, <r> is often pronounced as a linking sound when the following syllable begins with a vowel; for example, *the floor is wet* /ðəˈflɔrɪzˈwɛt/.

---

[3]iceberg = a very large piece of ice that floats in the ocean

[4]a loud shirt = a brightly colored shirt

[5]birdie = a small bird; in golf, one shot under par

It is best for non-native speakers living in North America to pronounce /ɚ/ whenever it occurs. It is considered more "correct" to pronounce your r's. Misunderstandings can be avoided in words like *cod, card, called, cord,* and *curd*. If a non-native speaker masters the vowel /ɚ/, he or she should have no trouble pronouncing the consonant /r/ and linking words ending in <r> to vowels.

Pronunciation of Vowels Followed by <r>

1.	fear	/fiɚ/	or	/fɪɚ/	6.	poor, pour	/pʊɚ/	or /pɔɚ/ (same as 5)
2.	fair, fare	/fɛɚ/	or	/feɪɚ/[6]		pure	/pyʊɚ/	or /pyuɚ/
3.	far	/fɑɚ/			7.	fire	/faɪɚ/	
4.	fur	/fɚ/			8.	flour, flower	/flaʊɚ/	or /ˈflaʊwɚ/
5.	for, four, fore	/fɔɚ/	or	/foʊɚ/	9.	foyer, employer	/fɔɪɚ/	or /ˈfɔɪyɚ/

Spelling of Vowels Followed by <r>

VOWELS #1 AND 2 + <r>: /iɚ/

Common spellings in stressed syllables:

    <ear>   fear, near, beard, dear

    <eer>   beer, cheer, queer, deer

    <ier>   pier, fierce, cashier

Other spellings:

        here, we're, sincere

        weird, irritate, satirical

VOWEL #6 + <r>: /ɑɚ/

Common spelling in stressed syllables:

    <ar>   far, start, hard, part, farm, large, dark, carton

Other spellings:

        heart, sergeant

VOWELS #10 AND 11 + <r>: /ʊɚ/ (OR /ɔɚ/)

Common spelling in stressed syllables:

    <ure>   sure, pure, cure, obscure, mature, jury

Other spellings:

        poor, tour, detour

VOWELS #3 AND 4 + <r>: /ɛɚ/

Common spellings in stressed syllables:

    <air>   air, hair, chair, fairy

    <are>   care, dare, scared

Other spellings:

        pear, wear, swear

        where, there, their, they're

VOWELS #8 AND 9 + <r>: /ɔɚ/

Common spellings in stressed syllables:

    <or>   forty, worn, port, force, afford

    <ore>   tore, wore, more, before, store

    <our>   four, pour, course, court

Other spellings:

        door, floor, board, drawer

        war, warm warn, ward, wardrobe, award, quart, quarter

---

[6]/fæɚ/ in some accents. In most accents, /æ/ doesn't occur in words which end in <r>. Words like *marry* and *carry* may be pronounced /ˈmæri/, /ˈkæri/ or /ˈmɛri/, /ˈkɛri/. Some people make no difference between *marry, merry,* and *Mary* in fast speech.

PRACTICE 10

The spelling patterns after <w> can be confusing. Stressed <or> is usually pronounced /ɔɚ/, and stressed <ar> is usually pronounced /ɑɚ/. However, in most words beginning with <w>, <wor> is pronounced /wɚ/, and <war> is pronounced /wɔɚ/. There are not many words like this, but they are very common. Say the following words aloud and make sure that the vowels sound the same in each column.

		1. /ɚ/	2. /ɔɚ/	3. /ɑɚ/
Regular spelling:	a.	burn	born	barn
	b.	stir	store	star
	c.	firm	form	farm
	d.	perk[7]	pork	park
After <w> and <qu>:	e.	were	war, wore	—
	f.	word	ward[8]	—
	g.	worm	warm	—
	h.	worse	wars	—
	i.	worship[9]	warship	—
	j.	—	warn, worn	—
	k.	work	—	—
	l.	world	—	—
	m.	worry	—	—
	n.	curt[10]	quart	cart

PRACTICE 11

Be sure to pronounce all the boldfaced words in column number 1 with /ɚ/ as in *were*.

	1. /ɚ/	2. /ɔɚ/ or /ɔ/
a.	They **were** unusual dresses.	They **wore** unusual dresses.
b.	What a long **word**!	What a long **ward**!
c.	Is that thing a **worm**?	Is that thing **warm**?
d.	The **worst** lasted two years.	The **wars** lasted two years.
e.	He wants to **worship**.	He wants the **warship**.
f.	She **worked** all night.	She **walked** all night.
g.	Do you like **working** a lot?	Do you like **walking** a lot?

---

[7]perk = to become lively and happy (to perk up); to percolate or make coffee

[8]ward = a large room or group of rooms in a hospital

[9]worship = to pray to God

[10]curt = abrupt, short, not polite (a curt answer)

EXERCISES FOR /ɚ/ AND VOWELS PLUS /ɚ/

A. Study the spelling patterns for /ɚ/, and write down at least two other words with the *same vowel sound* and *same major spelling pattern* as the examples. Memorize all the common words pronounced with /ɚ/ such as *word*, *work*, *earth*, etc., and try not to think of the spelling when you say them. Compare how /ɚ/ alone is spelled and how vowels followed by <r> are spelled.

B. Say the following words aloud and then write them in English spelling.

1. /wɚm/	**6.** /wɚd/	**11.** /hɚd/	**16.** /kɔɚt/
2. /wɔɚ/	**7.** /fɔɚm/	**12.** /sɚv/	**17.** /wɚs/
3. /lɚn/	**8.** /kɚl/	**13.** /wɛɚ/	**18.** /pyʊɚ/
4. /diɚ/	**9.** /fɚm/	**14.** /hɑɚd/	**19.** /ɚθ/
5. /fɑɚm/	**10.** /fiɚd/	**15.** /bɚn/	**20.** /wɔɚm/

C. How are the underlined letters pronounced in the following words? Divide into two groups: *farm, firm, burn, barn, hurt, heart, guard, carton, curtain, sugar.*

    1. /ɚ/ as in *fur* _____

    2. /ɑɚ/ as in *far* _____

D. How are the underlined letters pronounced in the following words? Divide into two groups: *hear, heard, beard, bird, first, fierce, earn, ear, girl, shirt.*

    1. /ɚ/ as in *fur* _____

    2. /iɚ/ as in *fear* _____

ADVANCED

E. How are the underlined letters pronounced in the following words? Divide into two groups: *were, where, wear, there, term, certain, earth, air, pear, pearl, learn.*

    1. /ɚ/ as in *fur* _____

    2. /ɛɚ/ as in *fair* _____

ADVANCED

F. How are the underlined letters pronounced in the following words? Divide into two groups: *wore, worn, worm, world, worry, award, coward, warning, work, worth, effort, afford.*

    1. /ɚ/ as in *fur* _____

    2. /ɔɚ/ as in *four* _____

ADVANCED

G. How are the underlined letters pronounced in the following words? Divide into two groups: *torn, turn, course, curse, cure, injure, nature, mature, journal, detour.*

    1. /ɚ/ as in *fur* _____

    2. /ʊɚ/ or /ɔɚ/ as in *poor* _____

SPANISH **H.** Record yourself reading the following sentences. Be sure to pronounce the underlined vowels in each sentence differently.

1. Birds don't have beards.
2. Did you hear what I heard?
3. She spent her earnings on new earrings.
4. I see fresh deer tracks in the dirt.
5. He fears being first.
6. Where were you last night?
7. Her hair was a mess.
8. People suffer many perils diving for pearls.
9. Warm air covered the earth.
10. Last term was terrible.
11. I usually walk to work.
12. Some wars are worse than others.
13. Do you know what the word *ward* means?
14. The worm wasn't warm.
15. The dress she wore wasn't worth much.

CHAPTER 5

Review of the Phonetic Alphabet and Vowels

5.1 Review Exercises

A. Write the phonetic symbol for the vowels in the following words. This can be done orally by giving the names of all the parts of the body.

1. face	8. eyeball	15. joint	22. back
2. mouth	9. pupil	16. hand	23. knee
3. lip	10. nose	17. palm	24. foot
4. tooth	11. nostril	18. finger	25. toe
5. tongue	12. head	19. thumb	
6. eye	13. neck	20. knuckle	
7. eyelash	14. body	21. nail	

B. Write the following words in English spelling.

1. /læf/	9. /ɔlˈdoʊ/	17. /lʊk/	25. /ləv/
2. /ˈfɔlɪŋ/	10. /θɪn/	18. /lɑɚdʒ/	26. /ʃrɪŋk/
3. /ˈmɛʒɚ/	11. /pliz/	19. /ʃaɪn/	27. /bɑks/
4. /ˈkələ/	12. /weɪst/	20. /tʃuz/	28. /dʒus/
5. /ʃɚt/	13. /ˈyuʒəli/	21. /dʒab/	29. /kæt/
6. /tʊk/	14. /waɪf/	22. /gɑt/	30. /ˈhæŋɚ/
7. /dək/	15. /ðɪs/	23. /lɔŋ/	31. /boʊθ/
8. /roʊz/	16. /maʊs/	24. /əˈvɔɪd/	32. /tətʃ/

ADVANCED **C.** Circle the word that doesn't rhyme (end with the same sound). If all the words rhyme, circle SAME. Write down the phonetic symbol for the vowel that is repeated.

	(a)	(b)	(c)	(d)		Symbol
EXAMPLE:	bead	feed	need	(bread)	SAME	/i/
1.	teen	mean	thin	scene	SAME	
2.	true	knew	zoo	do	SAME	
3.	food	would	good	should	SAME	
4.	higher	fire	liar	buyer	SAME	
5.	done	gone	son	fun	SAME	
6.	no	sew	toe	row	SAME	
7.	heard	board	third	word	SAME	
8.	much	such	touch	couch	SAME	
9.	lined	find	friend	signed	SAME	
10.	loan	phone	tone	none	SAME	
11.	shout	bought	taught	caught	SAME	
12.	head	red	said	dead	SAME	
13.	stays	raise	weighs	keys	SAME	
14.	crossed	lost	most	cost	SAME	
15.	laugh	safe	calf	graph	SAME	

D. Write the following words using the letters of the phonetic alphabet.

EXAMPLE: child = /tʃaɪld/

1.	boat	11.	there
2.	ring	12.	would
3.	sheep	13.	race
4.	think	14.	loud
5.	edge	15.	fight
6.	noise	16.	tie
7.	pleasure	17.	butter
8.	chew	18.	thought
9.	children	19.	cook
10.	hot	20.	tax

E. *Do in Groups.* The following words are among the 500 most frequently used words in English. Say each word aloud *very slowly,* stretch out the vowel sound, and try to isolate it (separate it from the word). Decide which of the 15 vowels each word contains and write the word in the proper column. For example, the word *eat* contains the vowel /i/, so it goes in column number 1; *hurt* contains the vowel /ɚ/ and goes in column number 12. When you are finished, read down each column and be sure all the words in that column contain the same vowel sound.

1. three	11. next	21. add	31. John	41. come	51. saw
2. most	12. would	22. who	32. work	42. like	52. out
3. point	13. mean	23. say	33. big	43. not	53. just
4. thought	14. home	24. look	34. through	44. first	54. find
5. down	15. built	25. place	35. black	45. does	55. turn
6. give	16. great	26. said	36. watch	46. dog	56. show
7. has	17. of	27. side	37. voice	47. piece	57. ran
8. stood	18. use	28. learn	38. why	48. found	58. put
9. leave	19. death	29. gone	39. young	49. friend	59. since
10. food	20. were	30. road	40. box	50. lived	60. change

ARE the Same

1 /i/ be	2 /ɪ/ sick	3 /eɪ/ day	4 /ɛ/ get	5 /æ/ fat	6 /ɑ/ stop	7 /ə/ up	8 /ɔ/ talk
eat 1 13	6 9 47 So used 15 built 33 big 59	16 23 25 60	26 said 11 19 49 friend	35 7 has 21 Add	31 John	17 39 young 45 53 41 come	36 40 43 46 51 29 gone

9 /ou/ no	10 /ʊ/ good	11 /u/ new	12 /ɚ/ her	13 /aɪ/ I	14 /au/ now	15 /ɔɪ/ boy
2 30 59 show 56 14 home	8 12 58 put 24	18 use 10 22 who 34 through	hurt 20 28 32 44 55	27 38 42 54	5 48 52	3 37

85.50

85
-90
5

890
145
15
-05

F. Write the phonetic symbol for the vowel sound of the underlined letters.

1. ———— a. Are you wri̲ting a letter?

   ———— b. I've already wri̲tten three letters.

2. ———— a. Who ta̲pped me on the shoulder?

   ———— b. I ta̲ped yesterday's lecture on my cassette recorder.

3. ———— a. I have to stop running. I'm out of bre̲ath.

   ———— b. I can't bre̲athe in here!

4. ———— a. I'm ho̲ping you can come to my party.

   ———— b. The girls are ho̲pping up and down on one foot.

5. ———— a. How many chi̲ldren do you have?

   ———— b. Do you know that chi̲ld's name?

6. ———— a. We enjoy sunba̲thing on the beach.

   ———— b. The dog needs a ba̲th.

7. ———— a. Put on your clo̲thes.

   ———— b. I'd like a piece of red clo̲th.

8. ———— a. I need to buy some fo̲od.

   ———— b. What happened to your fo̲ot?

G. Circle the letter of the word you hear.

1. (a. Leaving b. Living) is expensive.
2. Did you see the (a. cop b. cup)?
3. The sound wasn't (a. heard b. hard).
4. Would you like a (a. taste b. test)?
5. What happened to the (a. bowl b. ball)?
6. We've run out of (a. paper b. pepper) already.
7. The nurse will (a. feel b. fill) it.
8. The (a. suit b. soot) fell to the floor.
9. The (a. coast b. cost) is similar.
10. It was a rotten (a. peach b. pitch).
11. One of the (a. curtains b. cartons) is missing.
12. Where's the (a. boss b. bus)?
13. The (a. cat b. cot) doesn't look very good.
14. I think they need a (a. pool b. pull).
15. Where do they (a. work b. walk)?
16. Don't touch my (a. food b. foot)!
17. Did they find the (a. bag b. bog)?
18. It's a terrible (a. ward b. word).
19. The children (a. fail b. fell) a lot.
20. A white (a. color b. collar) is better.

5.2 Dialogues for Vowels

Write in the phonetic symbol of each underlined vowel if the spelling confuses you.

1. /ɪ/ *this,* /i/ *eat*

A: This fish is simply delicious.
B: I don't think so. Fish and chips is greasy.
A: Don't be silly. It's tender and crisp. Just eat a little.
B: But I'll be sick if I eat it.
A: You're kidding. You don't have to eat a big piece.
B: I don't have to eat any piece. We're not children.
A: You should at least try it. This is different.
B: This is ridiculous. I'm leaving.

2. /ɪ/ *live,* /i/ *leave*

A: Hello. May I please speak to Nick?
B: I'm afraid he isn't in.
A: Then may I leave him a message?
B: No. He doesn't live here any more.

3. /eɪ/ *cake,* /ɛ/ *best*

A: Who bakes better cakes? Betty or Trace?
B: Betty's cakes are great. They're tender and moist, and they definitely have a better flavor.
A: Trace makes all her cakes with fresh eggs and the best butter.
B: Is that why her cakes are so heavy?

4. /ə/ *love*

A: Your mother's so young and lovely.
B: Yes, I adore my mother and love to hug her.
A: And your younger brother is handsome and has so much money.
B: Yes, I just love my little brother.
A: Your uncle and cousins have also been very lucky.
B: They're such wonderful people and so much fun to be with.
A: But your other brother Bud has had some trouble.
B: Yes. Bud's out of the country and I hope he never comes back!

5. /ə/ *color,* /ɑ/ *collar,* /ɔ/ *cough*

A: I want my money back.

B: What's wrong?

A: Nothing much! It's the wrong color, it's uncomfortable, the collar's so tight it makes me cough, and the cuffs are too long.

B: May I see your sales receipt?

A: I haven't got it. But I bought it on Monday.

B: Then may I see the shirt? . . . Why, the collar's dirty, there are spots on the front, and the cuffs are covered with dust!

A: But I've only worn it once.

B: Once is enough!

Why, the collar's dirty, there are spots on the front, and the cuffs are covered with dust!

6. /oʊ/ *coast,* /ɔ/ *cost*

A: We just bought a boat and are moving to the coast in August.

B: But it costs so much to live on the coast.

A: We've thought it all over. We won't need many clothes because it's not so cold.

B: Please don't go. I'll be all alone and broken-hearted.

A: Don't get so choked up. You know it's only a few miles down the road.

7. /ʊ/ *good*

A: You're a good cook.

B: You like my cookies?

A: Mm. Especially your sugar cookies and your puddings.

B: How about the woman across the street, the butcher's wife?

A: She's good-looking, but you're the best cook in the neighborhood.

8. /ʊ/ *would,* /u/ *room*

A: I would like a double room for two nights.

B: What kind of room would you like?

A: A quiet room with a good view.

B: All our rooms have good views. They look out over a garden full of rose bushes, the pool, and the woods.

A: And could you provide a refrigerator full of food and two bottles of good wine?

B: That shouldn't be hard to do. By the way, who's that woman in the blue wool sweater?

A: That's my wife! Now would you mind getting back to the booking?

9. /ɚ/ *hurt*

A: Roll up your shirt sleeve. I promise you it won't hurt.

B: But will it work?

A: Certainly. You heard what the doctor said.

B: Nurse, are you perfectly sure it won't hurt?

A: I give you my word. You're awfully worried for a thirty-year old. You're not a little girl. Show some courage. Now turn around.

B: Ouch! That hurt! You got my nerve. That's the worst shot I've ever had.

A: And you're the worst patient I've ever had!

10. /ɚ/ *worm,* /ɔɚ/ *warm*

A: Earthworms love to bury themselves in the warm dirt.

B: And the birds can hear them. Early in the morning, they search and attack them without warning.

A: The poor worms make a worthless effort to get away, but the birds devour them without mercy.[1]

B: Unfortunately, it occurs everyday. There is war even in the world of nature.

11. /ɚ/ *early,* /ɛɚ/ *air,* /ɑɚ/ *far,* /ɔɚ/ *afford*

A: How far is it to the airport from here?

B: Well, it's about forty minutes by car if you go early in the morning.

A: How much does it cost to park there?

B: Thirteen dollars a day for long term parking.

A: I can't afford it. For a two-week trip, that's more than my airfare.

B: But it's worth it for a short journey. The hard part is finding a free space to park near the terminal.

A: I don't care about that. I walk to work every morning.

---

[1]devour /dɪˈvaʊɚ/ them without mercy = eat them up without showing any kindness

CHAPTER 6

Stress

Your driver's
license is invalid
in this state.

His grandmother is an invalid.

PREREADING QUESTIONS

How is the word *invalid* pronounced in these two sentences? In what way do they differ?

6.1 Stressed and Unstressed Syllables

English words can be made up of one syllable, two syllables, or many syllables. In all words of two or more syllables, one syllable is more prominent, louder, or more noticeable than the other syllables in that word. This strong syllable is **stressed** (accented), and the other weaker syllables are **unstressed** (unaccented).

Stressed syllables sound louder, are usually longer, and have clearer vowels and stronger consonants. In a word said in isolation, stressed syllables are higher pitched; in sentences, a pitch change (a change in melody from high to low or low to high) often occurs on stressed syllables.

Unstressed syllables sound softer, are usually shorter, and are frequently reduced or centralized. This means that the vowels tend to become /ə/, /ɪ/, /ɚ/, or /ʊ/, and the consonants are weaker. The pitch doesn't change direction on unstressed syllables.

PRETEST

How many syllables are in each of the following words? (See Sec. 6.3 if this is difficult for you.) Which syllable is stressed?

1. afford
2. offered
3. offering
4. develop
5. superstitious
6. distribute
7. distribution
8. television
9. promise
10. protect
11. preference
12. prefer
13. responsibility
14. refrigerator
15. characterizes
16. understand
17. misunderstand
18. unintelligible
19. individual
20. individuality

The English writing system does not tell you which syllables are stressed, although many other languages, such as Spanish, Italian, and Greek, use an accent mark to show stress. We will use the **symbol** /ˈ/ at the beginning of stressed syllables. For example, *beginning* /bɪˈgɪnɪŋ/ is stressed on the second syllable, and *syllable* /ˈsɪləbəl/ is stressed on the first syllable.

Stressing the correct syllable in a word is just as important as pronouncing the sounds correctly. Words and phrases can have different meanings depending on which syllable is stressed.

1. a. **in**valid /ˈɪnvəlɪd/ = a sick person
   b. in**va**lid /ɪnˈvælɪd/ = not valid or not correct

2. a. **Au**gust /ˈɔgəst/ = the name of the eighth month
   b. au**gust** /ɔˈgəst/ = majestic or grand

3. a. **per**sonal office /ˈpɚsənəl/ = a private office
   b. person**nel** office /pɚsəˈnɛl/ = the office where you apply for a job

4. a. **trus**ty /ˈtrʌsti/ = reliable or can be trusted
   b. trus**tee** /trʌsˈti/ = a person who manages someone else's property

5. a. **con**sole /ˈkɑnsoʊl/ = control panel in the front of a car
   b. con**sole** /kənˈsoʊl/ = to make someone feel better

Compare *innocence* /ˈɪnəsəns/, *in essence* /ɪnˈɛsəns/, and *in a sense* /ɪnəˈsɛns/. They are written differently, but in the spoken language, it is the location of stress that tells us which expression we mean.

6.2 Vowel Reduction

You may have already noticed that when we move the stress in English, we often change the vowel quality. When <a> in *invalid* is stressed, it is pronounced /æ/, but when <a> is unstressed, it is pronounced /ə/. This change in vowel quality from a stressed full vowel, such as /eɪ, ɛ, æ, ɑ, ɔ, oʊ, u/, to a short central vowel /ɪ/ or /ə/ (or sometimes /ʊ/ or /ɚ/) is called **reduction** or centralization of unstressed vowels. *Vowels in unstressed syllables immediately before or immediately after stressed syllables are usually reduced.* This is a very important characteristic of English, and it makes the difference between stressed and unstressed syllables very clear in the spoken language.

Non-native speakers are often not aware of vowel reduction because it is not indicated in the English writing system. Almost any vowel letter or group of letters may be pronounced as /ɪ/, /ə/, or /ɚ/ (before <r>) in unstressed syllables. Generally, the front vowels /i, ɪ, eɪ, ɛ/ (often spelled <i> or <e>) are reduced to /ɪ/ when they are unstressed; the low and back vowels /æ, ɑ, ɔ, oʊ, ʊ, u/ (often spelled <a>, <o>, <u>) are reduced to /ə/ when they are unstressed; and vowels followed by /ɚ/ (often spelled <er>, <ar>, <or>, <ure>) are reduced to /ɚ/ when unstressed.

Vowel Reduction

a	fast	breakfast
/ə/	ˈfæst	ˈbrɛkfəst/

Stressed	**Unstressed**
full vowel	**reduced vowel**

Compare the pronunciation of stressed and unstressed vowels in the following words.

Stressed Full Vowel		*Unstressed Reduced Vowel*	
1. ball	/ˈbɔl/	balloon	/bəˈlun/
2. fast	/ˈfæst/	breakfast	/ˈbrɛkfəst/
3. late	/ˈleɪt/	chocolate	/ˈtʃɑklɪt/
4. men	/ˈmɛn/	women	/ˈwɪmɪn/
5. social	/ˈsoʊʃəl/	society	/səˈsaɪəti/
6. recorder	/rɪˈkɔɚdɚ/	a record	/ə ˈrɛkɚd/

When vowels are reduced in unstressed syllables, it doesn't matter whether you use /ə/ or /ɪ/: you can say *below* as /bɪˈloʊ/ or /bəˈloʊ/, *decided* as /dɪˈsaɪdɪd/ or /dəˈsaɪdəd/, *Washington* as /ˈwɑʃɪŋtɪn/ or /ˈwɑʃɪŋtən/. For most non-native speakers, it is usually best to try to say /ɪ/.[1]

The vowels in many unstressed endings are reduced. Read the words in Table 6-1 aloud, and make sure to reduce the unstressed vowels. Don't think of the spelling.

---

[1]/ɪ/ is inherently short and easier for most students to say than /ə/ when it is unstressed. It is also perceptually more different from /ɑ/ and so brings out the fact that the reduced unstressed vowel is completely different from the full stressed vowel.

Table 6-1
Vowel Reduction in Unstressed Endings

Stress is on the *first* syllable of each word unless marked otherwise.

Spelling	Pronunciation	Examples
1. -ate	/ɪt/	climate, private, fortunate, accurate, chocolate (nouns and adjectives ending in \<ate\> only)
2. -ite	/ɪt/	definite, favorite, opposite, infinite
3. -age	/ɪdʒ/	garbage, beverage, cabbage, damage, marriage
4. -ive	/ɪv/	active, ag'gressive, negative, re'pulsive
5. -ace -ice	/ɪs/	furnace, menace, palace, terrace notice, office, ap'prentice, practice, promise
6. -ous	/əs/ OR /ɪs/	dangerous, jealous, fabulous, de'licious, sus'picious, re'ligious
7. -able -ible	/əbəl/	memorable, comfortable, de'pendable sensible, visible, ac'cessible, irre'sistible
8. -al -ile	/əl/	metal, personal, i'dentical, hori'zontal fertile, fragile, missile, sterile, imbecile
9. -cial -tial	/ʃəl/	social, special, arti'ficial, com'mercial, of'ficial influ'ential, partial
10. -ain	/ɪn/ OR /ən/	bargain, captain, certain, curtain, mountain (nouns and adjectives ending in \<ain\> only)
11. -ine	/ɪn/	engine, de'termine, discipline, e'xamine, famine, i'magine, medicine
12. -on	/ən/	carton, lesson, Jefferson, Washington
13. -tion -sion -gion	/ʃən/ /ʒən/; /ʃən/ /dʒən/	con'dition, revo'lution, communi'cation con'clusion, de'cision; per'mission region, re'ligion
14. -cian	/ʃən/	phy'sician, mu'sician, poli'tician
15. -ant -ent	/ənt/	instant, pleasant, im'portant, immigrant student, silent, moment, de'velopment
16. -cient -tient	/ʃənt/	ancient, ef'ficient, suf'ficient patient
17. -ance -ence	/əns/	entrance, distance, im'portance, ap'pearance silence, difference, e'xistence, residence
18. -ar -or -ure	/ɚ/	grammar, sugar, similar, pe'culiar major, color, tailor, visitor picture, nature, injure, furniture

EXERCISES

A. Read the following list of words and be sure to reduce the unstressed vowels. Underlined letters should all rhyme (have the same sound) regardless of their spelling.

1. /ɪt/   vis<u>i</u>t, lim<u>i</u>t, secr<u>e</u>t, clos<u>e</u>t, pil<u>o</u>t, min<u>u</u>te, bisc<u>ui</u>t, circ<u>ui</u>t, priv<u>a</u>te, chocol<u>a</u>te, fortun<u>a</u>te, favor<u>i</u>te, counterf<u>ei</u>t

2. /ɪs/   usel<u>ess</u>, weakn<u>ess</u>, off<u>i</u>ce, just<u>i</u>ce, prom<u>i</u>se, surf<u>a</u>ce, terr<u>a</u>ce, lett<u>u</u>ce, cris<u>i</u>s, bas<u>i</u>s, purp<u>o</u>se, religi<u>ou</u>s, danger<u>ou</u>s

3. /ə/   pharm<u>a</u>cy, emb<u>a</u>ssy, court<u>e</u>sy, jeal<u>ou</u>sy, pol<u>i</u>cy, com<u>e</u>dy, mel<u>o</u>dy, quant<u>i</u>ty

4. /ən/, /ɪn/,   brok<u>en</u>, doz<u>en</u>, rais<u>in</u>, reas<u>on</u>, butt<u>on</u>, urb<u>an</u>, fort<u>une</u>, eng<u>ine</u>,
   OR [n̩]   act<u>ion</u>, for<u>eign</u>, barg<u>ain</u>, mount<u>ain</u>

5. /əl/   midd<u>le</u>, unc<u>le</u>, trav<u>el</u>, lab<u>el</u>, loc<u>al</u>, met<u>al</u>, penc<u>il</u>, symb<u>ol</u>, caref<u>ul</u>,
   OR [l̩]   awf<u>ul</u>, soci<u>al</u>, fert<u>ile</u>, vin<u>yl</u>

6. /ɚ/   fing<u>er</u>, dang<u>er</u>, doct<u>or</u>, maj<u>or</u>, inj<u>ure</u>, pict<u>ure</u>, sug<u>ar</u>, popul<u>ar</u>, glam<u>our</u>

7. /əm/   it<u>em</u>, probl<u>em</u>, bott<u>om</u>, cust<u>om</u>, hands<u>ome</u>, alb<u>um</u>, aut<u>umn</u>,
   OR [m̩]   sol<u>emn</u>, rhyth<u>m</u>

B. Reduce the underlined vowel in the following words and make the unstressed syllable as short as you can. Check yourself in a mirror to make sure that you are not opening your mouth wide until you say the stressed syllable (the second syllable in these words) and that your lips are not rounded during <o> and <u>.

1. /ə/   <u>a</u>loud, <u>a</u>rrive, <u>a</u>ffect, <u>e</u>ffect, <u>e</u>nough, <u>o</u>'clock, <u>o</u>ffend, <u>u</u>nable, <u>u</u>ntil, <u>a</u>bove, <u>o</u>btain, <u>o</u>bserve, <u>a</u>dvice, <u>e</u>dition, <u>a</u>dmission

2. /tə/   t<u>o</u>day, t<u>o</u>night, t<u>o</u>morrow, t<u>o</u>gether, t<u>o</u>bacco, t<u>e</u>rrific

3. /sə/   s<u>u</u>ccess, s<u>u</u>ggest, s<u>e</u>lect, s<u>a</u>lute, c<u>e</u>ment, s<u>o</u>ciety, s<u>u</u>perior

4. /prə/   pr<u>e</u>pare, pr<u>e</u>fer, pr<u>e</u>vent, pr<u>o</u>nounce, pr<u>o</u>fessor, pr<u>o</u>fessional
   OR /prɪ/

5. /kən/, /kɪn/,   c<u>o</u>ntain, c<u>o</u>ntrol, c<u>o</u>nfuse, c<u>o</u>ntinue, c<u>o</u>ndition, c<u>o</u>nsider
   OR [kn̩]

C. Mark the stress and circle any underlined vowels that are reduced to /ə/ or /ɪ/.

1. t<u>a</u>ble, veget<u>a</u>ble, unfortun<u>a</u>te, rel<u>a</u>te, p<u>a</u>ge, cott<u>a</u>ge, r<u>ai</u>n, mount<u>ai</u>n, pl<u>a</u>ce, pal<u>a</u>ce, can<u>a</u>l, electric<u>a</u>l

2. <u>i</u>ce, just<u>i</u>ce, m<u>i</u>le, fert<u>i</u>le, eng<u>i</u>ne, f<u>i</u>ne, b<u>i</u>te, favor<u>i</u>te, al<u>i</u>ve, negat<u>i</u>ve

3. t<u>o</u>day, t<u>o</u>tal, m<u>ou</u>se, fam<u>ou</u>s, seas<u>o</u>n, al<u>o</u>ne, pl<u>a</u>nt, inst<u>a</u>nt, prev<u>e</u>nt, rec<u>e</u>nt

ADVANCED   **D.** *Exceptions.* Sometimes unstressed <i> is not reduced, but pronounced /aɪ/ in the endings <ine>, <ice>, <ite>, and <ile>. This often happens in compounds and academic words. Circle the underlined vowels that are reduced to /ɪ/ or /ə/.

1. exam<u>i</u>ne, outl<u>i</u>ne, determ<u>i</u>ne, Valent<u>i</u>ne, sunsh<u>i</u>ne, medic<u>i</u>ne, margar<u>i</u>ne

2. pract<u>i</u>ce, prejud<u>i</u>ce, sacrif<u>i</u>ce, parad<u>i</u>se, prom<u>i</u>se

3. satell<u>i</u>te, defin<u>i</u>te, appet<u>i</u>te, prerequis<u>i</u>te, paras<u>i</u>te, oppos<u>i</u>te

4. meanwh<u>i</u>le, miss<u>i</u>le, prof<u>i</u>le, percent<u>i</u>le, imbec<u>i</u>le, reconc<u>i</u>le

6.3 Dividing Words into Syllables CHINESE and JAPANESE

Non-native speakers whose language does not use the Latin alphabet sometimes have trouble deciding how many syllables are in a word. To figure out the number of syllables in a word, you need to *count the number of separate vowel sounds*. In most words, vowels alternate with consonants, so this is easy to do. For example, *develop* has three vowel sounds and three syllables. It does not matter to which syllable the medial consonants belong.[1] The word can be divided as /dɪ.ˈvɛ.ləp/, /dɪv.ˈɛl.əp/, or /dɪ.ˈvɛl.əp/. (The dictionary actually prefers the last way.) For pronunciation, a general way of dividing words into syllables is to divide between a vowel and following consonant or between two consonants in the middle of a word. The **symbol** /./ can be used to show the approximate syllable boundary. The important thing in English is the *number of syllables* and *which one is stressed*, not the precise location of the syllable boundary.

syl.la.ble	/ˈsɪ.lə.bəl/	CV.CV.CVC
ea.sy	/ˈi.zi/	V.CV
some.times	/ˈsəm.taɪmz/	CVC.CVCC
strong.ly	/ˈstrɔŋ.li/	CCCVC.CV
al.ter.nate	/ˈɔl.tɚ.neɪt/	VC.CV.CVC
pro.nun.ci.a.tion	/prə.nən.si.ˈeɪ.ʃən/	CCV.CVC.CV.V.CVC

There are two problems in trying to figure out the number of syllables from the English spelling system. First, you must know when the letter <e> is silent. Usually <e> at the end of a word is silent and therefore doesn't count as a syllable even when suffixes are added to the word. However, there are some exceptions. Adding <d> or <s> to certain words changes the number of syllables (see Chap. 14), and <le> after a consonant makes a new syllable.

<e> Silent	*<e> Makes a New Syllable*
typ~~e~~	may.be
for.tu.nat~~e~~	a.ble
for.tu.nat~~e~~.ly	
al.ter.nat~~e~~s	al.ter.na.ted
da.mag~~e~~	da.ma.ges
da.mag~~e~~d	

Secondly, you must know when a sequence of vowel letters stands for one vowel sound (one of the 15 vowels in Chap. 4) or two. Sequences of vowel letters that are *not* included in the spelling patterns in Chapter 4 are often pronounced as separate syllables.

<V + V> = One Syllable	*<V + V> = Two Syllables*
piece /pis/	sci.ence /ˈsaɪ.əns/
heat /hit/	cre.ate /kri.ˈeɪt/
peo.ple /ˈpi.pəl/	ge.o.gra.phy /dʒi.ˈɔ.grə.fi/

---

[1]Consonants that occur between two vowels in English belong to both syllables; that is, they are *ambisyllabic*.

The sequences <u + V> and <i + V> are typically pronounced as separate syllables, except in the unstressed endings in Secs. 6.2 and 6.4 (such as <tion> or in <qu + V, gu + V, su + V> where <u> = /w/). The vowels in all vowel sequences should be linked together smoothly. Use a short /w/ after back vowels and a short /y/ after front vowels for linking.

<u + V> = Two Syllables		*<i + V> = Two Syllables*	
gra.du.ate	/ˈgræ.dʒu.ʷeɪt/	ap.pre.ci.ate	/ə.ˈprɪ.ʃi.ʸeɪt/
si.tu.a.tion	/sɪ.tʃu.ʲʷeɪ.ʃən/	di.a.gram	/ˈdaɪ.ʸə.græm/
in.flu.ence	/ˈɪn.flu.ʷɪns/	ex.pe.ri.ence	/ɪk.ˈspi.ri.ʸɪns/
am.bi.gu.ous	/æm.ˈbɪ.gyu.ʷəs/	pe.ri.od	/ˈpi.ri.ʸəd/

EXERCISES

A. How many syllables are in the italicized words? Read each of the following sentences and be sure to pronounce the two italicized words differently.

1. I was never *hungry* when I traveled in *Hungary*.
2. *Please* do what the *police* say.
3. They cut *fiscal* expenditures for *physical* education.
4. Who's the *Senator* sitting in the *center*?
5. Did they *fix it*? Yes, it was *fixed*.
6. The audience *claps* when the tables *collapse*.
7. He plays the *organ* in a church in *Oregon*.
8. Are you *quite* sure the children were *quiet*?
9. She was *livid* when she found out he *lived* with another woman.
10. She wrote about her visit to the *dairy* in her *diary*.

B. How many syllables are in the italicized words? Which syllable is stressed? (Guess for now; see Sec. 6.4 for rules.) Practice saying the sentences aloud. Do not put a glottal stop (silence) between two vowel sounds in a row, but link them together smoothly.

1. My *niece* went on a *diet*.
2. He *reacted strangely* when he *reached* the end of the novel.
3. Every *individual* is *unique*.
4. The *officials appreciated* everyone's *cooperation*.
5. This *suit* is made of 100% *genuine* silk.
6. *Communism* started in the *Soviet Union*.
7. We must respond *immediately* to the *situation*.
8. You need to *punctuate* correctly and avoid using *abbreviations*.
9. Her answer was both *ambiguous* and *inappropriate*.
10. Is *creativity* encouraged in our *society*?

6.4 Stress Placement in Words of Two or More Syllables

How do you know which syllable is stressed in a word? You can look it up in a dictionary, you can remember how someone else said that word, or you can make an educated guess. The following general "rules" will help you to be able to stress the right syllable in most words. There are a number of exceptions, however.

In order to understand the rules, you need to know something about how words are made. Words are composed of prefixes (beginnings), suffixes (endings), and roots (base forms or stems).

> **Prefixes** are syllables added to the beginning of a word, such as <un-, de-, dis-, pre-, re-, micro-> as in *unhappy, decrease, disobey, predict, return, microscope.*
>
> **Suffixes** are syllables added to the end of a word, such as <-ly, -ment, -ness, -ful, -able, -logy> in *happily, development, kindness, careful, breakable, biology.*

Prefixes can change the meaning of a word (*unhappy* means not happy), and suffixes can change the meaning and the part of speech (*develop* is a verb, but *development* is a noun; *care* is a noun or verb, *careful* is an adjective, and *carefully* is an adverb; *biology* is the study of (<logy>) living things (<bio>) and it is a noun). A word can have several prefixes and/or suffixes.

The **root** is the center of a word, without prefixes and suffixes, and carries its basic meaning, such as *care* in *careful, carefully, careless, caring, carefree,* and *uncared-for.* Roots are generally one or two syllables long.

Compounds are words that have more than one root, each of which can exist as a word by itself, such as *newspaper* (*news + paper*), *policeman, baseball, lightbulb,* and *drugstore.* Many compounds are written as two words, such as *gas station, washing machine, tennis racket, pick out,* and *run into* (see Chap. 10).

Rules for Stress Placement in Words of Two or More Syllables

1. Stress the **first** syllable of two-syllable *nouns.*
   'table, 'mother, 'climate, 'record, 'insect, 'distance, 'preview

2. Stress the **root** of two-syllable *verbs* and *adjectives.*
   a. The second syllable is the root in:
      VERBS ap'pear, be'gin, con'clude, de'fine, dis'card, em'ploy, ex'plain, in'vent, pre'vent, pro'tect, to re'cord, re'serve
      ADJECTIVES a'live, com'plete, dis'tinct, e'nough, ex'treme, in'tense, pre'cise, re'mote
   b. The first syllable is the root in:
      VERBS 'harden, 'straighten, 'suffer, 'offer, 'finish, 'punish, 'baptize, 'damage, 'figure
      ADJECTIVES 'useful, 'cloudy, 'thirsty, 'pleasant, 'sudden, 'solid, 'jealous, 'active, 'proper, 'other
      Which pattern do you think is more common for verbs? for adjectives?
   c. Stress the root of other two-syllable words, such as adverbs and prepositions:
      a'bove, be'low, be'fore, be'sides, in'deed, un'til, per'haps, ex'cept, 'often, 'later, 'better, 'quickly

d. Some nouns are stressed on the root instead of the prefix and are exceptions to rule 1:[1] be'lief, de'sign, dis'pute, ex'cuse, mis'take, re'sult, sur'prise, suc'cess

3. Stress words of more than two syllables **according to their suffix**. See Table 6-2 for more examples.

   a. Stress the **suffix** in words ending in <*-ee, -eer, -ese, -ette, -esque, -ique*>, and verbs ending in <*-ain*>.
      emplo'yee, volun'teer, Vietna'mese, pictu'resque, enter'tain

   b. Stress the syllable **immediately before the suffix** in words ending with <*-ial, -ual, -ian, -ion, -cient, -ious, -eous, -uous, -ic, -ical, -ity, -ify, -itive, -itude, -logy, -graphy*>.
      of'ficial, per'mission, re'ligious, pro'ficient, e'lastic, 'practical, mi'nority, e'lectrify, re'petitive, 'attitude

   c. Stress the **second syllable before the suffix** in words ending with <*-ate, -ize, -ary*>.
      con'gratulate, un'fortunate, 'standardize, 'secretary

   d. Stress does not change but remains on the same syllable as other forms of the word, when most other suffixes are added, such as <*-able, -al, -ed, -en, -er, -est, -ful, -ing, -ish, ist, -ism, -less, -ly, -ment, -ness, -ous, -y*>, etc.
      pro'fessional (pro'fession), be'lievable (be'lieve), 'beautiful ('beauty), 'happiness ('happy), em'ployment (em'ploy), 'punishment ('punish), of'ficially (of'ficial), con'gratulated (con'gratulate)

4. Stress *compound nouns* on the first element (first *word*).
   'fireman, 'typewriter, 'gas station, po'liceman, 'wastepaper basket

5. Stress *two-word verbs* more strongly on the last word.
   pick 'up, turn 'off, drop 'out, put a'way, do 'over

6. Stress *reflexive pronouns* on the last syllable.
   my'self, your'self, him'self, them'selves, our'selves, your'selves

7. There is no sure rule for figuring out where to stress words of more than two syllables which do *not* fall into the above categories. In general, nouns and three-syllable adjectives tend to be stressed on the *first syllable* (an extension of rule 1). However, some long words may be stressed on the *first syllable of the root* (an extension of rule 2). This includes verbs beginning with prefixes such as <inter-, over-, under-, circum-, counter->. Other words simply follow rule 3d and are stressed on the same syllable as a shorter related word.

   a. Stress on the first syllable:
     ADJECTIVES: 'confident, 'difficult, 'excellent, 'possible, 'natural, 'negative, 'relevant, 'similar
     NOUNS: 'alphabet, 'benefit, 'character, 'democrat, 'energy, 'influence, 'interview, 'laboratory, 'microphone, 'origin, 'preference

   b. Stress on the first syllable of the root:
     bi'lingual, com'parative, circum'vent, contra'dict, de'velop, e'mergency, im'portant, inde'pendent, intro'duce, ir'regular, misunder'stand, over'come, un'natural

   c. Stress the same as a related word:
     de'clarative (de'clare), 'decorative ('decorate)

---

[1]Words borrowed from foreign languages are often stressed on the last syllable: *ci'gar, ga'rage, bro'chure, re'gime, mo'rale,* and *di'vine.*

Table 6-2
Stress Placement and Suffixes

Stressed syllables are in **boldface type**.

These suffixes are stressed:

-ain	/'eɪn/	(verbs only) enter**tain**, ascer**tain**, main**tain**
-ee	/'i/	emplo**yee**, refu**gee**, trai**nee**
-eer	/'iɚ/	volun**teer**, engi**neer**, ca**reer**
-ese	/'iz/	Japa**nese**, Portu**guese**, Chi**nese**
-ette	/'ɛt/	ciga**rette**, silhou**ette**, cas**sette**
-esque	/'ɛsk/	pictu**resque**, gro**tesque**
-ique	/'ik/	tech**nique**, u**nique**, an**tique**

Stress falls on the syllable immediately before these suffixes:

-ial	/iəl/	me**mor**ial, **triv**ial, pro**ver**bial
-cial	/ʃəl/	fi**nan**cial, arti**fi**cial, com**mer**cial
-tial	/ʃəl/	es**sen**tial, presi**den**tial, influ**en**tial
-ual	/uəl/	intel**lec**tual, indi**vid**ual, **vis**ual
-ian	/iən/	vege**tar**ian, pe**des**trian, Ca**na**dian
-cian	/ʃən/	phy**si**cian, poli**ti**cian, mathema**ti**cian
-sian	/ʒən/	Pa**ri**sian, Indo**ne**sian, **A**sian
-ion	/yən/	o**pin**ion, com**pan**ion, **mill**ion
-tion	/ʃən/	defi**ni**tion, demon**stra**tion, pro**duc**tion
-ssion	/ʃən/	pro**fes**sion, dis**cus**sion, per**mis**sion
-sion	/ʒən/	con**clu**sion, ex**plo**sion, oc**ca**sion
-cient	/ʃənt/	suf**fi**cient, ef**fi**cient, de**fi**cient, **an**cient
-tient	/ʃənt/	im**pa**tient
-ious	/iəs/	**cur**ious, lux**ur**ious, mys**ter**ious
-eous	/iəs/	simul**ta**neous, spon**ta**neous, **cour**teous
-cious	/ʃəs/	sus**pi**cious, de**li**cious, **con**scious
-tious	/ʃəs/	am**bi**tious, super**sti**tious, **cau**tious
-geous	/dʒəs/	advan**ta**geous, cou**ra**geous
-gious	/dʒəs/	re**li**gious
-uous	/yuəs/	am**big**uous, con**tin**uous, **stren**uous
-ic	/ɪk/	fan**tas**tic, re**al**istic, ener**get**ic
-ical	/ɪkəl/	**phys**ical, **class**ical, psycho**log**ical
-ity	/ɪti/	pub**lic**ity, pos**si**bility, hu**mid**ity
-ify	/ɪfaɪ/	(verbs) **class**ify, **terr**ify, hu**mid**ify
-itive	/ɪtɪv/	re**pet**itive, in**fin**itive, **sens**itive
-itude	/ɪtud/	**att**itude, **sol**itude, in**ep**titude
-logy	/lədʒi/	bi**ol**ogy, zo**ol**ogy, arche**ol**ogy
-graphy	/grəfi/	ge**og**raphy, autobi**og**raphy, pho**tog**raphy

Stress falls two syllables before these suffixes:

-ate	/eɪt/	(verbs) **op**erate, ap**pre**ciate, ex**ag**gerate
	/ɪt/	(adjectives and nouns) **del**icate, un**for**tunate, cer**tif**icate
-ize	/aɪz/	(verbs) a**pol**ogize, **crit**icize, **rec**ognize
-ary	/ɛri/ or /ɛɚi/	**sec**retary, con**tem**porary, vo**cab**ulary

Important exceptions:

-ee	com**mit**tee, **cof**fee
-ic	**Ar**abic, a**rith**metic, **Cath**olic /'kæθlɪk/, **lu**natic, **rhet**oric, **pol**itics
-ion	**tel**evision, **in**tersection
-ize	**reg**ularize, **char**acterize, **hos**pitalize, **per**sonalize, **nat**uralize
-tary /tri/	ele**men**tary /ɛlə'mɛntri/, supple**men**tary, docu**men**tary

EXERCISES

A. The following prefixes are often used in verbs. Write down at least two more *two-syllable verbs* (stressed on the root) for each prefix. Use your dictionary if necessary. Then practice saying the words aloud.

1. a-	/ə/	accuse, apply,	_____
2. ad-	/əd/	advise, admit,	_____
3. be-	/bɪ/	believe, behave,	_____
4. con-,	/kən/		
com-	/kəm/	convince, compare,	_____
5. de-	/dɪ/	decide, depart,	_____
6. dis-	/dɪs/	dismiss, discuss,	_____
7. en-,	/ɪn/		
em-	/ɪm/	enjoy, employ,	_____
8. ex-	/ɪks/	expect, excuse,	_____
9. in-,	/ɪn/		
im-	/ɪm/	involve, import,	_____
10. mis-	/mɪs/	mislead, misplace,	_____
11. ob-	/əb/	object, obtain,	_____
12. out-	/aʊt/	outlive, outdo,	_____
13. per-	/pɚ/	perform, permit,	_____
14. pre-	/prɪ/	prefer, prepare,	_____
15. pro-	/prə/	protect, propose,	_____
16. re-	/rɪ/	remove, reject,	_____
17. sub-,	/səb/		
sup-	/səp/	subtract, supply,	_____
18. un-	/ən/	undo, untie,	_____

B. The root is also stressed in longer verbs with the prefixes <inter>, <over>, and <under>, but nouns beginning with these prefixes are stressed on the first syllable: *inter'fere*, *over'sleep*, and *under'stand* (verbs), but *'interview*, *'overcoat*, and *'underwear* (nouns). Can you think of one more *verb* beginning with each prefix? (Note: *interpret* /ɪn'tɚprɪt/ is an exception.)

1. inter-	/ɪntɚ/	interfere, interact,	_____
2. over-	/oʊvɚ/	oversleep, overhear,	_____
3. under-	/əndɚ/	understand, underestimate,	_____

C. Which syllable is stressed in the following words? (Which are nouns? Which are verbs?)

1. captain, bargain, certain, complain, contain, detain
2. entertain, fountain, maintain, mountain, remain

ADVANCED

D. Which syllable is stressed in the following verbs? (Hint: Which have prefixes listed in Exercise A?)

    1. alter, defer, differ, enter, offer, order, prefer, refer, suffer, occur

    2. dictate, donate, frustrate, inflate, locate, relate, vacate, vibrate

E. Read through Table 6-2 (p. 69) aloud. Try to think of at least one more word for each suffix.

F. Mark the stress in the following words (or underline the stressed syllables).

    EXAMPLE: 'energy ener'getic

1. influence	**15.** courage
2. influential	**16.** courageous
3. office	**17.** boutique
4. official	**18.** proficient
5. bibliography	**19.** editor
6. bibliographical	**20.** editorial
7. mountaineer	**21.** demonstrate
8. referee	**22.** demonstration
9. elastic	**23.** identify
10. elasticity	**24.** identical
11. organize	**25.** necessary
12. organization	**26.** necessity
13. cassette	**27.** Vietnamese
14. superstitious	**28.** gratitude

G. Mark the stress in the following words (or underline the stressed syllables).

1. detain	**13.** moral
2. furious	**14.** morality
3. sensitive	**15.** substance
4. humid	**16.** substantial
5. humidity	**17.** origin
6. magnify	**18.** originate
7. magnification	**19.** optical
8. magnitude	**20.** optician
9. history	**21.** geology
10. historian	**22.** geological
11. compete	**23.** secondary
12. competitive	**24.** pioneer

H. Mark the stress in the following words.

1. local, location, locality, locally
2. electric, electricity, electrician, electrify, electrical
3. terror, terrible, terrify, terrific
4. magnet, magnetize, magnetic, magnetism
5. critic, critical, critique, criticism, criticize
6. technique, technical, technician, technology
7. commerce, commercial, commercialize, commercialization
8. certify, certificate, certification
9. memory, memorial, memorize, memorization
10. industry, industrial, industrialize, industrialization, industrious

 I. Mark the stress in the italicized words. Practice reading the sentences aloud and moving the stress. Record yourself and play it back.

1. The *mystery* was solved in a *mysterious* way.
2. The movie *terrified* the children, but the teenagers thought it was *terrific*.
3. Many *refugees* have found *refuge* in this country.
4. It's *possible* that he'll pass the course, but there's no *possibility* of his getting an A.
5. How large is the *magnetic* field of this *magnet*?
6. Those cookies are *perfect*; they're cooked to *perfection*.
7. I'm *confident* that they will not release this *confidential* information.
8. *Congratulations*! I *congratulate* you on a job well done.
9. A *mountaineer* is a person who climbs *mountains*.
10. How many *physicians* have studied *physics*?
11. The cars were widely *publicized*, but the *publicity* didn't improve sales.
12. You need an *electrician* to repair the *electrical* wiring.
13. He didn't *qualify* for the job because his *qualifications* weren't good enough.
14. Many *psychologists* use *psychological* tests.

CHAPTER 7

Stress (Advanced)

PREREADING QUESTIONS

How is the word *present* pronounced in the following sentences?
   a. I gave him a present.
   b. I'm going to present a paper at the meeting.

How is the word *separate* pronounced in the following sentences?
   a. We'd like separate rooms.
   b. We need to separate the desks.

7.1 Stress and Vowel Reduction in Noun–Verb Word Pairs

TWO-SYLLABLE NOUNS AND VERBS

Certain two-syllable words are stressed on the **first** syllable when they are **nouns** and on the **last** syllable (the root) when they are **verbs**. This is a special case of the first two stress placement rules.

PRACTICE 1

Read each word first as a noun and then as a verb. Be sure to *reduce* and *shorten* the vowel in the first syllable when it is unstressed.

		1. Noun	2. Verb
a.	record	/ˈrɛkɚd/	/rɪˈkɔɚd/
b.	conduct	/ˈkɑndəkt/	/kənˈdəkt/
c.	addict[1]	/ˈædɪkt/	/əˈdɪkt/
d.	protest	/ˈproʊtɛst/	/prəˈtɛst/
e.	progress	/ˈprɑgrəs/	/prəˈgrɛs/
f.	permit	/ˈpɚmɪt/	/pɚˈmɪt/
g.	increase	/ˈɪŋkris/	/ɪŋˈkris/
h.	conflict	/ˈkɑnflɪkt/	/kənˈflɪkt/
i.	desert[2]	/ˈdɛzɚt/	/dɪˈzɚt/
j.	contract[3]	/ˈkɑntrækt/	/kənˈtrækt/
k.	object	/ˈɑbdʒɪkt/	/əbˈdʒɛkt/
l.	subject[4]	/ˈsəbdʒɪkt/	/səbˈdʒɛkt/
m.	convict[5]	/ˈkɑnvɪkt/	/kənˈvɪkt/
n.	defect[6]	/ˈdifɛkt/	/dɪˈfɛkt/
o.	insult	/ˈɪnsəlt/	/ɪnˈsəlt/
p.	present	/ˈprɛzənt/	/prɪˈzɛnt/
q.	produce[7]	/ˈproʊdus/	/prəˈdus/
r.	rebel[8]	/ˈrɛbəl/	/rəˈbɛl/
s.	project	/ˈprɑdʒɪkt/	/prəˈdʒɛkt/
t.	suspect[9]	/ˈsəspɛkt/	/səsˈpɛkt/

---

[1]addict = (N) person who can't stop a harmful habit; (V) to have an uncontrollable habit

[2]desert = (N) very dry sandy area of land; (V) to leave completely. Note: *dessert* /dɪˈzɚt/, the sweet after a meal, is pronounced the same as the verb *desert*.

[3]contract = (N) written agreement; (V) to become smaller, to get an illness

[4]subject = (N) topic; person or animal in an experiment; (V) to cause to experience

[5]convict = (N) person sent to jail for a crime; (V) to find guilty of a crime

[6]defect = (N) something wrong; (V) to leave and join the opposing side

[7]produce = (N) fresh fruit and vegetables; (V) to make, grow

[8]rebel = (N) person who fights against;(V) to fight against anyone in power

[9]suspect = (N) person who might be guilty of a crime; (V) to believe to be true

PRACTICE 2

Now practice some of these words in sentences.

1. The band *re'corded* a new *'record* yesterday.
2. He *pre'sented* his wife with a beautiful *'present*.
3. They're *con'ducting* an investigation into his *'conduct*.
4. The criminal *'suspect* was *sus'pected* of robbing three banks.
5. The *'desert* is so dry that it is usually *de'serted*.

Related Forms.   When nouns are used like adjectives (before other nouns), they retain stress on the first syllable.

'Contract negotiations were completed last night.
There was a *'record* amount of rainfall this spring.

When <ing> or <ed> are added to verbs to make adjectives, stress remains on the second syllable.

The *re'cording* studio is closed.
He's a *con'victed* robber.

When other endings are added, such as <er> or <or>, the stress tends to be the same as the most closely related word.

A *con'ductor* is a person who *con'ducts* an orchestra.

Exceptions.   Not all two-syllable words that are both nouns and verbs follow this stress rule. Stress is on the *first* syllable for both the noun and verb form of *accent, comfort, purchase, promise,* and *rescue*. Stress is on the *second* syllable for both the noun and verb form of *control, surprise,* and many words beginning with the prefixes <de, dis, re>, such as *delay, demand, desire, dispute, report, result,* and *review*. Either syllable can be stressed in *research* and *detail*.

NOUNS, VERBS, AND ADJECTIVES ENDING IN <ate>

Words ending in <ate> that are three or more syllables long are stressed on the third syllable from the end. In **adjectives and nouns**, the <ate> ending is **reduced** to /ɪt/ (pronounced like the word *it*), but in **verbs**, the <ate> ending is pronounced as /eɪt/ (like the word *eight*).

PRACTICE 3

Read the following words both ways. Be sure to really shorten and change the vowel quality in adjectives and nouns, and be sure to put primary stress on the **third syllable from the end**, *not* on <ate>.

		1. Noun or Adjective <ate> = /ɪt/	2. Verb <ate> = /eɪt/
a.	graduate	/ˈgrædʒuɪt/	/ˈgrædʒueɪt/
b.	separate	/ˈsɛpərɪt/ → /ˈsɛprɪt/	/ˈsɛpəreɪt/
c.	estimate	/ˈɛstɪmɪt/	/ˈɛstɪmeɪt/
d.	duplicate[10]	/ˈduplɪkɪt/	/ˈduplɪkeɪt/
e.	approximate	/əˈpraksɪmɪt/	/əˈpraksɪmeɪt/
f.	alternate[11]	/ˈɔltɚnɪt/	/ˈɔltɚneɪt/
g.	moderate[12]	/ˈmadɚɪt/	/ˈmadɚeɪt/
h.	appropriate[13]	/əˈproupriɪt/	/əˈprouprieɪt/
i.	elaborate[14]	/əˈlæbɚɪt/ → /əˈlæbrɪt/	/əˈlæbɚeɪt/
j.	deliberate[15]	/dɪˈlɪbɚɪt/ → /dɪˈlɪbrɪt/	/dɪˈlɪbɚeɪt/
k.	accurate	/ˈækyərɪt/	—
l.	consulate	/ˈkansəlɪt/	—
m.	delicate[16]	/ˈdɛlɪkɪt/	—
n.	fortunate	/ˈfɔɚtʃənɪt/	—
o.	considerate[17]	/kənˈsɪdɚɪt/	—
p.	appreciate	—	/əˈpriʃieɪt/
q.	assassinate[18]	—	/əˈsæsɪneɪt/
r.	demonstrate	—	/ˈdɛmənstreɪt/
s.	exaggerate	—	/əgˈzædʒəreɪt/
t.	refrigerate	—	/rɪˈfrɪdʒəreɪt/

---

[10]duplicate = (N/ADJ) an exact copy; (V) to copy

[11]alternate = (N/ADJ) the second choice; (V) to take turns

[12]moderate = (N/ADJ) in the middle, not extreme; (V) to make less extreme

[13]appropriate = (ADJ) correct, suitable; (V) to set aside money for a purpose

[14]elaborate = (ADJ) detailed, complicated; (V) to add detail

[15]deliberate = (ADJ) on purpose; (V) to discuss, consider carefully

[16]delicate = finely made, sensitive, easily broken

[17]considerate = thoughtful of other people

[18]assassinate = to kill a person for political reasons

Related Forms. The vowel is also reduced in adverbs ending in <ately>, such as *for-tunately* /ˈfɔɚtʃənɪtli/. Be sure to keep the stress on the same syllable when suffixes that do not move stress, such as <ing>, <ed>, <ly>, and <or>, are added. This may result in the stress being on the fourth syllable from the end of the word. Of course, when suffixes like <tion> and others in Table 6-2 are added, the stress shifts.

PRACTICE 4 | SPANISH and GREEK |

Be sure that the main stress falls on different syllables in the following pairs of sentences.

1. It's a re**frig**erator.   It needs refrig**era**tion.
2. Where's the **op**erator?   When did she have an ope**ra**tion?
3. He con**gra**tulated her.   He offered his congratu**la**tions.
4. He was as**sas**sinated.   There was an assassi**na**tion.
5. What are they **cel**ebrating?   What's the cele**bra**tion?
6. It's ap**prox**imately $50.   It's only an approxi**ma**tion.
7. He treated her con**sid**erately.   He took it into conside**ra**tion.

EXERCISES

 A. Mark the stress in all words of two or more syllables and practice reading the sentences. Record yourself and play it back. Did you stress the proper syllable? Did you reduce unstressed syllables?

1. John Williams is conducting the concert tonight.
2. The students rebelled over the increase in tuition.
3. The rebels objected to their treatment by the authorities.
4. The Sahara Desert is increasing in size.
5. The union hasn't made any progress in getting a better contract.
6. They conducted a complete investigation of the project.
7. The police suspect that the convict is hiding in that deserted house.
8. He defected from the Democratic Party because of the conflict.
9. The criminal suspect protested that he wasn't informed of his rights.
10. Several subjects in the study contracted pneumonia /nəˈmoʊnyə/.
11. Because of the defects in construction, they didn't receive a permit.
12. The addict was convicted of selling drugs to support his addiction.

B. Circle the correct pronunciation of the <ate> ending and mark the stress in the underlined words.

1. A: Are you a grad<u>ate</u> student?   /eɪt - ɪt/

   B: Yes, and I hope to gradu<u>ate</u> next spring.   /eɪt - ɪt/

2. A: How much do they estim<u>ate</u> it will cost to fix your car?   /eɪt - ɪt/

   B: They gave me an estim<u>ate</u> of $500.   /eɪt - ɪt/

3. A: Has Susan separ<u>ated</u> from her husband?   /eɪt - ɪt/

   B: Yes, but I think it will be difficult for them to live separ<u>ately</u>.   /eɪt - ɪt/

4. A: I asked Professor Jones a question, and he elabor<u>ated</u> on it for ten minutes.   /eɪt - ɪt/

   B: Yes, he always gives elabor<u>ate</u> explanations.   /eɪt - ɪt/

5. A: My doctor told me to get a moder<u>ate</u> amount of exercise.   /eɪt - ɪt/

   B: You could try swimming and jogging on altern<u>ate</u> days.   /eɪt - ɪt/

   A: Or I could altern<u>ate</u> walking and driving to work.   /eɪt - ɪt/

6. A: Johnnie deliber<u>ately</u> tried to set the house on fire, but fortun<u>ately</u> I caught him just in time!   /eɪt - ɪt/   /eɪt - ɪt/

   B: I think you're exagger<u>ating</u>.   /eɪt - ɪt/

7. A: I need to send in duplic<u>ate</u> copies of my visa application to the French Consul<u>ate</u>.   /eɪt - ɪt/   /eɪt - ɪt/

   B: There's a duplic<u>ating</u> machine in my office. I can copy it for you.   /eɪt - ɪt/

   A: That's very consider<u>ate</u> of you. I'd really appreci<u>ate</u> it.   /eɪt - ɪt/   /eɪt - ɪt/

C. Mark the stress in all words of two or more syllables. Then read and record the paragraph.

A large demonstration was held this morning in front of the administration building. Students were protesting a 50% increase in tuition fees proposed by the trustees of the university. Both undergraduate and graduate students objected strongly to the proposal. They boycotted classes and marched in picket lines, demanding that administrators take action to relieve the drastic financial crisis. There were conflicting reports of the number of people involved in the protest, but some estimates were as high as 2,000. The Associate Dean said that the situation was very delicate and that increased efforts would be made to resolve the conflict.

7.2 Alternation of Reduced and Full Vowels

In English, there is a tendency to **alternate** full vowels and reduced vowels. In many long words, the stressed syllable and alternating syllables have full vowels, while the rest of the syllables have reduced vowels.

pho	to	graph	pho	**to**	gra	phy	pho	to	**gra**	phic
/ˈfoʊ	tə	græf/	/fə	ˈta	grə	fi/	/foʊ	tə	ˈgræf	ɪk/
☐	▫	☐	▫	☐	▫	☐	☐	▫	☐	▫
Full	Reduced	Full	Reduced	Full	Reduced	Full	Full	Reduced	Full	Reduced

Many dictionaries and English language books consider unstressed full vowels to have "secondary stress" and mark it with the symbol /ˌ/; for example, /ˈfoʊtəˌgræf/, /ˌfoʊtəˈgræfɪk/. If you have difficulty in pronouncing very long words, it might help you to think of these vowels as being a "little" stressed. Thus, you can break down a long word into two shorter words when you first try to say it: *ˈphoto ˈgraphic*. However, in continuous speech, full vowels with "secondary stress" are normally not stressed.

PRACTICE 5

Stress the syllables in **boldface** type and reduce the underlined vowels.

1. **pho**tograph   pho**to**graphy   pho**to**graphic
   /ˈfoʊtəgræf/   /fəˈtagrəfi/   /foʊtəˈgræfɪk/

2. **tel**egraph   te**leg**raphy   tele**graph**ic
   /ˈtɛləgræf/   /təˈlɛgrəfi/   /tɛləˈgræfɪk/

3. **dem**ocrat   de**moc**racy   demo**crat**ic
   /ˈdɛməkræt/   /dəˈmakrəsi/   /dɛməˈkrætɪk/

4. **dip**lomat   di**plo**macy   diplo**mat**ic
   /ˈdɪpləmæt/   /dɪˈploʊməsi/   /dɪpləˈmætɪk/

5. **pol**itics   po**lit**ical   poli**ti**cian
   /ˈpalɪtɪks/   /pəˈlɪtɪkəl/   /palɪˈtɪʃən/

6. **per**sonal   per**son**ify   perso**nal**ity
   /ˈpɚsənəl/   /pɚˈsanɪfaɪ/   /pɚsəˈnælɪti/

7. **com**petent   com**pet**itor   compe**ti**tion
   /ˈkampətənt/   /kəmˈpɛtɪtɚ/   /kampəˈtɪʃən/

8. **fam**ily   fa**mil**iar   fami**liar**ity
   /ˈfæməli/   /fəˈmɪlyɚ/   /fəmɪˈlyærɪti/

Exceptions. This principle of alternating full vowels and reduced vowels can help you to pronounce many new words; however, there are many exceptions. In long words, unstressed vowels immediately *after* stressed syllables are usually reduced to /ə/ or /ɪ/, but unstressed vowels immediately *before* stressed syllables are not always reduced, especially if the unstressed syllable is the first syllable of the word. Unstressed syllables in some words may be pronounced either way.

Reduced Unstressed Vowel			Full Unstressed Vowel	
delicious	/də'lɪʃəs/		nutritious	/nu'trɪʃəs/
majestic	/mə'dʒɛstɪk/		magnetic	/mæg'nɛtɪk/
fatality[1]	/fə'tælɪti/	OR	fatality	/feɪ'tælɪti/

Reduction is much more likely in very common words and at fast rates of speech. Also, many unstressed suffixes at the end of a word, such as <al>, <ant>, <ent>, <ness>, etc., are never pronounced with full vowels. Thus, the last syllable in all of the following words is reduced: *final, personal, important, inhabitant, darkness, happiness*.

EXERCISE

 A. Mark in the stress and circle the vowels that are reduced in the italicized words. Then practice the dialogue.

A: Who is the man in this *photograph*? He looks like a *politician* or a *diplomat*.

B: I believe that's Joe Moneybags, the *Democratic* congressman from Massachusetts. He's been in *politics* for a long time. He's very *diplomatic*. His *competitors* never seem to be able to defeat him.

A: You seem to be *familiar* with *politics*. Do you belong to a *political* party?

B: No, I'm neither a *Democrat* nor a Republican. But I take my *personal* duty as a citizen in a *democracy* very seriously and vote in every election.

---

[1]fatality = death from an accident, from *fatal* /'feɪtəl/ (adj.).

7.3 Disappearing Syllables

The vowel immediately after the stressed syllable is usually reduced. In some very common words, when two or three unstressed syllables follow a stressed syllable, the unstressed syllable immediately after the stressed syllable is dropped altogether. This is especially common before <r>.

PRACTICE 6

1. Read the following words aloud, omitting each vowel that is crossed out.

a.	interesting	/'ɪntrɪstɪŋ/	(some say /'ɪnə-rɛstɪŋ/)
b.	temperature	/'tɛmprətʃə-/	
c.	favorable	/'feɪvrəbəl/	
d.	miserable	/'mɪzrəbəl/	
e.	pleasurable	/'plɛʒrəbəl/	
f.	laboratory	/'læbrətɔri/	
g.	elementary	/ɛlə'mɛntri/	
h.	documentary	/dɑkyə'mɛntri/	
i.	separate	/'sɛprɪt/	(adjective only)
j.	deliberate	/dɪ'lɪbrɪt/	(adjective only)
k.	favorite	/'feɪvrɪt/	
l.	different	/'dɪfrɪnt/	
m.	restaurant	/'rɛstrɑnt/	
n.	aspirin	/'æsprɪn/	
o.	beverage	/'bɛvrɪdʒ/	
p.	comfortable	/'kəmftə-bəl/	(/ə-/ moves to the following syllable)
q.	reasonable	/'riznəbəl/	
r.	vegetable	/'vɛdʒtəbəl/	
s.	evening	/'ivnɪŋ/	
t.	chocolate	/'tʃɑklɪt/	
u.	family	/'fæmli/	
v.	naturally	/'nætʃrəli/	
w.	generally	/'dʒɛnrəli/	
x.	accidentally	/æksə'dɛntli/	
y.	awfully	/'ɔfli/	

2. The adverb ending <ically> is usually pronounced as /ɪkli/. (Compare this to the adjective ending <ical> /ɪkəl/.) Can you think of any other words that end in <ically>?

a.	physically	/'fɪzɪkli/	physical	/'fɪzɪkəl/
b.	practically	/'præktɪkli/	practical	/'præktɪkəl/
c.	economically	/ɛkə'nɑmɪkli/	economical	/ɛkə'nɑmɪkəl/

EXERCISE

 A. Cross out all the unstressed vowels that can be omitted. Then practice the dialogue.

A: Let's go to a different restaurant today. The food at Judie's has received favorable reviews in the paper and is reasonably priced. Besides, it's practically around the corner from the laboratory.

B: OK, let's try it. I'd like a pleasurable lunch.

A: Waiter, we'd like comfortable seats near the window, and please make out separate checks.

B: The menu looks basically interesting, but they don't have my favorite beverage, iced tea.

A: Oh well, they have several interesting vegetable dishes and five different chocolate desserts.

B: I don't know if I can eat anything. I'm really feeling miserable today. The students in my elementary class were deliberately causing problems.

A: Students periodically act up. Why don't you take some aspirin and forget about it. You'll feel better after you eat something.

CHAPTER 8

Rhythm

How could I have known that you don't like anchovies on your pizza?

PREREADING QUESTION

How are the words *have* and *that* pronounced in this sentence?

8.1 Stress in One-Syllable Words

When we speak naturally, words are parts of phrases and longer sentences. What we hear is a sequence of syllables in time, like notes in music. The time relationships among syllables make up the **rhythm** of language. Just as musical notes are of different lengths (1/2 notes, 1/4 notes, 1/8 notes, etc.) and are grouped together into measures (3/4 time, 7/8 time, etc.), syllables also make patterns that help us to figure out where words begin and end and which words are more important than others.

A clear example of rhythm in language is poetry. Listen to the following poem.[1] Try to tap your finger or your foot to it. Do all the syllables sound equal, or do some syllables stand out over others? On which syllables do taps occur? Is the rhythm regular and predictable?

---

[1]"Stopping by Woods on a Snowy Evening," from *The Poetry of Robert Frost* edited by Edward Connery Lathem. Copyright 1923, © 1969 by Holt, Rinehard and Winston. Copyright 1951 by Robert Frost. Reprinted by permission of Henry Holt and Company, Inc.

Whose woods these are I think I know
His house is in the village though;
He will not see me stopping here
To watch his woods fill up with snow.

My little horse must think it queer
To stop without a farmhouse near
Between the woods and frozen lake
The darkest evening of the year.

He gives his harness bells a shake
To ask if there is some mistake.
The only other sound's the sweep
Of easy wind and downy flake.

The woods are lovely, dark and deep,
But I have promises to keep,
And miles to go before I sleep,
And miles to go before I sleep.

Ordinary language also has a rhythm, but it is not as clear nor as regular as in poetry. Every language has its own rhythm. Consider the following two sentences. Which sentence sounds more natural in English? What is the difference between the two sentences? Is the rhythm of your native language more like (1) or more like (2)?

1. Big black dogs chase small white cats.

2. A big black dog is chasing a little cat.

As you probably guessed, (2) is more typical of English. In (1), all the syllables have about the same length, but in (2) some very short syllables alternate with longer syllables, and the syllables are clearly grouped into phrases.

The rhythm of English involves an alternation of strong or stressed syllables and weak or unstressed syllables. The stressed syllables are longer, clearer, and sometimes higher pitched; the unstressed syllables tend to be shortened and reduced. A stressed syllable is usually preceded or followed by one or two unstressed syllables. This alternation is not as strict as in poetry. In most ordinary speech, there may be from zero to four unstressed syllables between each stressed syllable.

Tap your finger to the following sentence.[2]

3. 'This is the 'house that 'Jack 'built.

---

[2]This example is used in David Abercrombie, *Studies in Phonetics and Linguistics* (London: Oxford University Press, 1965), p. 28.

Even though there are different numbers of unstressed syllables between the stressed syllables, the stresses fall at fairly regular intervals. Try to say the same sentence with a stress (tap) on *every* syllable.

> 4. 'This 'is 'the 'house 'that 'Jack 'built.

Now try to say the sentence very quickly, with all short unstressed syllables.

> 5. This-is-the-house-that-Jack-built.

Both (4) and (5) sound very bad to native speakers of English. They will have difficulty understanding sentences spoken too slowly, with all syllables long and stressed as in (4), or too quickly, with all short syllables as in (5). What kind of a rhythm do you use when you speak English?

In (3), all the words are one-syllable words, but some are stressed and some are unstressed. You learned rules for stressing longer words in the last chapter, but how do you know which one-syllable words are stressed and which are unstressed?

> One-syllable **content words** are usually **stressed**. Content words are nouns, verbs, adjectives, and adverbs. You can look them up in a dictionary and translate them. They carry the basic meaning of a sentence. In (3) *house*, *Jack*, and *built* are content words.
>
> One-syllable **function words** are usually **unstressed and reduced**. Function words include articles, prepositions, pronouns, conjunctions, and auxiliary verbs. They show grammatical relationships and are difficult to translate. Their meaning can change greatly depending on how they are used in a sentence. In (3) *is*, *the*, and *that* are function words.

In order to achieve a good rhythm in English, you need to *slow down, stretch out, and very clearly pronounce one-syllable content words* and the stressed syllables of longer words. And you must *reduce unstressed function words* and other unstressed syllables. The two most common mistakes made by non-native speakers are pronouncing one-syllable content words too quickly, by rushing them or dropping final consonants, and not reducing function words and unstressed syllables enough. As a result, the listener will have difficulty perceiving which syllables are stressed and which are unstressed. Since stress is the main cue to word boundaries in spoken language (equivalent to spaces in written language), the listener will therefore have problems figuring out where words begin and end. It is extremely important to make a clear difference between stressed and unstressed syllables when you are speaking English.

Good rhythm in English, as in any language, also means speaking at a regular speed with correct phrasing and pausing. Speaking at a regular rate allows your listener to predict where the next stress will fall. Grouping function words together with content words into phrases helps the listener establish grammatical units. Pausing (equivalent to punctuation marks in writing) lets the listener know where major grammatical units end and gives the listener time to figure out the meaning. If you've made some mistakes, the listener may need extra time to go back and "reprocess" what you've said. You shouldn't speak too slowly or suddenly change speed in the middle of a sentence. However, it's even worse to speak too quickly or to rush everything together without pausing long enough between sentences.

Rules for Stress in One-Syllable Words

The following one-syllable words are usually **unstressed**:

1. *Articles*: a, an, the, some
2. *Pronouns*: I, me, my, he, him, his, she, her, they, them, their, you, your, we, us, our, it, its
3. *Prepositions*: at, by, for, from, in, of, on, to . . .
   When they are followed by noun objects:
   We 'waited *for* a 'while.   I 'went *to* the 'party.
4. *Conjunctions*:
   a. and, but, so, or, nor
   b. that, where, which, who, as, if . . .
      When they introduce dependent clauses:
      The 'man *that* you 'met at the 'party is my 'uncle.
      Do you 'know *where* he 'went?
5. *Auxiliary Verbs*:
   a. am, is, are, was, were, be, been, have, has, had, do, does, did,
      can, will, would, could, should . . .
      When they are *affirmative* and *followed by a main verb*:
      'Mary *has* 'bought a 'dog.   Our 'friends *will be* 'coming 'soon.
   b. *be* as a *linking verb* (followed by an adjective or noun phrase):
      Our 'teacher *is* 'wonderful.   It *was* a 'waste of 'time.

The following one-syllable words are usually **stressed**:

1. *Nouns*: house, book, day, John, town, street . . .
2. *Adjectives*: big, small, round, blue, fat, thin, nice, more, most . . .
3. *Verbs*:
   a. *Main* verbs: eats, comes, came, go, went, gone, thought . . .
      want to, have to, has to, got to, used to . . .
   b. *Negative* auxiliary verbs: don't, can't, won't, aren't . . .
   c. Auxiliary verbs used *alone* (*not* followed by a main verb):
      'Yes, I '*do*.   I 'think we '*can*.
      He 'isn't 'coming, '*is* he?   'Yes, he '*is*.
4. *Adverbs*:
   a. fast, well, hard, loud . . . (answer the question "How?")
   b. now, here, soon, not, once, first . . . ("When? Where? How often?")
   c. up, down, on, off, in, out, through, back . . .
      Used *alone* or as the second part of a two-word verb:
      I'm 'going '*out*.   It 'rained '*off* and '*on*.
      'Hang it '*up*.   'Bring them '*back* to'morrow.
5. *Numbers*: one, two, three, four, five, six . . .
6. *Question Words*: what, where, when, how, who, why . . .
   When they are used *alone* to introduce questions:
   '*Where* did he 'go?   '*What* are you 'doing?
7. *Demonstratives*: this, that, these, those
   When they are used like adjectives or pronouns:
   '*That's* my 'car.   'Who told you '*that*?
   After '*that*, we 'left.   '*That* re'port is 'great.

EXERCISES

A. Tap your finger to the stressed syllables while you say the following sentences. Try to keep the same spacing between the "beats" (the stresses) by lengthening the stressed syllables when there are no unstressed syllables between them.

1. 'Susan will be 'talking to her 'boyfriend.
2. 'Susan will 'talk to a 'boy.
3. 'Sue 'talks to 'boys.
4. 'Bob 'writes 'long 'books.
5. 'Bobby's 'writing 'longer 'papers.
6. 'Bobby's been 'writing some 'beautiful 'articles.
7. 'Dogs 'chase 'cats.
8. A 'dog has 'chased the 'cat.
9. A 'dog has been 'chasing our 'cats.
10. A 'dog could have been 'chasing some of our 'cats.
11. 'Boys 'drink 'milk 'nights.
12. The 'boys would 'drink some 'milk at 'night.
13. The 'boys have been 'drinking some 'milk in the 'night.
14. The 'boys would have been 'drinking some of the 'milk into the 'night.

B. Mark the stress in the following sentences. Stress all content words.

1. I'd 'like some 'tea, 'please.
2. I love to look at the moon and stars at night.
3. At the beach, the sun is bright and the sand is hot.
4. They can't eat a lot of red meat.
5. We're late. We've got to rush to catch the bus.
6. Two men were robbed near the bank.
7. Where did you buy your new shoes?
8. They were on sale at a store in town.
9. This is the best car you can buy.
10. Do you know where she got them? Yes, I do.
11. He said that he would come at five or six o'clock.
12. You could call him up and talk to him now.

C. Mark the stresses in the following poem[3] and read it aloud.

> A bird came down the walk:
> He did not know I saw;
> He bit an angle-worm in halves
> And ate the fellow, raw.

---

[3]*Poems by Emily Dickinson*, second series, T. W. Higginson and M. L. Todd, eds. (Boston: Roberts Brothers, 1892) p. 140.

8.2 Weak Forms: Reducing Function Words

Many function words have two pronunciations, a strong form and a weak or reduced form. The **strong form** has a full vowel and is used only for emphasis or at the end of a sentence (before a pause).

I said "<u>to</u>" not "<u>at</u>".	to = /tu/	at = /æt/
You omitted the article "<u>a</u>".	a = /eɪ/	
What are you waiting <u>for</u>?	for = /fɔɚ/	

The unstressed **weak form** is normally used in the middle of a sentence or phrase. The vowel is reduced to /ə/, /ɪ/, or /ɚ/, initial <h> is dropped, and the whole word is very short.

I hope <u>to</u> see <u>him</u> <u>at</u> the meeting.	to = /tə/	him = /ɪm/	at = /ət/
Let's wait <u>for</u> <u>a</u> few minutes.	for = /fɚ/	a = /ə/	

In words that have /ə, i, aɪ/ as the vowel in the strong form (*some, from, she, we, I, my*), the vowel is shortened, but changes only a little in quality.

Using weak forms is *normal English*: it is not sloppy or "incorrect." Using weak forms regularly will greatly improve your rhythm in English and help people to understand you when you speak. The most common words with weak forms are as follows.

PRACTICE 1

Read the sentences aloud, making the weak forms as short as possible and linking them together with other words in the same phrase. Don't rush the stressed syllables.

1. *Articles:* a /ə/, an /ən/ or [n̩], the /ðə/, some /səm/ or [sm̩]

    a. *The* man sold me *a* hammer, *an* axe, and *some* nails.
       ðə   ə   ən   səm

2. *Pronouns:* he /i/, him /ɪm/, his /ɪz/, her /ɚ/, them /ðəm/, you /yʊ/ or /yə/, your /yɚ/, our /ɑɚ/

    a. Where did *he* go?   /ˈwɛɚdɪdi ˈgoʊ/
       i

    b. What's *his* name?   /ˈwətsɪz ˈneɪm/
       ɪz

    c. Take *your* time.   /ˈteɪkyɚ ˈtaɪm/
       yɚ

    d. Leave *them* alone.   /ˈlivðəmə ˈloʊn/
       ðəm   (→/əm/ in fast speech)

    e. Leave *him* alone.   /ˈlivɪmə ˈloʊn/
       ɪm

    f. I gave *her* the book.   /aɪ ˈgeɪvɚðə ˈbʊk/
       ɚ

    Note: When you drop /h/, be sure to link the pronoun to the previous word. Use the weak form without /h/ in the middle of a phrase, but pronounce /h/ at the beginning of a sentence or after any pause.

    g. *He* was late, wasn't *he*?   /hiwəz ˈleɪt ˈwəzəni/
       hi   i

(continued)

PRACTICE 1 (continued)

3. *Prepositions:* at /ət/, for /fɚ/, from /frəm/ or [frm̩], of /əv/, to /tə/ or /tʊ/

   a. I'll wait *for* the bus *at* the corner.
             fɚ   ət

   b. I'd like *to* have a cup *of* coffee.
            tə   əv   (/əv/ → /ə/ in fast speech before a consonant)

Note: Use the strong form at the end of a sentence, before a pause.

   c. What's he looking *for*?
                 fɔɚ

   d. He really wants *to*.
                  tu

4. *Conjunctions:* and /ən/ or [n̩], as /əz/, or /ɚ/, than /ðən/ or [ðn̩], that /ðət/, but /bət/

   a. Tom *and* Ann have more *than* they need.
         ən   ðən

   c. She's *as* quiet *as* a mouse.
          əz   əz

   b. He said *that* he was coming at one *or* two o'clock.
         ðət   ɚ

Note: The weak form of *that* is only used when it introduces a clause, not when it is used as a demonstrative.

   d. *That's* what I want.
      ðæts

   e. Did you see *that* girl?
                ðæt

5. *Auxiliary Verbs:* can /kən/ or /kɪn/ or [kn̩], have /əv/, has /əz/, had /əd/, do /dʊ/ or /də/, does /dəz/, am /əm/, are /ɚ/, was /wəz/ or /wz/, will /wəl/ or /əl/ or [l̩] . . .

   a. They *can* wait.   /ðeɪkən ˈweɪt/
         kən

   b. This class *has* been very helpful.
             əz

   c. You should *have* told me.
             əv (→ /ə/ in fast speech)

   d. I wouldn't *have* talked to her.
            əv (→ /ə/ in fast speech)

   e. What *do* they want?
           dʊ

   f. She *was* here a minute ago.
          wəz

   g. The guests *have* arrived.
           əv

   h. I wish Tom *had* bought more bread.
         əd

Note: Weak forms of auxiliary verbs are used when they are followed by another verb. After pronouns, weak forms reduce even further to contractions, *'d* /d/, *'ve* /v/, *'s* /z/ or /s/, *'ll* /l/. Strong forms are used in the negative, at the end of a sentence (as in short answers or tag questions), and when they are themselves used as main verbs rather than as auxiliaries.

   i. They *can't* wait.   /ðeɪ ˈkænt ˈweɪt/
        kænt

   j. Yes, I *have*.   /ˈyɛsaɪ ˈhæv/
       hæv

   k. He *has* a problem.   /hi ˈhæzə ˈprɑbləm/
       hæz

   l. What does he *do* for a living?   /ˈwətdəzi ˈdufɚə ˈlɪvɪŋ/
       du

PRACTICE 2

Non-native speakers often have difficulty pronouncing *can* and *can't*. *Can* has three different pronunciations. Practice the example sentences aloud.

1. /kən/, /kɪn/, or [kn̩]—*short unstressed* weak form
   Used normally in affirmative sentences when followed by a main verb. Stress the main verb and make *can* as short as possible.

   a. I can 'swim.
   b. We can 'hear the 'noise.
   c. 'Sharon can 'speak 'English.

   d. Can you 'help me?
   e. 'Where can we 'meet?

2. /ˈkænt/ or [ˈkɛnʔ]—*stressed* negative strong form

   Used in negative sentences. It is always stressed and often cut off sharply by a glottal stop (short silence) at the end.

   f. I 'can't 'swim.
   g. We 'can't 'hear any 'noise.
   h. I'm 'sorry, but I 'can't 'help you.

   i. 'Can't you 'do 'anything a'bout it? 'No, I 'can't.
   j. You can 'come, 'can't you?

3. /ˈkænn/ or [ˈkæən]—*long stressed* affirmative strong form
   Used before a pause or when emphasized for a special reason. It is very long and stressed.

   k. 'Yes, I 'can.
   l. Oh, 'dear. What 'can we do?
   m. I 'said that I 'can 'come. 'Didn't you under'stand me?

   n. They can 'come, and we 'can, 'too.

EXERCISES

A. What are some things you can or can't do? What are some things you can or can't do in your country? in the United States or Canada? at this school/company? at home? in your dormitory?

EXAMPLE: I can play the piano. I can dance. I can't play soccer.
In my country, you can't criticize the government.

B. *To* is reduced as a preposition and as part of an infinitive. Note the pronunciation of the following expressions:

have to /ˈhæftə/	has to /ˈhæstə/	ought to /ˈɔtə/
have got to /əvˈgatə/	has got to /əzˈgatə/	used to /ˈyustə/

1. I went to the movie.
2. I came to class late.
3. She needs to buy a book.
4. I have to leave now.
5. He has to go home.
6. She's got to do better.
7. He used to work here.

8. I wrote to my friend.
9. He drives to church.
10. I'd like to see you.
11. I ought to write a letter.
12. We have to improve.
13. They've got to finish it.
14. I used to get up early.

C. Long verb forms should sound like one word. Remember to stress only the main verb, or negative auxiliaries and the verb. In very long verb forms, such as *would have been taken, should have been studying, might have arrived,* the first word (the modal) may be stressed, but be sure to reduce *have: should have* /ʃʊdəv/, *might have* /maɪtəv/ (in fast speech /ʃʊdə/, /maɪtə/).

1. You should have talked to her.
2. I'm sure she would have helped you.
3. They couldn't have done it without help.
4. She must have forgotten about it.
5. They might have been stolen.
6. If I had known you were coming, I would have met you at the airport.
7. If he hadn't been sick, he would have done better on the test.

ADVANCED

D. Answer the following questions using *should have, could have, might have, must have,* and your own ideas. Be sure to reduce *have.*

1. Where was Roger on Friday? He wasn't in class.
   He should have been in class.
   He could have been sleeping.
   He might have been sick.
2. Who robbed the bank over the weekend?
3. What happened to flight 007? It disappeared last night over the Atlantic Ocean.
4. Chris is using crutches and has his leg in a cast. What happened?
5. Why doesn't Lisa have her books with her today?
6. The teacher looks very tired today. Why?
7. Mr. and Mrs. Smith's house burned down while they were away on vacation. How did the fire start?
8. Very few people came to my party Saturday night. I wonder why?

E. Because we use weak forms, the phonetic difference between certain function words may be very small or lost altogether. Both *have* and *of* are pronounced /əv/. A common mistake made by American children is to write *should of come* instead of *should have come.* You must know the grammar in order to distinguish the following similar-sounding words in conversational speech.

have - of - a	them - him - am	her - or - are ('re)
has - is - as - his	than - and - an	our - are
had - would ('d)	in - on	how are - how were

Circle the correct word and practice saying the sentences.

1. She (**has**/is) seen it already.
2. They took (**his**/is) chair.
3. Do (has/**as**) I say.
4. Give me a pencil (**and**/an) paper.
5. I want (are/**her**) to be happy.
6. One (are/**or**) two students were absent.
7. I would (**have**/of) told you if I (would/**had**) known about it.
8. I'd like a piece (**of**/a) cake.
9. Tomatoes cost a dollar (of/**a**) pound this week.
10. They (**would**/had) rather sleep late.

Your teacher or another student will read the following sentences quickly. Which word do you hear?

11. I met (him/them) at the store.

12. The boys (had/would) cut the lawn.

13. The station (had/would) broadcast the news at 5:00.

14. I'd rather have bacon (than/and) eggs.

15. Please put it (in/on) the desk.

16. Give her (a/the) cup of coffee.

F. *Dialogues for Weak Forms.*

1. and /ən/ → [n̩]

A: I love bacon *and* eggs.

B: I prefer toast *and* coffee.

A: How about hot dogs *and* baked beans?

B: Red beans *and* rice is much better.

A: Spaghetti *and* meatballs?

B: Fish *and* chips.

A: Ice cream *and* cake?

B: A peanut butter *and* jelly sandwich.

2. to /tə/

A: I'd like *to* speak *to* the manager.

B: I'm afraid the manager's gone out *to* lunch.

A: Can I speak *to* the assistant manager then?

B: I'm afraid the assistant manager has gone *to* a meeting.

A: Well I need *to* see someone who has the authority *to* give me a refund.

B: I'm afraid the store is about *to* close.

3. them /ðəm/ → [ðm̩], to /tə/

A: I want *them*. I want *them* now. I've got *to* have *them*.

B: But do you need *them*?

A: Of course I need *them*. I can't live without *them*.

B: Then I'll give *them to* you. But you've got *to* give *them* back *to* me tomorrow.

A: I have *to* return *them* so soon?

4. for /fɚ/

A: What are you doing?

B: I'm waiting *for* the bus. It's taking *for*ever to come.

A: How long have you been waiting?

B: *For* at least five minutes. I wish it would come on time *for* a change.

A: I wish you'd stop complaining *for* a change.

5. some /səm/ → [sm̩], for /fɚ/

A: I need *some* change. Do you have change *for* a dollar?

B: I have *some* nickels and dimes.

A: I need *some* quarters to get *some* soda from the machine.

B: Soda's not good *for* you anyway. You can get *some* juice *for* only 75 cents.

A: I asked *for* change, not *for* advice.

6. or /ɚ/, at /ət/

A: There are one *or* two things we have to get settled *at* once.

B: Certainly.

A: How long will you be staying *at* the hotel?

B: I'll be staying for three *or* four days. I'll be leaving on Monday *or* Tuesday.

A: And *at* what time on Monday *or* Tuesday will you be leaving?

B: Either in the morning *or at* night.

A: I see. That's very helpful.

B: Why don't we talk about it *at* lunch?

7. that /ðət/, can /kən/

A: I *can* see *that* you're upset, but I don't think *that* I *can* help you.

B: Why not?

A: The problems *that* you're having are in areas *that* are beyond my competence.

B: I know *that* you're not an expert, but isn't there something *that* you *can* do?

A: I *can* recommend *that* you call your mother.

8. than /ðən/ → [ðn̩]

A: It's faster *than* a speeding bullet.

B: More powerful *than* a locomotive.

A: Fiercer *than* a thunderstorm.

B: More mysterious *than* the night.

A: Able to leap tall buildings in a single bound.

B: It's a bird . . . it's a plane . . . it's superwoman!

9. as /əz/

A: She's *as* happy *as* a lark.

B: He's *as* quiet *as* a mouse.

A: She's *as* fast *as* the wind.

B: He's *as* slow *as* molasses.

A: She's *as* sweet *as* honey.

B: He's *as* hard *as* a rock.

A: She's *as* pretty *as* a picture.

B: He's *as* old *as* the hills.

A: They're *as* thick *as* thieves.

10. can /kən/ → /kɪn/, [kn̩]

A: *Can* you cook?

B: No, but I *can* eat out.

A: *Can* you sew?

B: No, I can't. But I *can* take my clothes to a tailor.

A: *Can* you clean house?

B: No, but I *can* ask my mother to do it.

A: Can't you do anything for yourself?

B: I *can* get married.

11. he /i/, him /ɪm/, his /ɪz/, her /ər/

A: What does *he* want *her* to do?

B: He wants *her* to wash *her* clothes, make *her* bed, clean *her* room, and do *her* homework every night.

A: What does she tell *him*?

B: She tells *him* that *he* should mind *his* own business.

A: But isn't *he her* father?

B: Yes, *he* is.

12. has /əz/, have /əv/

A: Betsy *has* failed the test, John *has* failed the test, and Michael *has* failed it.

B: Everyone *has* failed it. All year the class *has* been given impossible tests.

A: Some students *have* done well in the course.

B: That's impossible!

A: Not for me. My grades *have* all been A's.

13. have /əv/

A: You should *have* told me about it.

B: You shouldn't *have* said it didn't matter.

A: You should *have* at least warned me.

B: I might *have* said something if I'd known how upset you'd be.

A: You must *have* known *that* I'd be angry.

B: How could I *have* known *that* you don't like anchovies on your pizza? I guess I'll have to eat it all by myself.

14. was /wəz/ → [wz], *were* /wɚ/

A: I *was* just thinking . . . .

B: You *were* just thinking what?

A: I *was* just thinking that you and I . . . .

B: Go on. What *were* you thinking?

A: Well, I *was* thinking that you and I should . . . .

B: Should get married?

A: No—should stop interrupting each other.

8.3 Rhythmic Grouping: Pausing and Linking

PAUSING

Good rhythm in English involves not only making a clear difference between stressed and unstressed syllables but also grouping syllables together into larger units. That is, you must **pause** in the right places and **link** words together within a phrase. Where should you pause in the following paragraph?[1]

> In the morning the sun was up and the tent was starting to get hot. Nick crawled
>
> out under the mosquito netting stretched across the mouth of the tent, to look at the
>
> morning. The grass was wet on his hands as he came out. He held his trousers and his
>
> shoes in his hands. The sun was just up over the hill. There was the meadow, the river
>
> and the swamp. There were birch trees in the green of the swamp on the other side of
>
> the river.

Knowledge of English grammar and of the meaning of the passage are necessary to figure out where to pause. Pauses occur:

1. before punctuation marks (. , ; : ? ! "),
2. before conjunctions (*and, or, but, which, that, since* . . .), and
3. between grammatical units such as phrases, clauses, and sentences.

Phrases include prepositional phrases, noun subjects (article + adjective + noun), verbs with their objects and adverbs, gerund phrases (verb + <ing> and its objects), and infinitive phrases. Every pause group must contain at least one stressed syllable. Therefore, you cannot pause between unstressed function words (such as pronouns, auxiliary verbs, or conjunctions) and the content words they go with. Pauses can be marked with a verticle line (|).

Depending on how fast you speak,| pause groups will be longer,| with three to five stressed syllables,| or shorter,| with one or two stressed syllables.| If people have difficulty understanding you,| it is usually a good idea| to pause more frequently| and for a longer time.| In English,| syllables before pauses are lengthened.| In the middle of a sentence,| such as at the end of a prepositional phrase| or long subject,| many people lengthen the last word in the group| without coming to a complete stop.|

---

[1]Ernest Hemingway, *Big Two-Hearted River Part II*, in *The Complete Short Stories of Ernest Hemingway* (New York: Scribner's, 1987), p. 173.

LINKING

Within pause groups, words should be **linked or blended together** so that they sound like one word. In normal speech, there are no "white spaces" between closely connected words.

can serve = conserve	made him a steak = made a mistake
a loan = alone	love her = lover
find out = fine doubt	watch is = watches
an ice cream = a nice cream	dye it = diet

Linking means that *words should be joined smoothly to each other without adding extra sounds or omitting final consonants*. If you don't link words together, your speech sounds choppy, and it is difficult for your listener to know which words belong together in phrases.

Linking a Final Consonant to an Initial Vowel.   If a word ends in a consonant and the next word begins with a vowel, use the consonant to begin the syllable of the following word: do *not* insert a glottal stop (stop the air) between the two words.

1. in‿an‿airplane = /ɪ nə ˈnɛɚ pleɪn/, *not* [ɪn ʔən ʔɛɚ pleɪn]
2. live‿all‿alone = /ˈlɪ vɔ lə ˈloʊn/, *not* [lɪv ʔɔl ʔə loʊn]

Linking Two Vowels.   If a word ends in a vowel and the next word begins with another vowel, go from one vowel right into the other *without stopping your voice*. Use a short /y/ after front vowels, a short /w/ after back vowels, and /r/ after /ɚ/ to begin the following syllable. The word *the* is often pronounced as /ðɪ/ before words beginning with vowels.

3. go‿out = /goʊ ˈaʊt/ or [goʊ ʷaʊt], *not* [goʊ ʔaʊt]
4. the‿answer = /ðɪ ˈænsɚ/ or [ðɪ ʸænsɚ], *not* [ðɪ ʔænsɚ]

Linking Two Consonants.   If a word ends in a consonant and the next word begins with another consonant, go directly from one consonant to the next without releasing the first one (that is, without opening your mouth too wide) or adding a vowel sound like /ə/. (But don't omit the final consonant either. See Sec. 14.3 for pronouncing difficult consonant groups.) During the first consonant, begin moving your tongue silently inside your mouth into the position for the following consonant. If this is difficult for you, try to say the two consonants at the same time.

5. keep‿talking = /ˈkip ˈtɔkɪŋ/, *not* [kipʰ tɔkɪŋ], [kipə tɔkɪŋ], or [kitɔkɪŋ] (key talking)

If the two consonants are the same, just hold on to the first one a little longer.

6. bake‿cakes = /ˈbeɪ ˈkːeɪks/, *not* [beɪkʰ keɪks], [beɪkə keɪks], or [beɪ keɪks] (bay cakes)

PRACTICE 3

Practice linking words together in the following short sentences.

1. Linking C + V:

a. It's‿an‿apple.   /ɪt sə 'næ pəl/

b. Come‿in.   /kə 'mɪn/

c. It's‿all‿over.   /ɪt sɔ 'loʊ vɚ/

d. I give‿up.   /aɪ gɪ 'vəp/

e. He made‿a mess.   /hi 'meɪ də 'mɛs/

f. Cook‿a meal.   /'kʊ kə 'mil/

g. He robbed‿a bank.   /hi 'rɑb də 'bæŋk/

h. She baked‿a cake.   /ʃi 'beɪk tə 'keɪk/

i. She loves‿him.   /ʃi 'ləv zɪm/

j. He likes‿her.   /hi 'laɪk sɚ/

2. Linking V + V:

k. May‿I‿ask?   /meɪ ʸaɪ 'ʸæsk/

l. Do‿I know‿her?   /dʊ ʷaɪ 'noʊ ʷɚ/

m. I'll wear‿it.   /aɪl 'wɛɚ ʳɪt/

n. Did you see‿her?

o. They‿owe‿him money.

p. I‿always tie‿it.

q. His blue‿eyes were‿open.

r. Where‿is the‿office?

3. Linking C + C:

s. Keep‿talking.

t. You laugh‿too much.

u. Where does‿the bus‿stop?

v. I like‿black‿cats.

w. What‿time will you eat‿tonight?

x. His‿vacation was‿terrible.

y. Don't‿stop‿driving.

EXERCISES

A. Linking also helps the listener identify final consonants. Listen as your teacher reads each phrase, first without linking (cutting off each word sharply) and then with linking. Then listen to just one phrase from each group and try to identify it.

1. a. rope is   **2.** a. some is   **3.** a. rat up   d. racked up
      b. robe is   b. son is   b. rack up   e. wrapped up
                      c. sung his   c. wrap up

 B. Finish marking in the stresses and pauses in the following passage according to the way that you read aloud. Be sure that every pause group contains at least one stressed syllable. Then record yourself reading the passage aloud. Be sure to link words together within pause groups. Remember to drop unstressed, non-initial /h/ in function words.

[Nick is camping. He wakes up early in the morning and prepares to go fishing.]

Big Two-Hearted River[2]

In the 'morning| the 'sun was ‿'up| and the 'tent was 'starting to get 'hot.| 'Nick crawled ‿'out| 'under the mos'quito netting[3]| 'stretched ‿a'cross the 'mouth ‿of the 'tent,| to 'look ‿at the 'morning.| The 'grass was 'wet ‿on ‿his 'hands| as ‿he came ‿'out.| He 'held ‿his 'trousers(|) and ‿his 'shoes| in ‿his 'hands.| The 'sun was just ‿'up| over the 'hill.| There was the 'meadow,[4]| the 'river| and the 'swamp.[5]| There were 'birch trees[6](|) in the 'green ‿of the 'swamp| on the ‿'other 'side(|) of the 'river.|

The river was clear and smoothly fast in the early morning. Down about two hundred yards were three logs[7] all the way across the stream. They made the water smooth and deep above them. As Nick watched, a mink[8] crossed the river on the logs and went into the swamp. Nick was excited. He was excited by the early morning and the river. He was really too hurried to eat breakfast, but he knew he must. He built a little fire and put on the coffee pot.

---

[2]Ernest Hemingway, *Big Two-Hearted River Part II*, in *The Complete Short Stories of Ernest Hemingway* (New York: Scribner's, 1987), p. 173.

[3]mosquito netting /məˈskitoʊ nɛtɪŋ/ = a large net to protect you from mosquitoes, insects that bite

[4]meadow /ˈmɛdoʊ/ = a large field full of grass

[5]swamp /swɑmp/ = soft wet land; a marsh

[6]birch trees /ˈbɚtʃ triz/ = slender trees with white, paper-like bark

[7]logs /lɑgz/ = long, large pieces of wood; cut tree trunks

[8]mink /mɪŋk/ = a small animal with very warm brown fur that is used to make expensive coats

C. Mark the stresses and pauses in a paragraph or two of a book that you are reading or that represents the kind of English that you would like to be able to speak aloud. Read it aloud, paying attention to stress, pausing, and linking. Tape-record yourself and play it back.

D. *Oral Presentation: Description of a Place.* Prepare a short two-minute speech about a place that you like and that your classmates might want to visit some day. It could be your favorite city, your hometown, a resort, a place you have visited, or a place that you like to go to on weekends. Include an introduction, a detailed description, and a conclusion. Be sure to make it clear what is special about this place and why you like it. Write out your speech and mark in the stresses. Practice it aloud several times concentrating on stress, rhythm, and pausing. Go for smoothness, regularity, and clarity. When you give your speech in class, look up and talk to your audience. Put your main points on cards if necessary, but don't read.

E. *Dialogues for Linking.*

1. Consonant + Vowel

A: How do‿I make‿it?

B: You need‿an‿egg, an‿apple, an‿eggplant, an‿ounce of‿oatmeal, one‿onion, some‿apricots, some‿almonds, some‿orange juice, and some‿oil.

A: Anything‿else?

B: And‿an‿unripe banana.

A: That sounds like an‿incredible recipe. /ˈrɛsɪpi/

B: It may be an‿inedible[9] one. I just made‿it‿up.

2. Vowel + Vowel

A: Why‿are you so‿angry‿at me?

B: Well, you‿always‿argue‿about‿everything. I'm tired‿of‿it.

A: I don't‿argue‿all the time. I think you're‿being‿unfair.

B: There you go‿again.

3. Vowel + Vowel, Consonant + Vowel

A: (*Knock, Knock.*) Where‿is‿everyone? Is‿anyone‿at home?

B: Are you‿able to see‿anything?

A: No, it's‿okay. No‿one's‿around. Try the door.

B: It's‿open.

A: Good. Let's go‿in.

B: Wait‿a‿minute. I see‿a light‿inside. Somebody must be‿in. Let's get‿out‿of here—right‿away!

A: You're too‿anxious. It's‿only a cat.

B: If‿it's‿a cat, why‿is‿it picking‿up the phone?

---

[9]inedible /ɪn ˈɛdɪbəl/ = can't be eaten

4. One or Two Consonants + Vowel

A: It's_all right. Calm down.

B: I feel_okay now. Thanks.

A: Now tell_us_exactly how_it happened.

B: I was riding my bike when_he came_over and started yelling_at me.

A: What did_he say?

B: He said_I was ruining_his garden. Then_he suddenly turned_around, picked_up a rock, and hurled_it in my direction.

A: And what did you do?

B: I hit_him, kicked_him, and knocked_him down.

A: What_else?

B: And then I bit_him. That's when_he ran_away.

A: I see. It sounds like you got_off_easy.

5. Two Consonants + Vowel

A: She lives_at fifty-five_Atlantic_Avenue.

B: We'd better hurry. She likes_it when everyone_arrives_on time.

A: Do you have_a present?

B: Of course. I have_a nice bottle_of wine. She likes_it when_everyone brings_a gift.

A: She gives_awesome parties. She loves_it when we_all have_a good time.

B: She loves_it even more when_everyone leaves_early.

6. Consonant + Consonant

A: Stop_talking. I can't_drive if you keep_talking.

B: Stop_tailgating. If he stops_suddenly, you'll hit_him.

A: I'm warning you. I don't like_back_seat_drivers.

B: I don't like_poor drivers. You'd_better slow down.

A: Keep your trap_shut! You're not_driving.

B: Watch_out! That_car's_slowing down. (*Screech!*) Whew! I'm glad_I had my seat_belt_on.

A: Get_out! I can't_stand to hear your voice_anymore!

B: You might_at least_thank_me for preventing_an_accident.

Stop_talking. I can't_drive if you keep_talking.

CHAPTER 9

Rhythm (Advanced)

PREREADING QUESTIONS

What does it mean to stress the pronoun *I* in the following sentence?
    How did they find out? *I* didn't tell them.

Where is the stress in *New York* in the following sentences?
    a. They live in New York.
    b. They read the New York Times.

9.1 Breaking the Rules

STRESSING FUNCTION WORDS

Sometimes the rules for stressing one-syllable content words and not stressing function words are broken. In poetry, function words are sometimes stressed to maintain the regular rhythm of a line. In the Robert Frost poem (p. 84), *are* in the first line, *in* in the second line, and *will* in the third line are stressed to keep up the strict alternation of one unstressed syllable with one stressed syllable. In normal speech, *a function word may be stressed in order to emphasize it* or call attention to it for a special reason. (It also will be higher pitched; see Sec. 16.3.) In written English, this is generally indicated by writing the word in italics or underlining it.

1. 'Give it to '*me*, 'not to 'Sue.
2. 'Those are '*my* 'books, 'not '*your* 'books.
3. The 'word '*the* is an 'article.

It is important for non-native speakers to stress function words *only* when they really mean it. In (1) and (2) *me* and *my* are stressed because they are in contrast to *Sue* and *your*; normally they are not stressed. If you say

4. '*I* 'like it. (instead of I 'like it.)

with strong stress and high pitch on *I*, this means that you like it, but somebody else doesn't like it. If you stress *I* whenever you talk, you sound very egotistical (self-centered) to a native speaker, as if you do things differently from other people and your way is better. Stressing the auxiliary verbs as in

5. We '*have* 'read the 'last 'chapter.

means that you are arguing that you really read the last chapter against someone who doubts you. The simple present and past use the stressed auxiliary *do*, *does*, or *did* for this meaning.

6. He *does* love me; I'm sure of it.
7. I *did* turn in my paper; you just can't find it.

PRACTICE 1

Say each of the following sentences in two ways. First, say it normally, with unstressed and reduced function words (column 1). Then stress the italicized words (column 2). What is the meaning of the sentences in column 2? Can you identify which sentence is being read by your teacher or other students in the class?

1. Normal	*2. Emphatic or Contrastive Stress on Function Words*
a. I'm going home.	*I*'m going home.
b. He invited her to the party.	He invited *her* to the party.
c. Where's your house?	Where's *your* house?
d. Is she coming?	Is *she* coming?
e. Susan is happy.	Susan *is* happy.
f. I've got some money.	I've got *some* money.
g. The girls have finished.	The girls *have* finished.
h. Do you know her?	*Do* you know her?

REMOVING STRESS

In conversational speech and especially fast speech, *one-syllable content words* and common *two-syllable function words* (*into*, *over*, *under*, *because*, *before*, *after*, *until*, *whether*, . . .) are *sometimes not stressed* in order *to improve the rhythm* of a sentence that has several stressed syllables in a row. Native speakers prefer an alternation of stressed and unstressed syllables rather than a long series of stressed syllables. Thus, an English speaker might only stress every other word in the following sentence.

    1. 'Big black 'dogs chase 'small white 'cats.

This can happen whenever there is a sequence of stressed syllables. Of course, good writers and speakers try to avoid long sequences of stressed syllables like this by changing the grammar and vocabulary. When words that are normally stressed lose their stress, they *are not reduced*. In fact, people might disagree about whether the words are stressed or not (they are considered to have secondary stress). A lot depends on the speed of speech and on what kind of rhythm the speaker has already set up. A fast speaker would probably say each of the following sentences without pausing and omit the stresses in *book, after, get, next, boy, into,* and *about*.

    2. 'This book is 'better than 'that one.
    3. I'm 'going to 'bed after 'dinner.
    4. He's 'planning to get 'married next 'year.
    5. 'One boy 'got into 'trouble about 'smoking.

In general, it's best for a non-native speaker to stress every content word unless you speak quite fluently, are careful not to drop final consonants, and do not shorten vowels too much in words like *book, next,* and *boy*. However, not stressing two-syllable function words will improve your rhythm. Some of these words have reduced forms: *because* or *'cause* /bɪkəz/ or /kəz/, *until* or *till* /əntɪl/ or /tɪl/, *into* /ɪntʊ/ or /ɪntə/.

    A good example of words losing their stress to improve the rhythm of a sentence is how we say numbers, dates, and abbreviations. Although each number or letter may be stressed in slow speech, at faster speeds we usually stress the first and last number or letter and omit the stress in the middle. The strongest stress is on the last word. We also tend to pause after these expressions.

6.	1903	'nineteen oh 'three
7.	$500	'five hundred 'dollars
8.	$10.99	'ten dollars and 'ninety-nine 'cents
9.	3000 miles	'three thousand 'miles
10.	8.3	'eight point 'three
11.	545-0329	'5 4 '5 I '0 3 2 '9
12.	F.B.I.	/'ɛf bi 'aɪ/
13.	Y.M.C.A.	/'waɪ ɛm si 'eɪ/
14.	452 B.C.	/'fɔɚ fɪfti 'tu bi 'si/

Note: The letters of the alphabet are pronounced as follows:

A /eɪ/	F /ɛf/	K /keɪ/	P /pi/	U /yu/
B /bi/	G /dʒi/	L /ɛl/	Q /kyu/	V /vi/
C /si/	H /eɪtʃ/	M /ɛm/	R /ɑɚ/	W /'dəbəyu/
D /di/	I /aɪ/	N /ɛn/	S /ɛs/	X /ɛks/
E /i/	J /dʒeɪ/	O /ou/	T /ti/	Y /waɪ/
				Z /zi/

EXERCISES

A. Abbreviations are very common in American English. Be sure to slow down when you say abbreviations and stress them properly. Remember to use the article *an*, not *a*, before the letters A, E, F, H, I, L, M, N, O, R, S, or X since the name of these letters begins with a vowel sound.

1. The criminal was finally caught by the F.B.I.
2. How long have you lived in the U.S.A.?
3. Scotland is part of the U.K.
4. Dr. Smith got his Ph.D. from U.C.L.A.
5. He's getting either an M.A. or a B.A. from N.Y.U.
6. Is the football game being broadcast by NBC, CBS, or ABC?
7. WGBH, a public radio station, plays classical music at 7 A.M.
8. In many colleges, a 4.0 is an A average.
9. K.L.M. flight 307 leaves J.F.K. at 9:30 P.M.
10. We have an R.C.A. TV, a Sony VCR, and an I.B.M. PC.

B. Ask other class members questions about themselves and write down the answers after hearing them *only once*.

1. What's your phone number?

   _____

2. What's your social security number?

   _____

3. What's your ID number?

   _____

4. What's your address?

   _____

5. When were you born?

   _____

6. How do you spell your last name?

   _____

7. What degree are you studying for?

   _____

8. What are the numbers of the courses you are taking?

   _____

9. How much did your textbook cost?

   _____

10. (Make up your own question with numbers or abbreviations that you commonly use.)

   _____

9.2 Words with Variable Stress

The stress in some compounds and words stressed on the last syllable can move depending on their location in a sentence. Before a pause they are stressed on the last syllable, but when followed by a stressed syllable, their stress moves to the first syllable to create an alternating rhythm.

NUMBERS, COMPOUND ADJECTIVES, COMPOUND ADVERBS, NOUNS WITH FINAL STRESS

Stress the *last* syllable (or last "word") when it occurs at the *end of a sentence* or phrase; that is, before a pause or a possible pause. This is the normal, or dictionary location, of primary stress in these words.

Stress the *first* syllable (or first "word") when it is immediately *followed by another word in the same phrase*. This usually happens when the word is functioning as an adjective and is followed by a noun stressed on the first syllable.

1. a. He's 'only *four*'*teen*.
   b. He's '*fourteen* 'years 'old.

2. a. He's *fifty*-'*five*, and his 'wife is *twenty*-'*nine*.
   b. It 'costs '*fifty-five* 'dollars and '*twenty-nine* 'cents.

3. a. 'All their 'cakes are *home*-'*made*.
   b. '*Home-made* 'pies are de'licious.

4. a. His 'suit is *dark* 'blue.
   b. He 'wore a '*dark blue* 'suit.

5. a. His 'age is *un*'*known*.
   b. He 'died from an '*unknown* 'cause.

6. a. It's 'hot and 'humid *out*'*side*.
   b. I'd 'like an '*outside* 'cabin.[1]

7. a. They 'went *down*'*stairs* to 'look for their 'toys.
   b. The '*downstairs* 'bedrooms are 'cool and 'comfortable.

8. a. 'Good *after*'*noon*. 'All *after*'*noon* it 'rained.
   b. My '*afternoon* 'class was 'cancelled.

9. a. He 'lives in *New* '*York*. *New* '*York* is a 'large 'city.
   b. The '*New York* 'Times is a 'well-known 'newspaper 'published in '*New York* 'City.

10. a. I 'speak *Japa*'*nese*.
    b. I 'ate at a '*Japanese* 'restaurant.

---

[1]outside cabin = a room in a ship with a window

TWO-WORD VERBS

A **two-word verb** is a verb plus adverb ("preposition" or "particle") that has a special meaning. Which of the following are two-word verbs?

1. a. *Look out*! A car is coming.
   b. I'm *looking out* the window.
2. a. I *ran into* Susan at the supermarket.
   b. He *ran into* the house when it started to rain.

In these examples, two-word verbs are found in (a): *look out* means to be careful; *run into* means to meet unexpectedly. You must look them up in the dictionary to find out their meanings; you cannot translate them word for word. The verb plus adverb acts like a single verb. Some two-word verbs can be followed by another preposition (to drop *out of* school). English has many two-word verbs such as *wake up*, *put on*, *put off*, *put away*, *pay back*, *do over*, *turn down*, *hand in*, *figure out*, *get along (with)*, and *run out (of)*. Can you think of any others?

Stress *both* words of a two-word verb *when they are separated*.

1. I 'put my 'books a'way.
2. I 'picked it 'up 'yesterday.
3. She 'tried some 'dresses 'on at the 'store.
4. Did you 'turn the 'lights 'off?
5. 'Yes, I 'turned them 'off.

When the verb and adverb are *not* separated, one of the stresses is lost: they become one "word" with one stress. Stress the *adverb* when it occurs *at the end of a sentence or phrase*. This is the normal location of stress for two-word verbs.

6. My 'books are 'all *put a'way*.
7. You'd 'better *look 'out*.
8. His 'dog was *run 'over* by a 'truck.
9. The 'lights are *turned 'off* 'now.
10. The 'dresses she *tried 'on* were ex'pensive.

When the verb and adverb are *not* separated and they are *followed by a noun object*, *either* the *verb or* the *adverb* can be stressed according to the overall rhythm of the sentence.

11. I've 'put away my 'books al'ready.
12. I've 'just *put a'way* my 'books.

CHAPTER 10

Stress in Compound Nouns

a black board

a blackboard

PREREADING QUESTION

What is the difference in pronounciation between *blackboard* and *black board*?

10.1 Compound Nouns

A **compound noun** is a sequence of two or more words that together have a new meaning and function as a single noun. The second element or "word" of the compound is a noun; the first element is usually a noun but may also be another part of speech. A compound noun may be written as one or two words.

roommate	newspaper	school bus	wastepaper basket
popcorn	highway	travel agent	amusement park
greenhouse	wash cloth	shaving cream	computer program

The first element describes the second noun, and it is always *singular*.

a flower garden = a kind of garden that contains flowers (*not* flowers garden)
a garden flower = a kind of flower that is grown in a garden

A compound noun is pronounced like a single word. There is only *one main stress*, which falls on the *first element* (usually the first syllable). The stressed syllable is higher in pitch than the other syllables when the word is said by itself or at the end of a statement.

107

my **sun'**glasses   /maɪ ˈsənglæsɪz/   the **'post** office   /ðə ˈpoʊstɔfɪs/

The syllable that is normally stressed in the second noun when it appears alone (ˈglasses, ˈoffice) loses its stress, but retains its vowel quality.[1] That syllable is said to have secondary stress, and it is marked in dictionaries with /ˌ/: /ˈsənˌglæsɪz/, /ˈpoʊstˌɔfɪs/. Compare the following words.

weekend   /ˈwikɛnd/   compound noun with unstressed, *unreduced* syllable
weakened   /ˈwikənd/   verb with unstressed, *reduced* syllable

EXERCISES

A. Fill in the blanks with compound nouns, and read the sentences aloud.

1. Juice made from oranges is called _____ orange juice _____.
2. A pool used for swimming is a _____ swimming pool _____.
3. A card that gives you credit is a _____.
4. A machine used for washing clothes is a _____.
5. Balls of snow are called _____.
6. A store that has many departments is called a _____.
7. An extinguisher that puts out fires is a _____.
8. Beans from the coffee plant are called _____.
9. A watch that you wear on your wrist is a _____.
10. A garden that contains vegetables is a _____.
11. A recorder that plays tapes is called a _____.
12. A center in which you do your shopping is a _____.

B. Mark the primary stress and practice reading the following longer compounds.

1. This *air conditioner* isn't working.
2. Where's the *Psychology Department* located?
3. Take your *application form* to the *administration building*.
4. Throw those old *textbooks* in the *wastepaper basket*.
5. My old *English professor* now works at an *employment agency*.
6. Many *traffic accidents* were reported over the *weekend*.
7. I think he's a *newspaper reporter*, but he might be a *magazine editor*.
8. The *unemployment office* is crowded with *factory workers*.

---

[1]In a few common words, the vowel in the second noun is reduced, as in *fireman* /ˈfaɪɚmən/, *police-man* /pəˈlismən/. When this happens, the word begins to sound more like a word with a suffix than a compound.

C. Write down five other compound nouns.

1. _____

2. _____

3. _____

4. _____

5. _____

10.2 Introduction to Intonation

The alternation of stressed and unstressed syllables creates the beat or rhythm of English. **Rhythm** is the **time pattern** of speech. **Intonation** is the **melody**, the tune, or the changes in the pitch of the voice. In singing, notes can be high or low, and the voice can jump or glide either up or down. In speaking, syllables can be spoken on a higher or lower pitch, and the voice can rise, fall, or remain the same during the production of syllables.

TO DO

A sequence of syllables can have the same rhythm, but a different intonation pattern. Try tapping to a sequence of alternating long and short syllables, such as /'da də 'da də 'da də/. This same sequence can be said with various intonation patterns, or even whispered, and the rhythm remains the same.

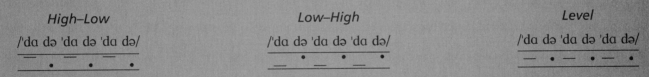

High–Low	*Low–High*	*Level*
/'da də 'da də 'da də/	/'da də 'da də 'da də/	/'da də 'da də 'da də/

Say a vowel such as /ɑ/ with different intonation patterns. First jump between two syllables; then slide or glide continuously over one long syllable. If you put your hand on your larynx, you may feel that it moves up for a rise and down for a fall. This can be seen easily in men who have a large Adam's apple (place that sticks out on the throat).

	Fall *(High–Low)*	*Rise* *(Low–High)*	*Level* *(No Change)*
Jump	ɑ ɑ	ɑ ɑ	ɑ ɑ
Glide	ɑ:	ɑ:	ɑ:

PRACTICE 1

Now try the same with some words, first over two syllables, and then over one syllable. In English, the fall or rise *begins on the stressed syllable* and is continued in any following unstressed syllables. Preceding unstressed syllables are mid or low, so that the *fall* begins by *jumping up* to the stressed syllable. Can you identify which pattern your teacher or another student is producing?

	1. Fall (Ends Low)	*2. Rise (Ends High)*	*3. Level*
Jumps:			
a.	'uh oh	'uh oh	'uh oh
b.	'see you	'see you	'see you
c.	'nothing	'nothing	'nothing
d.	a 'woman	a 'woman	a 'woman
e.	im'possible	im'possible	im'possible
Glides:			
f.	'oh	'oh	'oh
g.	'no	'no	'no
h.	'yes	'yes	'yes
i.	a 'man	a 'man	a 'man
j.	an engi'neer	an engi'neer	an engi'neer

Which of these three patterns (fall, rise, or level) is usually used in English when asking a question? Which pattern is used when making a statement? Which pattern is used in the middle of a sentence when you aren't finished speaking? Listen to the intonation patterns in the word *coming* in the following sentences.

1. Are you *coming*?
2. I think he's *coming*.
3. I think he's *coming* tomorrow, but I'm not sure.
4. When is he *coming*?

As you probably guessed, a rise is typically used at the end of questions (1), a fall is usually used at the end of statements (2), and very little change in pitch is used in the middle of a sentence (3). In English, a rise occurs on yes–no questions (questions beginning with an auxiliary verb such as *is*, *was*, *do*, *did*, *have*, etc.), but a fall, like in statements, is used at the end of information questions (questions beginning with question words like *who*, *what*, *where*, *when*, etc.). Thus both (2) and (4) end in a fall.

Intonation and stress are closely related. Not only do we need to know the *direction* of the change in pitch (rise or fall) if any, but we also need to know *where* the pitch change takes place. In English, every pause group contains **one major fall or rise in pitch** that begins on a stressed syllable. Normally, the fall or rise occurs **on the last stressed syllable before a pause**. This combination of stress and major pitch change is called **sentence stress**. Since stress occurs on content words, this means that the sentence stress or major pitch change usually occurs in the last content word before a pause. **Boldface type** will be used on syllables that receive sentence stress.

Fall on the Last Stressed Syllable	*Rise on the Last Stressed Syllable*
5. I'll 'see you to'**mor**row.	Will I 'see you to'**mo**rrow?
6. I'd 'really 'like to 'see you.	Would you 'really 'like to 'see me?
7. I 'think she's '**beau**tiful.	Do you 'think she's '**beau**tiful?
8. It was a 'beautiful '**day**.	Was it a 'beautiful '**day**?

This basic intonation pattern, a rise or fall beginning on the last stressed syllable before a pause, is the normal pattern of English. There are other intonation patterns where the pitch pattern and/or its location are different, but they have special meanings. In Section 9.1 we mentioned putting strong stress and high pitch on *I* at the beginning of a sentence, which means '*I,* not someone else'. More of these special patterns and more details on intonation will be discussed in Chapter 16. For now, it is best to practice putting the sentence stress on the last stressed syllable before a pause.

10.3 Compound Versus Non-compound Constructions ADVANCED

Sentence stress is important in showing the difference between a compound noun and a sequence of words, such as an adjective plus a noun or a verb plus a noun.

A compound noun is pronounced like one word. It is stressed on the first element only. When compound nouns occur at the end of a sentence, the *first element* receives *sentence stress*. In a phrase made up of an adjective plus a noun, *both* words are stressed and the *last word* receives *sentence stress*. This same pattern is also used in other sequences of two words before a pause, as in verbs followed by nouns.

	Compound Noun	*Adjective + Noun*	*Verb + Noun*
1.	a 'train station	a 'nice 'station	'finish 'dinner
2.	a 'baseball player	a 'famous 'player	de'liver 'papers
3.	the 'summertime	a 'wonderful 'time	'go 'home
4.	an a'musement park	an a'musing 'park	'play 'ball

Sometimes the same combination of words can be used either as a compound noun with a special meaning or as an ordinary sequence of two words. There is a difference in both rhythm (one versus two stress beats) and intonation (major pitch change on the first or last word).

Falling Intonation

Compound:	a '**black**board	(the large slate the teacher writes on with chalk)
Non-compound:	a 'black '**board**	(any board or piece of wood which is black) Adjective + Noun
Compound:	They're '**wash**ing machines.	(they are special machines that wash clothes)
Non-compound:	They're 'washing ma'**chines**.	(people are cleaning some machines) Verb + Noun

Rising Intonation

Compound: Is it a 'blackboard?   Jump up; *board* is short, very high,
                   . . . — •   and weak

Non-compound: Is it a 'black 'board?   Long rise on *board*
                   . . . — ⁄

PRACTICE 2

Use both rhythm and intonation to make a difference between compound and non-compound expressions. First, read the underlined words, and then read the sentences. Your teacher will then read either (1) or (2): which do you hear? The questions (k–n) are difficult; listen for a jump up in compounds and a long rise on the last word in non-compounds.

	1. Compound	*2. Non-compound*
a.	'Those are 'greenhouses. (glass buildings where plants are grown)	'Those are 'green 'houses. (houses that are green in color)
b.	He 'entered the 'darkroom. (the room that photographers develop pictures in)	He 'entered the 'dark 'room. (any room that is dark)
c.	We 'saw some 'yellow jackets. (large yellow and black bees that can sting)	We 'saw some 'yellow 'jackets. (yellow coats)
d.	They 'look like 'hot dogs. (long pork sausages served in rolls)	They 'look like 'hot 'dogs. (dogs which are hot)
e.	They're 'cheapskates. (people who don't like to spend any money)	They're 'cheap 'skates. (inexpensive skates)
f.	They 'looked at a 'toy store. (a store that sells toys)	They 'looked at a 'toy 'store. (a tiny store that is a toy, not a real one)
g.	We 'visited the 'White House. (the place where the U.S. President lives)	We 'visited the 'white 'house. (a house that is white)
h.	They're 'playing cards. (cards for playing games like bridge, poker, etc.)	They're 'playing 'cards. (people are playing games using cards)
i.	He's a 'famous 'English teacher. (a person who teaches English as his job)	He's a 'famous 'English 'teacher. (a teacher who comes from England)
j.	'Where's the 'new 'blackboard? (board the teacher writes on)	'Where's the 'new 'black 'board? (black piece of wood)
k.	Are they 'washing machines? (machines that wash clothes)	Are they 'washing 'machines? (is someone cleaning machines?)
l.	Did you 'see the 'bluebird? (a kind of bird with a red breast and blue feathers)	Did you 'see the 'blue 'bird? (any bird that is blue in color)
m.	Have you ever seen a 'boardwalk? (a raised wooden walkway along the beach)	Have you ever seen a 'board 'walk? (a board that walks)
n.	Do you 'know of a 'freeway to 'get there? (a wide road for driving quickly)	Do you 'know of a 'free 'way to 'get there? (a method that doesn't cost any money)

EXERCISES

A. Mark the stress in the following sentences, and practice reading them with correct rhythm and sentence stress.

1. **a.** The President lives in the White House.
   b. My friend lives in a white house.

2. **a.** I bought a new yellow jacket.
   b. He was stung by a yellow jacket.

3. **a.** We were afraid to enter the dark room.
   b. We developed our pictures in the darkroom.

4. **a.** A hot dog would taste good right now.
   b. The hot dog is really panting.

5. **a.** The story had a weak end.
   b. We had a wonderful weekend.

6. **a.** You shouldn't be so careless.
   b. I'm not interested; in fact, I couldn't care less.

7. **a.** Where's the bus stop?
   b. Where does the bus stop?

8. **a.** He's egotistical. In other words, he's selfish.
   b. You should express your idea in other words.

B. In each pair of sentences, one expression is a compound noun and the other is not. Underline the compound noun. Record yourself reading the sentences, and listen to see if you said them differently. CHINESE students need to be especially careful to pronounce the non-compound expressions correctly.

1. **a.** It's a paper clip.
   b. It's a paper bag.

2. **a.** I want an orange shirt.
   b. I want some orange juice.

3. **a.** It's a fire engine.
   b. It's a fine engine.

4. **a.** They're snow shoes.
   b. They're new shoes.

5. **a.** It's a diamond ring.
   b. It's a wedding ring.

6. **a.** It's an enormous building.
   b. It's an apartment building.

7. **a.** That's a defective story.
   b. That's a detective story.

8. **a.** I need a light bulb.
   b. I need a large bulb.

9. **a.** He lives on a main road.
   b. He lives on Main Street.

10. **a.** That's drinking water.
    b. They're drinking water.

CHAPTER 11

Review of Stress and Rhythm

11.1 Reading Passages

 A. Listen and mark the stresses in the following paragraph. Then record yourself reading it aloud, remembering to reduce unstressed syllables. Be 'sure to 'mark a 'stress on 'every 'word of 'two or 'more 'syllables and on 'every 'one-syllable 'content word. The first sentence is done for you.

Motion[1]

We shall be'gin our 'study of 'physics and 'chemistry with an a'nalysis of 'motion: 'what it 'is, 'how 'things 'move, and 'why they 'do so. For several reasons this is the logical point of departure from the casual realm of our daily lives to the precise realm of science. Everything in the universe is in ceaseless movement, from the most minute[2] constituents[3] of atoms to the immense galaxies of stars that populate space, and this movement is an essential factor in the structure and evolution of the physical world. Another consideration is the simplicity of the phenomena involved in motion, which permits us to become familiar with the methods

---

[1]Arthur Beiser and Konrad Krauskopf, *Introduction to Physics and Chemistry* (New York: McGraw-Hill, 1964), p. 2.

[2]minute = very small

[3]constituent = part of something

of science before applying these methods to more complicated situations. And, as a historical note, modern science had its genesis[4] in the study of motion. The classic conflict between the Ptolemaic and Copernican concepts of the solar system brought into clear focus the relative nature of motion, while Galileo's observations on moving bodies, which contradicted ancient but unfounded beliefs, showed the power and primacy of measurement in the exploration of nature.

B. Listen and mark the stresses in the following passage. Then record yourself reading it aloud.

The Scientific Method[5]

'Scientists, like 'other 'human 'beings, 'have their 'hopes and 'fears, their 'passions and de'spondencies[6]—and their strong emotions may sometime interrupt the course of clear thinking and sound practice. But science is also self-correcting. The most fundamental axioms[7] and conclusions may be challenged. The prevailing hypotheses[8] must survive confrontation with observation. Appeals to authority are impermissible. The steps in a reasoned argument must be set out for all to see. Experiments must be reproducible.

The history of science is full of cases where previously accepted theories and hypotheses have been entirely overthrown, to be replaced by new ideas that more adequately explain the data. While there is an understandable psychological inertia[9]—usually lasting about one generation—such revolutions in scientific thought are widely accepted as a necessary and desirable element of scientific progress. Indeed, the reasoned criticism of a prevailing belief is a service to the proponents[10] of that belief; if they are incapable of defending it, they are well advised to abandon it. This self-questioning and error-correcting aspect of the scientific method is its most striking property, and sets it off from many other areas of human endeavor where credulity[11] is the rule.

---

[4]genesis = beginning, starting point

[5]Carl Sagan, *Broca's Brain: Reflections on the Romance of Science* (New York: Random House, 1974), p. 82.

[6]despondency = feeling discouraged and without hope

[7]axiom = statement accepted as true

[8]prevailing hypothesis = widespread idea that explains the facts, explanation believed by everyone

[9]inertia = resistance to change, desire not to change

[10]proponent = person who argues in favor of

[11]credulity = willingness to believe without proof

C. Mark the stresses in the following passage on your own. Then read it aloud in groups to check your answers. Stress in the following words can not be predicted from the rules: dis'plays, a'lert, 'Yankee, Wis'casset.

Severe Sun Storm Threatens Utilities[12]

A severe disturbance of the Earth's magnetic field, caused by temporary changes in solar activity, began on Tuesday night, threatening electric utility equipment and communication systems, Government scientists said yesterday.

The storm, which on Tuesday produced displays of the northern lights as far south as Pennsylvania, is expected to persist for several days and may intensify.

Utility managers around the country were notified yesterday to remain on alert, because such storms can interrupt electrical transmissions and damage transformers at generating stations. Some officials have questioned whether such a storm in April might have caused explosions and a fire at the Maine Yankee nuclear plant in Wiscasset.

11.2 Review Exercises

A. Mark the stresses in the following imaginary paragraph. Review the rules for stress placement in Section 6.4 if necessary.

(**1.**) A prestigious company published an influential book, which became a commercial success. (**2.**) It contained grotesque pictures of corrupt politicians entertaining beautiful actresses in luxurious surroundings. (**3.**) The public was disgusted yet fascinated by the sight of government employees acting so outrageously. (**4.**) Critics said that the descriptions of their conduct were exaggerated and not realistic, and that the publicity caused by these revelations could potentially damage their careers. (**5.**) A presidential commission is investigating the matter and will report its findings in the newspaper when it has gathered all relevant information.

---

[12]*New York Times,* June 6, 1991, sec. A, p. 16. Copyright © 1991 by The New York Times Company. Reprinted by permission.

B. Mark the stresses and circle the best phonetic transcription for the underlined syllables. Review Chapters 6, 7, and 8, if necessary.

EXAMPLE: It's 'fortunate that she ar'rived on 'time.
(neɪt/n̄ɪt)(ðæt/ðət)

1. Where <u>can</u> I buy some pho<u>to</u><u>gra</u>phic equipment?
(kæn/kən)   (toʊ/tə)(græ/grə)

2. You <u>can't</u> play re<u>cords</u> late at night in the dormitory.
(kænt/kənt) (kɔɚdz/kɚdz)

3. <u>Do</u> you <u>ob</u>ject to her <u>con</u>duct? Yes, I <u>do</u>.
(du/dʊ)(ɑb/əb)   (kɑn/kən)   (du/dʊ)

4. I got <u>an</u> esti<u>mate</u> for repairing the electri<u>cal</u> wiring in <u>our</u> house.
(æn/ən)(meɪt/mɪt)   (kal/kəl)   (aʊɚ/ɑɚ)

5. They plan to oper<u>ate</u> as soon <u>as</u> possible.
(reɪt/rɪt)   (æz/əz)

6. <u>That</u> bookstore is <u>hav</u>ing a sale on contemporary novels.
(ðæt/ðət)   (hæv/əv)

7. He <u>was</u> forced <u>to</u> resign because of his unpo<u>pu</u>larity.
(wɑz/wəz)   (tu/tə)   (pyu/pyə)

8. The Minister <u>for</u> Industries is <u>con</u>ducting an official survey.
(fɔɚ/fɚ)   (kɑn/kən)

9. Jane <u>and</u> Ted <u>have</u> been gradu<u>ate</u> students for three years.
(ænd/ən)(hæv/əv)   (eɪt/ɪt)

10. We asked <u>them</u> to <u>pre</u>pare us a deli<u>cious</u> meal.
(ðɛm/ðəm)(pri/prɪ)   (sius/ʃəs)

11. You should a<u>po</u>lo<u>gize</u> to her yourself.
(pɑ/pə)(lɔ/lə)

12. Did <u>you</u> know <u>that</u> he was assassi<u>na</u>ted?
(yu/yʊ)   (ðæt/ðət)   (neɪ/nɪ)

13. <u>He</u> realized that <u>he</u> wasn't prepared for the examination.
(hi/i)   (hi/i)

14. The service <u>at</u> our local gas station is very effi<u>cient</u>.
(æt/ət)   (sient/ʃənt)

15. What <u>are</u> you waiting <u>for</u>?
(ɑɚ/ɚ)   (fɔɚ/fɚ)

C. Mark the stresses and circle the best phonetic transcription for the underlined syllables.

1. He collects antiques, doesn't he?
(hi/i)(kɔ/kə)   (hi/i)

2. The desert is a desolate place.
(sɔ/sə)(leɪt/lɪt)

3. You can buy toothpaste at a drugstore, but you can't buy tennis balls.
(kæn/kən)   (kænt/kənt)

4. He removed his clothes from the washing machine and put them away.
(hɪz/ɪz)   (ðɛm/ðəm)

5. Many Vietnamese refugees have immigrated here to escape persecution.
(greɪ/grɪ)   (ɛ/ə)   (sɛ/sə)

6. People typically criticize others more than themselves.
(saɪz/sɪz)   (ðæn/ðən)

7. It was a delicate operation, but they expect the patient to make
(keɪt/kɪt)

sufficient progress to be able to go home tomorrow.
(siɛnt/ʃənt)(prɑ/prə)   (tu/tə)

8. They suspected that the volunteers had permitted the stranger to come in.
(su/sə)   (hæd/əd)   (tu/tə)

9. He became jealous when he saw his wife with the famous actor.
(lus/ləs)   (tɔɚ/tɚ)

10. Politicians often get votes for their personality, not for their views.
(pɑ/pə)   (næ/nə)   (fɔɚ/fɚ)

11. Presidential candidates tend to exaggerate their qualifications.
(tiɑl/ʃəl)   (reɪt/rɪt)

12. News of the scandal was devastating to the political contest.
(wɑz/wəz)   (pɑ/pə) (kɑn/kən)

13. Congress deliberated for over an hour before coming to a decision.
(kɑŋ/kəŋ)   (reɪ/rɪ)   (æn/ən)

14. Have they identified the problem? No, they haven't.
(hæv/həv/əv)   (hæv/həv/əv)

15. We need some black boards to make ourselves a bookcase.
(aʊɚ/ɑɚ)   (keɪs/kəs)

CHAPTER 12

Consonant Overview

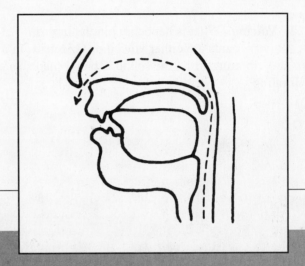

PREREADING QUESTIONS

What sound is being made? Can you explain how to make it?

1. nose
2. nasal cavity
3. upper lip
4. upper teeth
5. tooth ridge
6. hard palate
7. soft palate (velum)
8. lower lip
9. lower teeth
10. tip of the tongue
11. front of the tongue
12. back of the tongue
13. larynx
14. vocal folds
15. glottis

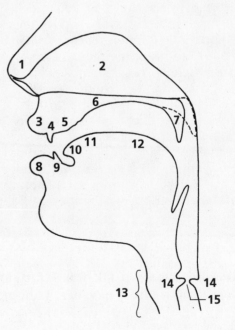

FIGURE 12-1
Side View of the Speech Organs

12.1 Production of Consonants

Vowels can be described by the position of the tongue (high or low, front or back) and lips (rounded or unrounded). In vowels, the air flows out of the mouth continuously; the tongue and lips simply shape the air flow. *Consonants* are sounds that interrupt or restrict the flow of air. We can describe any consonant by answering the following five questions about it.

1. Voicing. What is happening in the larynx?

All consonants are either voiced or voiceless. In a **voiced** sound, the vocal folds in the larynx are vibrating while the sound is being made. In a **voiceless** sound, the vocal folds are not vibrating.

TO DO

Take a deep breath; then exhale and make a long /ɑ/. Put your hand over your larynx (the place on your throat that sticks out the most) and try it again. You should feel the vibration of your vocal folds. Now take a deep breath and just exhale with your mouth open, making a long /h/. You should feel that nothing is happening in your larynx. Take a deep breath and alternate /ɑhɑhɑh/ continuously several times until you run out of breath. You should be able to feel with your hand the difference between voiced /ɑ/ and voiceless /h/. Another way to test for voicing is to put your hands over your ears. During voiced /ɑ/, you will hear a loud buzzing noise, but not during /h/. In order to gain control over your vocal folds, try taking deep breaths and alternating between /ɑ/ and /h/ at different speeds. When the teacher points to his or her larynx, turn on voicing for /ɑ/; as soon as he or she takes his or her hand away, turn off the voicing to produce /h/.

Try making some other sounds, still holding your hand on your larynx. Take a deep breath and exhale with a long /s/. Is it voiced or voiceless? How about /z/? Alternate between voiceless /s/ and voiced /z/ continuously (don't stop the breath between them). Try alternating /sszzsszz/ again as the teacher points toward and away from his or her larynx at different speeds. Can you make the sound voiced or voiceless exactly when you want to? In normal speaking, we are constantly turning voicing on and off at very short time intervals. If you can gain control of voicing while making /s/ and /z/, you will be able to apply that skill to producing other sounds that might be more difficult for you.

Using a similar procedure, decide whether the following consonants are voiced or voiceless. Then alternate between each pair, being careful not to change anything except voicing: /ffvvffvv/; /θθðð θθðð/; /ʃʃʒʒ ʃʃʒʒ/.

Make a long /lll/. Is it voiced or voiceless? It's voiced. Can you make it voiceless? (Take a deep breath because you will run out of air quickly.) How about /r/? Try to make it voiceless. In English, we use voiceless /l/ and /r/ in the words *place*, *clean*, *price*, and *cream*. Try /m/. If you make it voiceless, you should feel air coming out your nose. Voiceless /m/ is sometimes used in the expressions *hm* (="is that so?") and *uh hm* (="yes, I'm listening"). Go through the rest of the consonants and find out for yourself whether they are voiced or voiceless: /n, ŋ, p, t, k, w, y, b, d, g/.

The *voiceless* consonants are /p, t, k, f, θ, s, ʃ, tʃ, h/.
The *voiced* consonants are /b, d, g, v, ð, z, ʒ, dʒ, m, n, ŋ, l, r, w, y/.

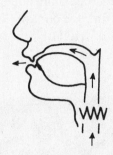

Voiced /z/:
the vocal folds are vibrating.

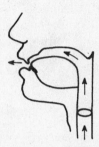

Voiceless /s/:
the vocal folds are not vibrating.

FIGURE 12-2
Voicing

2. Manner of Articulation. How is the sound made? How close do the two articulators come together?

To **articulate** means to make a sound. The **articulators** are the organs in the mouth, such as the tongue or lips, that approach each other in order to produce a sound. The articulators may stop the air completely or let a relatively small or large amount of air pass through.

In the **stops** /p, t, k, b, d, g/ and [ʔ], the articulators come together tightly and *stop the air flow completely*. No air escapes during the production of a stop.

TO DO

Say /ɑpɑ/ a few times, holding the /p/ a little longer each time. Try it again and hold the /p/ for a very long time, /ɑppp/. What happened? While you were holding the /p/, you couldn't breathe because /p/ stops the air completely. You finally had to release it (open your mouth). Try /ɑbɑ/, /ɑdɑ/, /ɑgɑ/. Note that in English the voiced consonants /b, d, g/ must stop the air completely.

In the **fricatives** /f, θ, s, ʃ, v, ð, z, ʒ, h/, the articulators come very close together but do not completely stop the air flow. The air must squeeze out through a very small channel, so it becomes turbulent and creates a *hissing noise* or **friction**.

TO DO

Make a long /fff/, /sss/, /ʃʃʃ/, and /θθθ/, and listen to the friction. Which is louder, /f/ or /s/? Which makes a higher pitched sound, /s/ or /ʃ/? Can you feel your tongue squeezing when you make /s/? To feel the narrow air channel, try *sucking the air in* instead of exhaling when you make /s/; you should feel a jet of cold air between your tongue and the roof of your mouth. Try to suck the air in while saying /ʃ/. For which sound, /s/ or /ʃ/, is the air channel narrower? You should feel a narrower channel for the higher pitched /s/.

Now try each of the voiced fricatives, /vvv, zzz, ððð, ʒʒʒ/ and listen: you will hear two sounds, the voicing produced at the larynx and the friction produced in the mouth, which you can also feel. Be sure to take a deep breath and squeeze the articulators together as you force the air out. Without enough air pressure, you will not be able to produce both voicing and friction. Try each pair, /ffvv/, /sszz/, /ʃʃʒʒ/, /θθðð/ and be sure that the *only change* you make is adding voicing. Look in a mirror to make sure that the voiced and voiceless sounds look exactly the same. Compare /p/ and /f/ (*a pan, a fan*), /b/ and /v/ (*a ban, a van*), to feel the difference between a stop and a fricative.

The **affricates** /tʃ/ and /dʒ/ are sequences of a stop plus a fricative: the stop is immediately released into a fricative made at the same place.

TO DO

Make and compare the following sequences of sounds, /ɑtɑ/, /ɑʃɑ/, /ɑtʃɑ/. In /ɑtɑ/ feel how the air is stopped and then, as soon as it is released, the vowel begins. In /ɑʃɑ/, the air is never stopped completely; the air path is just narrowed and then opened up again. In /ɑtʃɑ/, first the air is stopped, then the articulators open a very little bit and produce friction before opening up completely into the vowel. Compare /ɑdɑ/, /ɑʒɑ/, and /ɑdʒɑ/.

In the **approximants** /r, l, w, y/, the articulators approach each other, but they create no friction. These sounds are similar to vowels. The consonant /r/ is produced like the vowel /ɚ/; it is considered to be a consonant when it begins a syllable.

TO DO

Compare /r/ and /z/ (*rip, zip*), /w/ and /v/ (*wine, vine*), /y/ and /ʒ/ (*mayor, measure*), to feel the difference between a smooth approximant and a noisy fricative. Compare /r/ in *rain, train,* and *drain.* After /t/ and /d/, /r/ becomes a fricative.

In the **nasals** /m, n, ŋ/, the articulators come together completely and stop the air from coming out of the mouth, but the air is allowed to flow smoothly out the nose. The velum or soft palate, the very back part of the roof of the mouth, is lowered to let the air enter the nasal cavity. In all other English consonants, the velum is raised to prevent air from escaping out the nose.

A *stop* stops the air completely.

A *fricative* lets a little noisy air pass out.

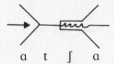

An *affricate* first stops the air, then lets a little noisy air pass out.

An *approximant* lets a lot of air flow out.

FIGURE 12-3
Manner of Articulation

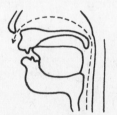

Nasal /n/:
air flows out the nose.

FIGURE 12-4
Nasal

TO DO

Try to say the sequence /**dndndn**/ without inserting any vowels between the sounds. Try it silently. Can you feel something moving in the back of your mouth? Try the same thing with /**bmbmbm**/, then /**gŋgŋgŋ**/. The only difference between the stops /b, d, g/ and the nasals /m, n, ŋ/ is that the air exits out the nose during the nasals. We pronounce many words ending in /dən/ or /tən/ by going directly from the stop to the nasal without inserting a vowel. The nasal itself acts like a vowel and forms a syllable, /ən/ = [n̩]. Try pronouncing the following words this way: *sudden* ['sədn̩], *harden*, *didn't*, *couldn't*, *button* ['bəʔn̩], *certain*, *suddenly*, *certainly*.

3. Air Path. Does the air travel down the center or the sides?

Most consonants are **central**; there is a single air path down the middle. However, for the **lateral** /l/, the air travels around one or both sides of the tongue.

TO DO

Make a long /lll/. Then exhale and make an /l/ *sucking the air in*. Where do you feel cold air? Make /sss/ while inhaling. Can you feel the cold air go over the center of the tongue for /s/ and around the sides for /l/?

Try saying /dldldl/ without inserting a vowel between the sounds. Do it again silently. You should feel that the tip of the tongue stays fixed while the sides of the tongue go down and up. Feel this transition between /d/ and /l/ while slowly and silently saying *sadly*, *gladly*, and *rapidly*. Then try saying the words

handle, middle, needle, and *medal* without inserting a vowel between /d/ and /l/. The lateral /l/ acts like a vowel in these words and forms a syllable, /əl/ = [ļ].

Make /r/ on an inhalation. The air flows over the center of the tongue, and the tip of the tongue does not touch any part of the roof of the mouth. However, in /l/, the tip of the tongue touches behind the teeth and stays there for the whole sound, while the air comes out one or both sides. Alternate silently then aloud between /r/ and /l/ to feel this difference.

/d/ No air escapes during the stop.

/l/ Air passes out around sides of tongue.

/r/ Air passes out over center of the tongue.

FIGURE 12-5
Lateral versus Central Air Path

4. Timing. Can the sound be held or prolonged?

Most sounds are maintainable: you can hold or prolong the sound as long as you have breath. However, the consonants /w, y/ and [ɾ] (fast /d/ between vowels) are essentially **momentary** or brief sounds; if you try to hold them, they become a different sound.

TO DO

Say /awa/ and /aya/ several times, prolonging /w/ and /y/. /awa/ now sounds like the sequence /a.u.a/, and /aya/ sounds like /a.i.a/. /w/ and /y/ are quick versions of the vowels /u/ and /i/.

Try saying the sequence /ada/ faster and faster, making the /d/ as short as you can until your tongue just briefly and lightly hits or taps

the roof of the mouth. You now have made /d/ into a **tap** [ɾ], which is one kind of [r] in many languages. This sound is often used in North American English for /t/ or /d/ in unstressed syllables. Try pronouncing the following words using a tap: *riding, writing, ladder, latter, thirty, party, lady, phonetic, editor.*

5. Place of Articulation. Where is the sound made? Which two articulators approach each other?

Look in a mirror while you say the consonants in each group, both aloud and silently, in order to see, hear, and feel them. Refer to Figure 12-1 (p. 119).

Lower Lip and Upper Lip — /p, b, m, w/

TO DO

Say /p, b, m, w/ silently and feel the two lips. For which sound do the lips make a different shape? The lips close completely for /p, b, m/, but they are rounded and still open for /w/ (and the back of the tongue is raised as in the vowel /u/). Look in the mirror while you say the following groups of words and make sure that each group looks exactly the same: *pop, Bob, mom*; *pat, bat, mat*; *lap, lab, lamb*; *wrap it, rabbit.*

Inside of Lower Lip and Upper Teeth — /f, v/

TO DO

Look in a mirror and say, first aloud and then silently, /afa/. Notice how the lower lip moves up to touch the upper teeth; the upper lip does not move (and should have no rounding). Be sure that the *inside* of the lower lip lightly touches the edges of the teeth. Now try /ava/ silently, then aloud, and be sure that it looks exactly the same as /afa/. While looking in the mirror, alternate /ffvvffvv/ keeping the air stream going the whole time. Make sure that /f/ and /v/ have exactly the same articulation. Keep the fricative noise going during /v/. Do not add any lip rounding, and keep the upper lip out of the way. Look in the mirror to be sure that /f/ and /v/ look the same in the following words: *fairy, very*; *fail, veil*; *safer, saver*; *leaf, leave.*

Tip of Tongue and Upper Teeth — /θ, ð/

TO DO

Looking in your mirror, move the tip of the tongue up until it lightly touches the cutting edge of the upper teeth. Then take a breath and blow air out between the tongue and teeth to make a long /θθθ/. Do not press the tongue too tightly against the teeth; air must be able to pass out since /θ/ is a fricative, not a stop. You should be able to see only a little bit of your tongue (don't stick your tongue out). Try /aθa/ several times, first silently, then aloud. While looking in the mirror, try some words that use /θ/: *author, healthy, a thought, thick, thank, mouth, cloth.* Now alternate /θθððθθðð/ keeping the air flowing out continuously and check in your mirror to make sure that your articulation stays exactly the same throughout. Try /aða/ several times, silently and aloud, being sure to keep the air flowing the whole time (relax; /ð/ is a very soft sound). Then try some words that use /ð/: *other, another, mother, this, that, them, breathe.*

Tip of Tongue and Tooth Ridge — /t, d, n, l, s, z/ and [ɾ]

TO DO

Slide the tip of your tongue slowly back from the upper teeth *along the roof of the mouth as far back as you can* and feel it. Just behind the teeth is a a rough area that curves up and then becomes smooth. The rough area just behind the teeth is called the **tooth ridge** or alveolar ridge. Try silently saying /t, **d**, **n**, l/ and feel where your tongue touches. Look in the mirror while saying /t, d/ silently. Can you see the tip of your tongue? In English, these consonants are made with the tongue tip firm-ly pressing the tooth ridge and not the teeth, so you shouldn't see the tip of your tongue in the mirror (you may see a little bit of the underside of your tongue). If you can see the tip of your tongue, try sliding it back until you can't see it anymore. Alternate /t/ and /s/ and feel your tongue. Usually /s/ and /z/ are made with the tongue tip down (behind the lower teeth), and the air is squeezed through a small channel between the area just behind the tip of the tongue and the tooth ridge.

Front of the Tongue and Hard Palate — /ʃ, ʒ, tʃ, dʒ, r, y/
(with some lip-rounding for /ʃ, ʒ, tʃ, dʒ, r/)

TO DO

When you slide your tongue along the roof of your mouth, you'll feel a curve and smoothness behind the tooth ridge. This area behind the tooth ridge is the **hard palate** /ˈpælɪt/. /ʃ, ʒ, tʃ, dʒ/ are made with the front of the tongue approaching the hard palate. From /s/, slowly slide your tongue back a little to /ʃ/. /ʃ/ is articulated a little further back on the tongue than /s/, and the tongue tip comes up a little. If you just move your tongue, however, your /ʃ/ will not sound exactly like an English /ʃ/. You also need to push the sides of the lips together a little. Try sliding from /s/ to /ʃ/ and then from /z/ to /ʒ/ looking in the mirror and rounding the lips slightly as you move your tongue back. You will notice that the addition of lip rounding increases the difference between the sounds by lowering the pitch of the hissing sound of /ʃ/ and /ʒ/. You should also feel that /ʃ/ and /ʒ/ are *softer* sounds than /s/ and /z/. Alternate /ʃʃʒʒʃʃʒʒ/ a few times looking in the mirror to make sure that the *only* change you are making is in voicing. Then try a few words that use these sounds: *fashion, nation, shop, she, wash, wish; pleasure, Asia, garage, rouge*. In /tʃ/ and /dʒ/, the front of the tongue touches the front of the hard palate and completely stops the air before opening up into /ʃ/ and /ʒ/. Try a few words with /tʃ/ and /dʒ/: *choose, cheap, church, watch; joke, jump, George, age*.

In /y/, the center of the tongue is raised up toward the center of the hard palate, and the tip of the tongue is behind the lower teeth as in the vowel /i/. The air is not stopped completely (as in /dʒ/), and there is no friction (as in /dʒ/ and /ʒ/). Compare /ɑyɑ/ and /ɑdʒɑ/. Try a few words with /y/: *beyond, yes, year, use, reunion*.

The consonant /r/ is produced like the vowel /ɚ/: the tip of the tongue is lifted up slightly and points to the front of the hard palate, the back of the tongue is raised, and the lips are slightly rounded. Look in your mirror and compare the lip positions of /r/ and /ʃ/ as in *rock, shock; rip, ship; train, chain*. You should see that the lips come closer together for /r/ than for /ʃ/. Compare the lip positions of /r/ and /w/ as in *right, white; red, wed*. You should see that the lips come even closer together for /w/ than for /r/. Try pronouncing some words with /r/ making sure that the tongue tip *does not touch* any part of the roof of the mouth: *road, right, red, around, arrive.* (See Fig. 4.4, p. 47.)

Back of the Tongue and Soft Palate — /k, g, ŋ/

TO DO

Slide the tip of the tongue back as far as you possibly can along the roof of the mouth. You should feel that after the smooth hard palate, it gets soft. This is the **soft palate**. Try saying /k, g, ŋ/ silently a few times, and try to feel the back of your tongue going up and touching the soft palate. Look in the mirror to see that the tongue is in the same place for /ŋ/ as it is for /k/ and /g/. Look in the mirror and say *kick*, *king*, *gag*, and *gang*. Be sure that you stop the air completely when you say /g/, as in *big*, *bigger*, *dog*, and *doggie*.

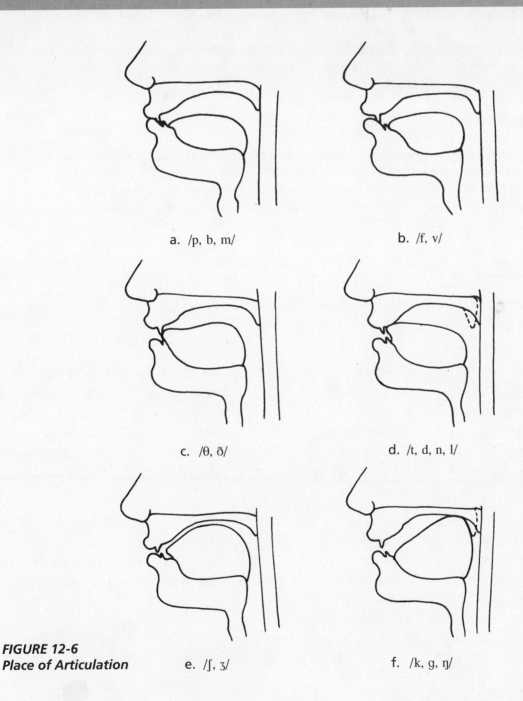

a. /p, b, m/

b. /f, v/

c. /θ, ð/

d. /t, d, n, l/

e. /ʃ, ʒ/

f. /k, g, ŋ/

FIGURE 12-6
Place of Articulation

Glottis (inside the larynx) — /h/ and [ʔ]

TO DO

Take a deep breath and breathe out. The sound that you made when you exhaled is /h/. The **glottis** (the space between the vocal folds in the larynx) is open and allows the air to pass out freely. Try /h/ between different vowels: /ɑhɑ/, /ihi/, /oho/. The mouth is shaped for the following vowel during the production of /h/; no other special movement in the mouth is made for /h/. Say *ahead*, *behind*, *he*, and *who*.

Take a deep breath and hold it a while. When you hold your breath, your glottis is closed. This is called a **glottal stop** [ʔ]. It is used in the middle of the exclamation *uh oh* [ʔə ʔoʊ], which Americans say when they discover they've made a mistake. Try this exclamation a few times; then see if you can stop in the middle and hold it. People often make a glottal stop when they are about to lift something very heavy. The glottal stop is used in American English together with or in place of /t/ in certain words like *button, certain, can't go,* and *it was*. It is *not* normally used, however, to start words beginning with vowels.

Now that you have experimented with all the places of articulation, can you quickly and easily slide from one to the other? Try slowly and continuously the sequence /fθsʃ/ and then /vðzʒ/. Close your eyes and try to feel the movement of your tongue. In normal speech, you must be able to go directly from one consonant to any other within words and phrases.

PRACTICE 1

Practice going smoothly and continuously from one place of articulation to another in the following phrases.

1. /f/ + /s/
   a. laughs a lot
   b. enough sun
   c. rough seas
   d. eats fish
   e. a nice fit

2. /f/ + /θ, ð/
   a. math final
   b. fifth floor
   c. tough things
   d. cough then
   e. breathe freely

3. /θ/ + /s, z/
   a. health service
   b. tenth season
   c. south central
   d. says things
   e. the girls think

4. /v/ + /ð, θ/
   a. live there
   b. love them
   c. of the
   d. give thanks
   e. both voices

5. /v/ + /z, s/
   a. themselves
   b. leave silently
   c. sees very well
   d. is vacant
   e. a nice voice

6. /ð/ + /z, s/
   a. sees them
   b. plays those
   c. knows the
   d. likes that
   e. smooth sailing

7. /ʃ/ + /θ, ð/
   a. both shoes
   b. fourth shot
   c. wash them
   d. wish that

8. /v/ + /z/ + /ð/
   a. loves them
   b. lives there
   c. arrives then
   d. saves these

EXERCISES

A. *Consonant Warmup* [to be done at the beginning of class each day]. Say all the consonants in nonsense syllables. Sometimes make the consonants initial /pɑ, bɑ, tɑ, dɑ . . ./; sometimes make them final /əp, əb, ət . . ./; sometimes make them medial /əpi, əbi, əti . . ./.

1.	p	b	t	d	k	g	tʃ	dʒ
2.	f	v	θ	ð	s	z	ʃ	ʒ
3.	m	n	ŋ	l	r	w	y	h

B. Decide if the following sounds are *voiced* or *voiceless*, and give an *example word* for each sound.

1. /l/	**5.** /ð/	**9.** /ə/	**13.** /ʃ/	**17.** /θ/
2. /z/	**6.** /f/	**10.** /s/	**14.** /v/	**18.** /ŋ/
3. /m/	**7.** /ʒ/	**11.** /dʒ/	**15.** /tʃ/	**19.** /b/
4. /k/	**8.** /d/	**12.** /p/	**16.** /æ/	**20.** /w/

C. Complete the following chart of consonants that have the same place and manner of articulation, but differ in voicing.

	Voiceless	Voiced	Voiceless	Voiced
1.	p	_____	_____	v
2.	_____	d	_____	ð
3.	_____	g	s	_____
4.	tʃ	_____	ʃ	_____

D. Decide if the underlined letters represent a *stop* (does the air stop completely?), *fricative* (is a noise produced in the mouth?), *affricate* (does the air stop before a noise is produced?), *approximant* (is it a smooth, continuous sound?), or *nasal* (does air come out the nose?). Give the phonetic symbol for each.

1. e<u>ff</u>ort	**6.** e<u>v</u>er	**11.** di<u>sh</u>es	**16.** au<u>th</u>or
2. mea<u>s</u>ure	**7.** mo<u>th</u>er	**12.** di<u>tch</u>es	**17.** da<u>dd</u>y
3. ba<u>b</u>y	**8.** a<u>w</u>ay	**13.** ea<u>s</u>y	**18.** ma<u>j</u>or
4. <u>a</u>round	**9.** be<u>c</u>ome	**14.** si<u>ng</u>er	**19.** be<u>y</u>ond
5. fu<u>nn</u>y	**10.** su<u>pp</u>er	**15.** bi<u>gg</u>er	**20.** su<u>mm</u>er

E. Observe your classmate while he or she *silently* forms the following consonants. Is the place of articulation correct?

1. /f/	**3.** /t/	**5.** /ʃ/	**7.** /v/	**9.** /ð/
2. /b/	**4.** /θ/	**6.** /z/	**8.** /w/	**10.** /g/

F. How would you help a fellow student who pronounced the following words incorrectly as shown in brackets []? What should he or she change?

EXAMPLE: *thought* as [tɔt] instead of /θɔt/
Answer: Move the tongue forward so that the tip lightly touches the upper teeth. Loosen the contact between the tongue and teeth to let the air pass out continuously (/θ/ is a fricative, not a stop).

1. sun as [sən] instead of /sən/
2. love as [ləf] instead of /ləv/
3. yes as [dʒɛs] instead of /yɛs/
4. that as [dæt] instead of /ðæt/
5. very as ['bɛri] instead of /'vɛri/
6. catch as [kæʃ] instead of /kætʃ/
7. mouth as [maʊs] instead of /maʊθ/
8. measure as ['mɛʃɚ] instead of /'mɛʒɚ/

G. Read the words for each consonant in Sec. 12.2. Note the ways that each consonant is spelled and the exceptions. Record yourself reading the sentences in Sec. 12.3 and play the recording back. Write down the phonetic symbols for the consonants that you are having difficulty producing or hearing consistently.

12.2 American English Consonant Sounds

Not means that this sound does not occur in the words in parentheses. Major spelling patterns are underlined.

1. /p/ pan, played, cap, rope, happy, open, camping, help
(*not* psalm, psychology, pneumonia, pseudonym, receipt, cupboard, raspberry, coup, corps)

2. /b/ ban, blade, cab, robe, rubber, baby, number, bulb
(*not* debt, doubt, subtle, lamb, comb, dumb, climb, bomb, plumber)

3. /t/ tan, try, bat, late, night, cigarette, crystal, missed, Thomas, thyme, pizza
(*not* listen, fasten, soften, often, Christmas, whistle, castle, mortgage, ballet, fillet, buffet, bouquet, gourmet, depot)

4. /d/ Dan, dry, bad, made, ladder, handle, needed, played, raised, robbed
(*not* handkerchief, handsome, Wednesday)

5. /k/ can, king, cream, back, take, occur, muscular, box, quarter, frequent, technique, chemistry, school, echo, stomach, headache, chronological, zucchini
(*not* knee, know, knife, muscle, indict)

6. /g/   go, green, bag, struggle, finger, ghost, guest, dialogue, exist
(*not* sigh, night, caught, though, weigh, neighbor, campaign, sign,
foreign, diaphragm, gnat, singer, tongue)

7. /f/   fan, leaf, effort, off, enough, laugh, cough, rough, photograph, alphabet,
sphere

8. /v/   van, voice, leave, develop, every, carve, of

9. /θ/   thin, three, breath, month, south, method, birthday, athlete

10. /ð/   then, these, father, other, although, breathe, southern, smooth
(*not* clothes, asthma)

11. /s/   sin, bus, glass, this, place, city, cease, science, states, tax, smell, loose,
the use, the advice
(*not* island, isle, aisle, debris, bourgeois, Illinois, corps)

12. /z/   zoo, buzz, these, diseases, easy, cousin, dogs, plays, moves, baptism, is,
was, has, scissors, dessert, to lose, to use, xerox

13. /ʃ/   shoe, she, wish, fashion, tradition, cautious, social, delicious, ocean,
permission, tissue, pressure, sure, sugar, machine, Chicago

14. /ʒ/   measure, casual, seizure, beige, garage, regime, occasion, Asian

15. /tʃ/   chew, which, watch, achieve, nature, actual, situation, question, cello
(*not* yacht, architect, chef)

16. /dʒ/   juice, major, adjust, injure, George, edge, age, exaggerate, region,
magic, energy, gradual, educate, soldier, margarine

17. /m/   make, some, simmer, smile, socialism, comb, climb, autumn,
diaphragm

18. /n/   no, son, sinner, knock, know, snack, button, sign, gnaw, pneumonia
(*not* autumn, hymn, condemn, column, damn)

19. /ŋ/   sung, tongue, singer, belonging, think, finger, anxious, handkerchief

20. /l/   low, pilot, hello, tall, fly, cloud, please, little, real, fool
(*not* colonel, half, salmon, psalm, chalk, talk, always, folk)

21. /r/   row, pirate, hurry, fry, crowd, drive, true, throw, prepare, street, wrong,
rhythm
(*not* Mrs., iron)

22. /w/   woman, away, what,[1] quiet, squeeze, suite, language, twelve, one,
choir
(*not* who, whose, whole, answer, sword, two, write, wrong, wrist)

23. /y/   yes, beyond, unit, Europe, music, few, fuel, huge, million, beauty

24. /h/   how, behave, hotel, who, whole, inherit, adhesive
(*not* hour, honor, honest, heir, exhibit, exhaust, ghost, vehicle, Graham,
Chatham, neighbor, rhyme; *not* in unstressed non-initial he, him, his,
her, have, has, had)

---

[1]In some accents of English, /hw/ (voiceless /w/) in *whale, which,* and *where* is different from /w/ in *wail, witch,* and *wear* in careful speech. However, this difference often
disappears at conversational speeds.

12.3 American English Consonant Sounds in Sentences

1.	/p/	Peter plans to pick up a jump rope in the department store.
2.	/b/	Bob bought a pair of brown rubber boots for his baby.
3.	/t/	The teacher told us to try to write eighteen sentences every night.
4.	/d/	Those bad children seldom did what their daddy told them to do.
5.	/k/	The cook is baking six carrot cakes with cream cheese frosting.
6.	/g/	The ugly dog has been digging up all the grass in the garden.
7.	/f/	They laughed at the awful photograph of Fred falling off a fence.
8.	/v/	We voted in favor of a law to give everyone five days of vacation.
9.	/θ/	The wealthy author will be thirty-three on his birthday next month.
10.	/ð/	It's hard for either of them to breathe smoothly in this weather.
11.	/s/	My sister sent six small presents to our house this Christmas.
12.	/z/	My crazy cousin always loses his gloves and his keys.
13.	/ʃ/	She wished he would shine his shoes and wash the dishes.
14.	/ʒ/	Two Asians were injured in an unusual explosion at the garage.
15.	/tʃ/	After church, the children will watch a nature program on channel seven.
16.	/dʒ/	The religious judge majored in education in college.
17.	/m/	Some of them have promised not to smoke at the meeting.
18.	/n/	His son is not one of the well-known citizens in this town.
19.	/ŋ/	The young singer sang a beautiful English song.
20.	/l/	Do you believe the careful pilot will fly through those low clouds?
21.	/r/	The professor really hurried through the crowd and arrived before it started to rain.
22.	/w/	We wished the woman would walk more quietly while we worked.
23.	/y/	You could spend a year visiting the fabulous museums in Europe.
24.	/h/	He's happy when his handsome son Henry behaves himself.

CHAPTER 13

Differences Between Voiced and Voiceless Consonants

Which pig would you like?

PREREADING QUESTIONS

How do you pronounce *pig*? How does it differ from *big* and *pick*?

It is an oversimplification to say that the vocal folds vibrate during the production of voiced consonants and that they do not vibrate during voiceless consonants. This is true in the middle of a word, but there are other important differences between voiced and voiceless consonants at the beginnings and ends of words.

13.1 Aspiration of Initial Voiceless Stops /p t k/

The *voiceless stops* /p, t, k/ are **aspirated** at the *beginning of stressed syllables*.[1] This means that there is a *period of voicelessness, like breath or /h/,* after the stop is released and before the vocal folds begin to vibrate for the following vowel. This period of voicelessness or **aspiration** can be indicated by [ʰ] appearing after the consonant. Thus, the words *pie*, *take*, and *cold* can be written as [pʰaɪ], [tʰeɪk], and [kʰoʊld].

---

[1]However, /p, t, k/ are not aspirated after /s/, as in *speak*, *stop*, *scare*, *split*, *strong*, and *scream*.

133

To understand better what is happening, look at Figure 13-1. The top line indicates what is happening in the mouth: first the mouth is open for the vowel, then closed completely for the stop, and then open again for the following vowel. The bottom three lines indicate what can happen at the same time in the larynx. A wavy line means voicing (vocal folds are vibrating); a straight line means voicelessness (vocal folds are not vibrating). In (1), for a *fully voiced stop* [ɑbɑ], the vocal folds vibrate continuously the whole time. In (2), for a *voiceless unaspirated stop* [ɑpɑ], the vocal folds begin to vibrate *as soon as* the mouth opens. (In order to do this, the vocal folds need to be narrowed or closed during the stop.) In (3), for a *voiceless aspirated stop* [ɑpʰɑ], the vocal folds begin to vibrate a short period *after* the mouth has opened. (The vocal folds are open during the stop phase, so it takes a while for the air pressure to start them vibrating.)

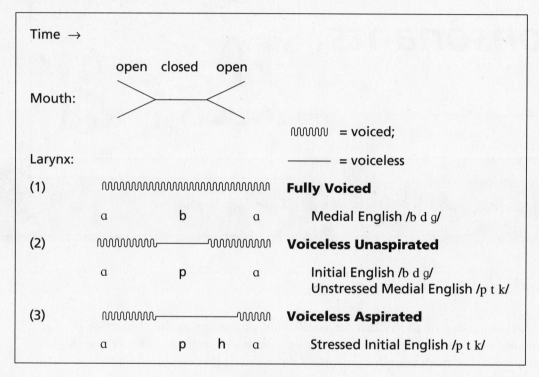

FIGURE 13-1
Aspiration

Some languages (e.g., Thai) have all three types of stops. Languages such as French have only two types, fully voiced (1) and voiceless unaspirated (2). In English, /b, d, g/ are fully voiced (1) in the middle of words (*symbol, rubber*), but they tend to be voiceless unaspirated (2) in initial position (*buy, bear*).[2] /p, t, k/ are voiceless aspirated (3) at the beginning of stressed syllables (*pie, repair*) and voiceless unaspirated (2) in other positions

---

[2]Actually, initial /b, d, g/ are partially voiced. Voice onset time can vary continuously from fully voiced to strongly aspirated. See Catford (1988:57–59) and Ladefoged (1975: 124–125).

(*up, simple, spy*). Think of your own language and compare. The spelling may be confusing; it's sometimes helpful to try pronouncing English /b, d, g/ as if they were spelled <p, t, k> in your own language.

TO DO

Take a deep breath and exhale a few times to produce /hhh/ and feel the openness in your larynx. Take another breath and as you are exhaling, close and open your mouth to make a series /hphphphhh/. Then try just /phh/ a few times. Now take a breath and very slowly add /ɑ/ after /phh/ while your are exhaling to make /**phhɑɑ**/. Be sure to keep the same soft, relaxed feeling in your larynx. If you put your hand in front of your mouth, you should feel your breath. Now try a few words beginning with <p>: *pie, pay, pack*. Say them very slowly, as if you were sighing, to get lots of aspiration. Do the whole series with /hthh/ → /thhɑɑ/ → *tie, town, take*, and /hkhh/ → /khhɑɑ/ → *car, come, cold*.

PRACTICE 1

Aspirate the initial voiceless stops in column 1. Pay special attention to /p/.

	1. *Voiceless (Aspirated)* /p, t, k/		2. *Voiced (Unaspirated)* /b, d, g/
a.	I think it's **cold**.	[kʰoʊld]	I think it's **gold**.
b.	Do you have the **time**?	[tʰaɪm]	Do you have the **dime**?
c.	I need to go **pack**.	[pʰæk]	I need to go **back**.
d.	Her **curls** are lovely.	[kʰɚlz]	Her **girls** are lovely.
e.	He's going to **tie** it.	[tʰaɪ]	He's going to **die**t.
f.	The **peas** are terrible.	[pʰiz]	The **bees** are terrible.
g.	They **came** for a swim.	[kʰeɪm]	They're **game** for a swim.
h.	They're in **town** now.	[tʰaʊn]	They're **down** now.
i.	He's quite a **pig**.	[pʰɪg]	He's quite **big**.

In English, voiceless stops at the beginning of stressed syllables are still aspirated when they are followed by /r/, /l/, or /w/. This means that /r, l, w/ begin *voiceless* (like /h/) *after /p, t, k/*. Think of saying /h/ *at the same time* as /r/, /l/, or /w/. We can indicate **voicelessness** by a small circle (representing the open glottis) under the consonant; thus, *crowd*, *class*, and *quick* can be written as [k̥raʊd], [k̥læs], [kʷɪk]. Aspiration helps to distinguish the following words.

	Voiceless /l/ or /r/		Fully Voiced /l/ or /r/	
1.	please	[pl̥iz]	police	[pə'lis]
2.	claps	[kl̥æps]	collapse	[kə'læps]
3.	train	[tr̥eɪn]	terrain[3]	[tə'reɪn]
4.	prayed	[pr̥eɪd]	parade	[pə'reɪd]

TO DO

Take a breath and exhale with /phh/, /khh/, /thh/. Then try exhaling **[phr̥r̥]**, **[khr̥r̥]**, **[thr̥r̥]**, **[phl̥l̥]**, **[khl̥l̥]**, **[khʷw̥]**, adding voiceless /r, l, w/ as if you were whispering. Now try to add a vowel at the end of the sequence: [phr̥ɑ], [khr̥ɑ], [thr̥ɑ], [phl̥ɑ], [khl̥ɑ], [khʷɑ]. Can you still feel a puff of air in front of your mouth? You should feel very *relaxed* when you do this. Try to get the same feeling in your larynx in the following series of words: *keen, clean, cream, queen; tie, try; pay, pray, play.*

PRACTICE 2

Aspirate the initial stops in column 1 and make the following /r, l, w/ voiceless. CHINESE students should be careful not to omit /r/ or /l/. Begin /r/ and /l/ during the stop and make them long enough to be clearly heard. See Sec. 15.9, Exercise A, to compare *pray, play, pay; brand, bland, band; grass, glass, gas.*

1. Voiceless (Aspirated) /pr, tr, kr/		2. Voiced (Unaspirated) /br, dr, gr/
a. They're already **crowing**.[4]	[kr̥oʊɪŋ]	They're already **growing**.
b. Where's the **train**?	[tr̥eɪn]	Where's the **drain**?[5]
c. Have you no **pride**?	[pr̥aɪd]	Have you no **bride**?
d. Is it **cream**?	[kr̥im]	Is it **green**?
e. There's a **trunk** in the street.	[tr̥əŋk]	There's a **drunk** in the street.
f. You should **praise** them.	[pr̥eɪz]	You should **braise**[6] them.
g. It's a land **crab**.	[kr̥æb]	It's a land **grab**.
h. Please **try** it.	[tr̥aɪ]	Please **dry** it.
i. It's **pressed** meat.	[pr̥est]	It's **breast** meat.

(continued)

---

[3]terrain = ground, an extent of land (rocky terrain)
[4]crow = to make a loud cry like a rooster or black bird
[5]drain = place where water goes down
[6]braise = to cook in a liquid

PRACTICE 2 (continued)

	1. Voiceless (Aspirated) /pl, kl/		*2. Voiced (Unaspirated)* /bl, gl/
j.	The **class** was large.	[kl̥æs]	The **glass** was large.
k.	It was **planned**.	[pl̥ænd]	It was **bland**.
l.	Do you have any **clue**?	[kl̥u]	Do you have any **glue**?
m.	They're **pleading**[7] too much.	[pl̥idɪŋ]	They're **bleeding** too much.
n.	They're light **clothes**.	[kl̥oʊz]	Their light **glows**.[8]
o.	It's an ugly **plot**.[9]	[pl̥ɑt]	It's an ugly **blot**.[10]

	/kw/	
p.	Please be **quiet**.	[kw̥aɪət]
q.	He left **quickly**.	[kw̥ɪkli]

PRACTICE 3

You will note that /r/ after /t/ and /d/ is a fricative: a noise similar to /ʃ/ is produced when the tongue pulls away from the roof of the mouth. (The tongue tip should not go back up and hit the tooth ridge again.) Compare the following words.

	1. /tʃ/	*2.* /tr/	*3.* /dr/	*4.* /dʒ/
a.	chain	train	drain	Jane
b.	chip	trip	drip	gyp[11]
c.	chill	trill	drill	Jill
d.	chew	true	drew	Jew

---

[7]plead = to beg, ask for
[8]glow = to shine
[9]plot = a plan or scheme, usually to do something bad
[10]blot = a spot, stain
[11]gyp = (slang) to cheat, to have someone take your money

13.2 Vowel Length and Final Consonants

Stressed vowels are **lengthened** *before final voiced consonants*. This is especially noticeable in one-syllable words. Extra **length** can be indicated by the symbol [ː] after the sound; thus, *bag* and *live* can be written as [bæːg], [lɪːv]. When you lengthen the vowels /ɪ, ɛ, æ, ə, ɔ, ʊ/, relax and flatten the tongue, moving in the direction of /ə/ so that you will keep them distinct from /i, eɪ, ɑ, oʊ, u/. *Live* [lɪːv] or [lɪəv] should not sound like *leave* or *leaf*.

PRACTICE 4

Make each vowel in column 2 at least one and a half times longer than the vowel in column 1 *without changing its quality.*

	1. *Voiceless Consonants* /p t k f θ s ʃ tʃ/		2. *Voiced Consonants* /b d g v ð z ʒ dʒ/	
	Short *preceding* **vowel**		**Long** *preceding* **vowel**	
a.	cup	[kʰəp]	cub[1]	[kʰəːb]
b.	bet	[bɛt]	bed	[bɛːd]
c.	plate	[pl̥eɪt]	played	[pl̥eɪːd]
d.	pick	[pʰɪk]	pig	[pʰɪːg]
e.	leaf	[lif]	leave	[liːv]
f.	proof	[pr̥uf] (noun)	prove	[pr̥uːv] (verb)
g.	teeth	[tʰiθ] (noun)	teethe[2]	[tʰiːð] (verb)
h.	loss	[lɔs]	laws	[lɔːz]
i.	rich	[rɪtʃ]	ridge	[rɪːdʒ]
j.	backs	[bæks]	bags	[bæːgz]
k.	raced	[reɪst]	raised	[reɪːzd]
l.	lift	[lɪft]	lived	[lɪːvd]

---

[1]cub = a baby bear or lion

[2]teethe = to grow teeth (the baby is teething)

When /m, n, ŋ, l, ɚ/ are followed by a voiceless consonant, the entire syllable is very short. When /m, n, ŋ, l, ɚ/ occur *at the end of a word* or are followed by voiced consonants, the *whole syllable is long*. Think of words like *man* [mæːnː] or [mæənː], *time* [tʰaɪːmː], *fell* [fɛːlː] or [fɛəlː] as taking up the time of two syllables.

PRACTICE 5

Make a clear difference in length between the words in column 1 and column 2. CHINESE and JAPANESE speakers should be especially careful not to shorten and cut off words ending in nasals.

	1. Voiceless Consonant after /m, n, ŋ, l, ɚ/		*2. No Consonant or Voiced Consonant after /m, n, ŋ, l, ɚ/*	
	***Short** syllable*		***Long** syllable*	
a.	think	[θɪŋk]	thing	[θɪːŋː]
b.	lamp	[læmp]	lamb	[læːmː]
c.	can't	[kænt]	can	[kæːnː]
d.	felt	[fɛlt]	fell	[fɛːlː]
e.	short	[ʃɔɚt]	shore	[ʃɔːɚː]
f.	sent	[sɛnt]	send	[sɛːnd]
g.	lunch	[lənt ʃ]	lunge³	[ləːndʒ]
h.	plants	[plænts]	plans	[plæːnz]
i.	bumps⁴	[bəmps]	bums⁵	[bəːmz]
j.	false	[fɔ(l)s]	falls	[fɔː(l)z]
k.	heart	[hɑɚt]	hard	[hɑːɚd]

---

³lunge = to move forward suddenly

⁴bump = a rounded, raised area; to hit suddenly

⁵bum = a person without a job or home

13.3 Final Voiceless Consonants

Final voiceless *stops* are *not aspirated* in normal speech. They are cut off very quickly before a pause or linked to following sounds.

Aspirated /p, t, k/ *beginning of stressed syllables*	*Unaspirated* /p, t, k/ *elsewhere*
pan, u'pon	'open, up‿and, up
tan, ba'ton[1]	'button, but‿he, but
key, o'kay	'lucky, luck‿is, luck

Final voiceless *fricatives* and *affricates* have *longer and stronger friction* (that is, they are noisier) than final voiced fricatives and affricates. A common mistake is to make final voiced fricatives too strong or too long in an effort to pronounce them clearly. Lengthen the vowel *before* these voiced consonants and then let them die out. Thus, when a word ends in a *voiceless* consonant, a short vowel is followed by a relatively long consonant. When a word ends in a *voiced* consonant, a long vowel is followed by a relatively short consonant.

Final /f, θ, s, ʃ, tʃ/ *Short preceding vowel and longer, stronger friction*	*Final* /v, ð, z, ʒ, dʒ/ *Long preceding vowel and shorter, weaker friction*
safe	save
teeth	teethe
price	prize
raced	raised
plants	plans
wash	garage
'h'	age

Before a pause, the difference between voiced and voiceless consonants in English is signaled more by vowel length and the differences discussed above than by an actual difference in voicing. Final "voiced" consonants may in fact be completely voiceless. If you have difficulty pronouncing any of the voiced consonants in final position (such as /g, v, z, ʒ, dʒ/), try lengthening the vowel and substituting a weak version of its voiceless counterpart (/k, f, s, ʃ, tʃ/).

---

[1]baton = short thin stick used by a conductor to lead an orchestra

PRACTICE 6

Practice making a clear difference between the words in column 1 and column 2 through changes in vowel length and the quality of the final consonant.

	1. Voiceless	*2. Voiced*
a.	Please take this **back**.	Please take this **bag**.
b.	Has he used his **bet**?	Has he used his **bed**?
c.	I need a **cap**.	I need a **cab**.
d.	Where are your **plants**?	Where are your **plans**?
e.	Give him a **cart**.	Give him a **card**.
f.	You can take your **pick**.	You can take your **pig**.
g.	She's going to **sink**.	She's going to **sing**.
h.	I wish I had blue **ice**.	I wish I had blue **eyes**.
i.	I found ten **bucks**.[2]	I found ten **bugs**.[3]
j.	How much have they **spent**?	How much did they **spend**?
k.	It was a wonderful **safe**.	It was a wonderful **save**.[4]
l.	Are those baby's **teeth**?	Do those babies **teethe**?
m.	What happened to his **lamps**?	What happened to his **lambs**?
n.	He made a nice **batch**.[5]	He made a nice **badge**.[6]
o.	They **lift** over there.	They **lived** over there.
p.	He **let** them in.	He **led** them in.
q.	How many **laps**[7] did he run?	How many **labs**[8] did he run?
r.	They often **duck**[9] behind his car.	They often **dug** behind his car.
s.	Only two **seats** are left.	Only two **seeds** are left.

---

[2]buck = slang word for *dollar* (it cost ten bucks)

[3]bug = an insect

[4]save = (noun) in sports, a good play that prevents the other team from scoring

[5]batch = a group or quantity of something (a batch of cookies, of letters, of computer commands)

[6]badge = a piece of metal that a person wears to show his or her position (a police officer's badge)

[7]lap = one complete trip around a track or across a swimming pool

[8]lab = short for *laboratory* (the language lab)

[9]duck = (verb) to move down quickly (duck your head under a low doorway)

13.4 North American English /t/ ADVANCED

Syllable *final /t/ before a pause*, *consonant*, or unstressed /ən/ ([n̩]) is often replaced by or pronounced together with *a glottal stop* [ʔ]. This may happen at the ends of words or within words. It makes final /t/ easier to pronounce in common words such as *it*, *what*, *at*, *but*, *not*, *about*, *out*, *get*, *might*, *can't*, and *right*. It is particularly important not to aspirate or strongly release the /t/ in these words when they are unstressed.

PRACTICE 7

Use a glottal stop in place of or together with final /t/ in the following sentences.

1. I saw a black cat.
2. Where did he sit?
3. He can't do it.
4. What can you do about it?
5. Let me go.
6. It rained.
7. Sit down.
8. It was nice.
9. Come here at once.
10. He might not come.
11. I've already eaten.
12. Button your buttons.
13. Are those mittens made of cotton?
14. Great Britain has many mountains.

/t/ *and /d/* after a vowel and *before an unstressed vowel* (including /ɚ/ and /əl/) are not pronounced differently in normal speech. They both sound like a very fast /d/; that is, they are pronounced as a *voiced tap* [ɾ].[1] This may happen within a word or between words in the same pause group. Thus, *leader, liter* and *lead her* are all pronounced as ['liɾɚ].

This is one of the main differences between North American English and other varieties of English. It is not necessary for a non-native speaker to pronounce /t/ in this way, but you need to be able to hear it in order to understand native speakers. You can't expect /t/ always to be voiceless, and you must be careful not to mix up /t/ or /d/ with /r/ (which may be pronounced as a tap in your language). Whatever you decide, you should should try to be consistent. If you already pronounce medial /t/ and /d/ as taps, be careful not to make the tap so short that you drop it: *united* has three syllables; *better, study, little*, and *thirty* have two syllables.

---

[1]The rule is actually more complicated. It does not apply to /t/ and /d/ at the beginning of syllables with secondary stress, e.g., *arithmetic, amputate, dormitory, secretary*. For a discussion, see Kreidler (1989:108–112).

PRACTICE 8

In the following words and sentences, try to pronounce medial /t/ and /d/ as a tap (very short /d/).
Can you think of other words like these?

1. leader = liter
2. ladder = latter
3. Adam = atom
4. medal = metal
5. raided = rated
6. rider = ride her
7. letter = let her
8. build it = built it

9. He invited her to a party.
10. The editor's at a meeting.
11. He bet all his money.
12. We're out of milk.
13. You can get a bottle for me.
14. It'll be fine.
15. Thirty or forty people came.
16. I'd like a little butter.

A common mistake by non-native speakers is to shorten and cut off words that end in vowels, <r>, <n>, or <l> (*see, day, car, men, bell*). In these words, you should *lengthen* the vowel and *link* the final vowel or voiced consonant *smoothly* to any following words. If you cut them off with a glottal stop, a native speaker might hear them as ending in /t/.

PRACTICE 9

Listen to your teacher say each sentence pair. Notice how words ending in /t/ connect differently to following words than words ending in vowels. Then practice the sentences.

	1. Short Vowel	*2. Long Vowel*
	/t/ = [tʔ] *or* [ʔ]	*Link Smoothly*
a.	I don't know what he **sought**.[2]	I don't know what he **saw**.
b.	They can **seat** you.	They can **see** you.
c.	Did you have a good **date**?	Did you have a good **day**?
d.	He's going to **bite** that pencil.	He's going to **buy** that pencil.
e.	Did you see her **goat**?	Did you see her **go**?
f.	Did he talk about his **plant**?	Did he talk about his **plan**?
g.	Where's my **belt**?	Where's my **bell**?
h.	His **cart** was stolen.	His **car** was stolen.
	/t/ = [ɾ][3]	*Link Smoothly*
i.	I don't know what he **sought** in her.	I don't know what he **saw** in her.
j.	They can **seat** us.	They can **see** us.
k.	It isn't the **date** I want.	It isn't the **day** I want.
l.	He's going to **bite** it.	He's going to **buy** it.
m.	Did you see her **goat** over there?	Did you see her **go** over there?

---

[2]sought = past tense of *seek*, to look for (seek freedom)
[3]/t/ = [ɾ] in these sentences only when there is *no pause* after the example words. If one pauses after /t/, then /t/ = [tʔ].

13.5 Exercises for Voiced and Voiceless Consonants

A. Circle all *aspirated* consonants (or transcribe the words and write in [ʰ] after all aspirated consonants).

EXAMPLE: ⓟay or [pʰeɪ]

1. price	**5.** glued	**9.** apple	**13.** please
2. duck	**6.** cream	**10.** appear	**14.** pretend
3. cake	**7.** study	**11.** beer	**15.** become
4. tight	**8.** pepper	**12.** title	**16.** agree

B. Underline all vowels that should be *lengthened* (or transcribe the words and write [ː] after lengthened vowels).

EXAMPLE: d<u>ea</u>d or [dɛːd]

1. tie	**5.** rich	**9.** heat	**13.** club
2. take	**6.** half	**10.** buzz	**14.** shirt
3. map	**7.** have	**11.** fall	**15.** fun
4. large	**8.** red	**12.** big	**16.** race

C. How would you help a fellow student who pronounced the following words incorrectly as indicated? What should he or she change?

1. *Big* sounds like *bick*.
2. *Time* sounds like *dime*.
3. *Car* sounds like *cart*.
4. *Ice* sounds like *eyes*.
5. *Crow* sounds like *grow*.
6. *Save* sounds like *safe*.

ADVANCED

D. In which words would <t> or <tt> usually be pronounced as a *glottal stop* [ʔ] or [tʔ]? In which words would it be pronounced as a *voiced tap* [ɾ] or short /d/?

1. mountain	**5.** writing	**9.** atom	**13.** today
2. maintain	**6.** written	**10.** atomic	**14.** can't come
3. write	**7.** faster	**11.** hitting	**15.** return
4. writer	**8.** little	**12.** fitness	**16.** dirty

ADVANCED

E. Read the following poem aloud pronouncing <t> and <tt> as an American or Canadian would.

> Betty Botter bought some butter
> But, said she, this butter's bitter
> I'll buy a bit of better butter
> To make my batter better.
> So she bought a bit of better butter
> And made her batter better.

F. Read each sentence using one of the two words in parentheses—either (a) with a voiced consonant, or (b) with a voiceless consonant. Have your partner or teacher guess which word you said.

1. Do you need a   (a. cab   b. cap)?
2. What happened to those   (a. bees   b. peas)?
3. Your   (a. plans   b. plants)   are unusual.
4. She   (a. led   b. let)   me in.
5. Are you going to   (a. braise   b. praise)   them?
6. Did you get a good   (a. card   b. cart)?
7. Do you hear the   (a. buzz   b. bus)?
8. It looks like it's   (a. gold   b. cold).
9. I'm afraid he's going to   (a. sing   b. sink)   if we don't stop him.
10. Ten   (a. dimes   b. times)   are not enough.
11. I bought a   (a. big   b. Bic)   pen.
12. Did you have a good   (a. day   b. date)?
✗ 13. Only a few   (a. seeds   b. seats)   are left.
14. It was terribly   (a. bland   b. planned).
15. They didn't like the   (a. prize   b. price)   at all.
16. It was an enormous   (a. badge   b. batch).
17. Leave my   (a. bag   b. back)   alone.
18. It was a terrific   (a. save   b. safe).
19. Won't you   (a. dry   b. try)   it?
✗ 20. Where did those   (a. bums   b. bumps)   come from?
21. She hasn't made her   (a. bed   b. bet).
✗ 22. I don't have any   (a. glue   b. clue).
23. Can you   (a. see   b. seat)   him now?
24. I didn't know they were   (a. falls   b. false).
25. The   (a. robe   b. rope)   is in my closet.

G. *Dialogues for Voiced and Voiceless Consonants.*

1. bag [bæːg], *back* [bæk]

A: I'm taking this *bag back*.

B: Don't take it *back*. It's such a beautiful *bag*.

A: But on the *back* of the *bag*, there's a scratch.

B: Why don't you give the *bag* to me.

2. pig [pʰɪːg], *pick* [pʰɪk]

A: Which *pig* would you like? *Pick* out any one you want.

B: I like this little *pig*. Can I *pick* it up?

A: You can't have that *pig*. It's not big enough.

B: But you said I could *pick* any *pig* I wanted!

3. bed [bɛːd], bet [bɛtʔ]

A: I *bet* that *bed* is uncomfortable.

B: I *bet* you never heard of futons before. A futon makes a wonderful *bed*.

A: Let me try it . . . This *bed* is hard.

B: Firm. A soft *bed* is bad for your back. I *bet* you didn't know that.

4. thing [θɪːŋ], think [θɪŋk]

A: I *think* that *thing* is ugly.

B: What a *thing* to say. I *think* you're horrible.

A: What do you want that *thing* for anyway? I bet it stinks.

B: It's not a "*thing*"; it's a baby skunk. I *think* it will make a wonderful pet.

5. cub [kʰəːb], cup [kʰəp]

A: They're feeding the *cub* a *cup* of milk.

B: I didn't think *cubs* could drink from *cups*.

A: Well that *cub* can. Look at him. He's so cute.

B: Yeah, he's a real cute *cub*. He just knocked the *cup* out of the zookeeper's hand, and now he's trying to bite him.

6. eyes [aɪːz], ice [aɪs]

A: What beautiful *eyes*! They're *ice* blue.

B: I don't trust people with blue *eyes*. Their hearts are like *ice*.

A: But your *eyes* are blue!

B: Opposites attract. Your *eyes* are brown. My *ice* melts in your warm *eyes*.

7. peach [pʰitʃ], beach [bitʃ]

A: I love the peace and quiet at the beach.

B: The beach makes me hungry for a juicy peach.

A: Look! A seagull has stolen your peach. It's on the other side of the beach.

B: And here come the bees! What happened to our peace?

8. pride [pʰaɪːd], bride [braɪːd]

A: Bruce has too much pride. He'll never take Prudence as his bride.

B: Why not? Prudence is pretty and prosperous. He should be proud of such a bride.

A: Prudence is the president of her company, and Bruce is only a vice-president.

B: Hm. That could cause problems.

CHAPTER 14

<ed> and <s> Endings

A man robbed a bank downtown. He walked in and passed a note to the teller.

PREREADING QUESTION

How is the <ed> ending pronounced in *robbed, walked,* and *passed?*

14.1 Adding <ed>

PRETEST

Say each of the following words aloud. How many syllables (vowel sounds) are in each word? How is the <ed> ending pronounced?

1. changed	3. waved	5. decided	7. bombed	9. noticed
2. expected	4. washed	6. confused	8. clapped	10. carried

The <ed> or <d> that is added to a regular verb to form the past tense in English is pronounced in different ways depending on how the verb ends. The <ed> ending is pronounced as a *separate syllable /ɪd/ only in verbs that end in /d/ or /t/* (spelled <d, dd, de, t, tt, te>). *In all other verbs, the <e> is silent,* and only the sound /d/ or /t/ is added.

PRACTICE 1

Read the following examples making sure that the <ded> or <ted> at the ends of the words in *group 1* is pronounced as *a complete syllable* /dɪd/ or /tɪd/; do not shorten it too much or make the vowel voiceless. Note that <ded> sounds the same as the word *did*: *needed = knee did*. You may pronounce the first /t/ or /d/ as a voiced tap (short /d/) when it follows a vowel, so that *waited = waded*[1] ['weɪɾɪd]. In group 2, be sure that you do not pronounce <e>. Can you think of any other examples of words that belong in group 1?

1. Pronounce <e> <ed> = /ɪd/ after /t/ or /d/		2. <e> is Silent <ed> = /d/ or /t/ only after other sounds	
a. needed	/'nidɪd/	workéd	/wɚkt/
b. added	/'ædɪd/	stoppéd	/stɑpt/
c. attended	/ə 'tɛndɪd/	plannéd	/plænd/
d. exploded	/ɪk 'sploʊdɪd/	removéd	/rɪ 'muvd/
e. wanted	/'wəntɪd/	watchéd	/wɑtʃt/
f departed	/dɪ 'pɑɚtɪd/	enjoyéd	/ɪn 'dʒɔɪd/
g. visited	/'vɪzɪtɪd/	promiséd	/'prɑmɪst/
h. accepted	/ək 'sɛptɪd/	developéd	/dɪ 'vɛləpt/
i. admitted	/əd 'mɪtɪd/	preferréd	/prɪ 'fɚd/
j. separated	/'sɛpəreɪtɪd/	organizéd	/'ɔɚɡənaɪzd/

In group 2 above, how do you know when the <ed> ending is pronounced /d/ and when it is pronounced /t/? Remember that /d/ is voiced and /t/ is voiceless. *When <ed> or <d> is added to a verb that ends in a voiceless sound* (except /t/), *it is pronounced /t/;* when it is added *to a verb that ends in a voiced sound* (except /d/), *it is pronounced /d/.*

PRACTICE 2

Remember that /t/ after a consonant is not aspirated and that stressed vowels before /d/ should be lengthened. Adding <ed> often results in a group of two or more consonants; go right from one consonant into the next one without releasing the first consonant. That is, don't open your mouth and insert [ʰ], [ə], or [ɪ] between the consonants; instead, try saying both consonants at the same time. Can you think of any other example words for each group?

1. <ed> = /t/ after voiceless consonants /p, k, f, θ, s, ʃ, tʃ/		2. <ed> = /d/ after voiced sounds /b, g, v, ð, z, ʒ, dʒ, m, n, ŋ, l/ and all vowels	
a. hopped	/hɑpt/	robbed	/rɑbd/
b. thanked	/θæŋkt/	begged	/bɛgd/
c. laughed	/læft/	loved	/ləvd/
d. divorced	/dɪ 'vɔɚst/	surprised	/sɚ 'praɪzd/

(continued)

---

[1]wade = to walk in water (to wade across a river)

PRACTICE 2 (continued)

1. <ed> = /t/ after voiceless consonants /p, k, f, θ, s, ʃ, tʃ/		2. <ed> = /d/ after voiced sounds /b, g, v, ð, z, ʒ, dʒ, m, n, ŋ, l/ and all vowels	
e. finished	/ˈfɪnɪʃt/	engaged	/ɪŋ ˈgeɪdʒd/
f. watched	/watʃt/	changed	/tʃeɪndʒd/
g. marched	/maɚtʃt/	returned	/rɪ ˈtɚnd/
h. helped	/hɛlpt/	called	/kɔld/
i. relaxed	/rɪ ˈlækst/	borrowed	/ˈbɑroʊd/
j. asked	/æskt/	married	/ˈmærid/

ADJECTIVES ENDING IN <ed>   ADVANCED

An *exception* to the above rule is the pronunciation of certain old-fashioned adjectives ending in <ed>. Most adjectives formed from verbs, such as in *a married woman*, *a divorced man*, and *a borrowed book*, are pronounced the same as the verbs. However, in a small number of adjectives that are very old words in the English language, <ed> is pronounced as a separate syllable /ɪd/: *naked* /ˈneɪkɪd/ *crooked* /ˈkrʊkɪd/ *rugged* /ˈrəgɪd/. <ed> is also pronounced as a separate syllable in adverbs ending in <edly>: *supposedly* /sə ˈpoʊzɪdli/ *allegedly* /ə ˈlɛdʒɪdli/, *markedly* /ˈmaɚkɪdli/.

PRACTICE 3   ADVANCED

Match the italicized words with their meanings. Then say the sentences aloud and pronounce <ed> as a separate syllable.

1. The child is *naked*.
2. It's a *crooked* street.
3. The beggar is wearing *ragged* clothes.
4. We're having *wretched* weather.
5. They're afraid of the *wicked*[2] witch.
6. Those are *rugged* mountains.
7. He was a very *learned* man.
8. He's sitting *cross-legged*.
9. He *allegedly* stole $10,000.
10. Your pronunciation has improved *markedly*.
11. *Supposedly*, he's sick today.
12. She *deservedly* won first prize.
13. He's been absent *repeatedly*.

a. rough and strong
b. terrible, awful
c. evil, very bad
d. educated
e. torn, in rags
f. with his legs crossed
g. wearing no clothes, nude
h. not straight, with bends
i. over and over again
j. noticeably, quite a lot
k. they say (with no proof)
l. it appears that
m. rightly

---

[2]*wicked* also means *great*, *wonderful*, and *very* in current slang (a wicked shot, a wicked good week).

EXERCISES

A. Cross out the <e> in the <ed> ending whenever it is *not* pronounced.

1. blinked	**4.** opened	**7.** avoided	**10.** handicapped
2. improved	**5.** attached	**8.** charged	**11.** discovered
3. pointed	**6.** allowed	**9.** omitted	**12.** delighted

B. *Adding a Syllable*. Answer the following questions using the past tense of the verb followed by *to* and another verb. Do not release the /t/ or /d/ before *to*, but say the sequence /tt/ or /dt/ together (*need_to* /ˈnidtə/, *needed_to* /ˈnidɪdtə/).

1. When did he need to come?   *He needed to come yesterday.*
2. What did she want to do?
3. Where did they decide to go?
4. What did she start to do?
5. When did he expect to be there?
6. When did they intend to arrive?
7. When did you start to learn English?
8. Why did you want to come to the United States?
9. When did you decide to come here?
10. When did you need to apply for a visa?
11. What did you hate to do when you were a child?

C. *Adding a Syllable*. Answer the following questions using the past tense of the verb. Don't drop medial /t/: *started* doesn't sound the same as *starred*.

1. When did you start looking for an apartment?
2. What did your advisor suggest doing?
3. What did you end up telling your advisor?
4. How did your roommate first treat you?
5. Who did you visit over the weekend?
6. How did your mother sound over the phone?
7. How many times did your teacher repeat the instructions?
8. Who did the teacher point at?
9. What did you avoid doing over the weekend?
10. How long did you attend high school?

D. *Linking onto Vowels*. Answer the following questions using the past tense of the verb and be sure to *link* the final /t/ or /d/ to the following word. Remember that /h/ in *him* and *her* is *silent* when the pronoun is linked to the preceding word.

1. What did you talk about last night?
2. Who did the class laugh at?
3. Who did the teacher stare at angrily?
4. Which room did you walk into by mistake?
5. Why did the teacher turn around?

6. When did he ask her out?

7. Who did you introduce him to?

8. What sports did you play in high school?

9. When did you help your roommate?

10. When did your father marry your mother?

E. Listen to the following sentences and circle the verb form (past or present) that you hear (or write PA or PR).

1. The stores   (closed / close)   at 6 P.M. on Saturday.

2. Your chocolate cake   (tasted / tastes)   great.

3. I think that they   (lived / live)   in Miami.

4. The movie   (started / starts)   at eight o'clock.

5. They   (received / receive)   a lot of money from their parents.

6. We   (counted / count)   the money before leaving.

7. The children   (needed / need)   to go to the bathroom.

8. We   (studied / study)   in the library every afternoon.

9. After work, I usually   (walked / walk)   home.

10. I   (called / call)   him up every Sunday.

11. She really   (loved / loves)   her children.

12. My parents   (wanted / want)   me to go to college.

F. Change the following verbs to the past tense. Write /ɪd/ (extra syllable), /t/, or /d/ to show how to pronounce the past tense <ed> ending. (Optional: Put each word in a short sentence.)

1. open	15. relate
2. refuse	16. remember
3. attend	17. control
4. climb	18. ask
5. persuade	19. pretend
6. prefer	20. die
7. hurry	21. shout
8. charge	22. watch
9. arrive	23. explain
10. last	24. sew
11. correct	25. slip
12. relax	26. exchange
13. hope	27. remind
14. enjoy	28. hug

G. Tell a partner what you did over the weekend, yesterday, last night, or this morning. *Use the past tense consistently.* Your partner should listen carefully and tell you (or write down) whenever it sounded like you used the present instead of the past tense to talk about a past event. If you don't have a partner, tape-record yourself and play the recording back.

H. In your daily conversations in English, make an effort to use the past tense whenever you mean it.

 I. *Reading for <ed> Ending.* Write /ɪd/, /t/, or /d/ below each <ed> ending to show how it is pronounced. Check your answers in pairs or groups. Then read the passage aloud, record it, and play it back. Remember to link words in the same phrase.

EXAMPLE: need*ed*   walk*ed*   rain*ed*
　　　　　/ɪd/　　　　/t/　　　　/d/

Howard's Morning

The clock radio play*ed* soft music, but it sound*ed* far away to Howard. At last,

he open*ed* his eyes, roll*ed* over, and look*ed* at the clock. He turn*ed* away and start*ed*

to go back to sleep when suddenly he realiz*ed* that it was already eight o'clock. He

was late. He jump*ed* out of bed, quickly shav*ed*, brush*ed* his teeth, comb*ed* his hair,

and got dress*ed*. He'd want*ed* to take a shower, but decid*ed* that there wasn't

enough time. He rush*ed* down the stairs and into the kitchen. He hat*ed* being late.

Hurriedly, he fix*ed* breakfast—coffee and a toast*ed* English muffin (no time for his

usual fri*ed* egg)—and rac*ed* out the door. He start*ed* his car and had just pull*ed* out

the driveway when the thought popp*ed* into his mind: it was Saturday; he didn't

have to go to work after all. He slowly return*ed*, climb*ed* the stairs, chang*ed* his

clothes, and went back to bed again.

How is the <ed> ending most commonly pronounced?

14.2 Adding <s>

PRETEST

Say each of the following words aloud. How many syllables (vowel sounds) are in each word? How is the <es> ending pronounced?

1. lives	3. prizes	5. manages	7. niece's	9. decides
2. finishes	4. writes	6. ourselves	8. likes	10. toes

The <s>, <es>, or <'s> that is added to a noun or verb to form the plural, possessive, or third person singular present tense in English is pronounced in different ways depending on how the word ends. <s>, <es>, or <'s> is pronounced as a *separate syllable* /ɪz/ *only in nouns or verbs that end in* /s, z, ʃ, ʒ, tʃ, dʒ/ (spelled <s, ss, se, z, zz, ze, sh, ch, tch, ge, ce, x>). *In all other words, the <e> is silent*, and only the sound /s/ or /z/ is added.

PRACTICE 4

Read the following examples making sure that the <es> or <'s> at the ends of the words in *group 1* is pronounced as *a complete syllable* /ɪz/; do not shorten it too much or make the vowel voiceless. <es> or <'s> in these words sounds the same as the verb *is*: *judges = judge's = judge is*. In group 2, be sure that you do not insert a sound between a consonant and final <s>. Can you think of any other examples of words that belong in group 1?

1. Pronounce <e>		2. <e> is Silent	
<es>, <'s> = /ɪz/ *after* /s, z, ʃ, ʒ, tʃ, dʒ/		<es, s, 's> = /s/ or /z/ *after other sounds*	
a. classes	/ˈklæsɪz/	takes	/teɪks/
b. dances	/ˈdænsɪz/	smiles	/smaɪlz/
c. washes	/ˈwɑʃɪz/	hopes	/hoʊps/
d. suitcases	/ˈsutkeɪsɪz/	chocolates	/ˈtʃɑklɪts/
e. apologizes	/ə ˈpɑlədʒaɪzɪz/	magazines	/mægə ˈzinz/
f. sandwiches	/ˈsænwɪtʃɪz/	decides	/dɪ ˈsaɪdz/
g. languages	/ˈlæŋgwɪdʒɪz/	themselves	/ðəm ˈsɛlvz/
h. relaxes	/rɪ ˈlæksɪz/	replies	/rɪ ˈplaɪz/
i. Alice's	/ˈælɪsɪz/	Mike's	/maɪks/
j. James'[1]	/ˈdʒeɪmzɪz/	Jane's	/dʒeɪnz/

In group 2 above, how do you know when the ending is pronounced /s/ and when it is pronounced /z/? *When <s>, <'s>, or <es> is added to a word that ends in a voiceless sound* (except /s, ʃ, tʃ/), *it is pronounced* /s/; *when it is added to a word that ends in a voiced sound* (except /z, ʒ, dʒ/), *it is pronounced* /z/.

---

[1]If a noun already ends in <s>, only an apostrophe is added, not <'s>: Thomas' house, the girls' books, Mr. Jones' dog.

PRACTICE 5

Lengthen the vowels in group 2. Can you think of any other examples of words in each group?

	1. <s, es> = /s/		*2. <s, es> = /z/*
	after voiceless consonants		*after voiced sounds*
	/p, t, k, f, θ/		*/b, d, g, v, ð, m, n, ŋ, l/*
			and all vowels
a.	hopes	/hoʊps/	robes	/roʊbz/
b.	beets	/bits/	beads	/bidz/
c.	docks	/dɑks/	dogs	/dɔgz/
d.	laughs	/læfs/	loves	/ləvz/
e.	bumps	/bəmps/	comes	/kəmz/
f.	departs	/dɪ ˈpaɚ-ts/	delivers	/dɪ ˈlɪvɚ-z/
g.	thinks	/θɪŋks/	things	/θɪŋz/
h.	states	/steɪts/	stays	/steɪz/
i.	results	/rɪ ˈzəlts/	animals	/ˈænɪməlz/
j.	Mark's	/maɚ-ks/	Martha's	/ˈmaɚ-θəz/

Note that <s> in the following common words is pronounced /z/: *is, was, has, does, goes, says, his, hers, theirs, yours, ours, always, sometimes*. When the verb *is* or *has* is contracted to <'s>, it also follows the above rules: *it's* /ɪts/, *that's* /ðæts/, *she's* /ʃiz/, *there's* /ðɛɚ-z/.

EXERCISES

A. Cross out the <e> in the <es> ending whenever it is *not* pronounced.

1. refuses	**4.** replaces	**7.** pages	**10.** compares
2. rides	**5.** matches	**8.** tomatoes	**11.** cigarettes
3. gloves	**6.** knives	**9.** foxes	**12.** headaches

B. *Adding a Syllable*. Answer the following questions using the plural form of the italicized word. Be sure to *add a complete syllable* in making the plural of these longer words.

1. How many *sandwiches* did you order?

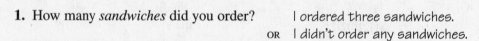

OR I didn't order any sandwiches.

2. How many *sentences* did you have to write?

3. How many *languages* did you study in school?

4. How many *exercises* did the teacher assign for homework last night?

5. How many pairs of *sunglasses* do you own?

6. How many *apartment complexes* are there nearby?

7. How many *differences* have you noticed between classes here and in your country?

8. How many *surprises* did you have on your last birthday?

9. How many bad *experiences* have you had here?

10. How many *advantages* are there to jogging everyday?

C. *Possessives.* Write /s/, /z/, or /ɪz/ to show how the possessive ending is pronounced in the following words. Then use the words to answer the following question (or make up your own question beginning with *whose*). Continue with names of students in your class.

Whose books are those? They're —————— books.

1. Barbara's	**4.** Alex's	**7.** Miss Smith's	**10.** Steve's
2. Liz's	**5.** Mary's	**8.** Mr. Jones'	**11.** Michael's
3. Heather's	**6.** Philip's	**9.** Ms. Thompson's	**12.** George's

ADVANCED

D. A common use of the plural is in the expression *one of . . .* , as in *one of my friends*, *one of his favorite books*, *one of the men*, or *one of the best restaurants in town*. Make up a short sentence using the plural form of each of the following words after *one of*.

1. (teacher)   One of my teachers is always late to class.
   OR   I saw one of my teachers at the movies last night.

2. (friend)	**4.** (player)	**6.** (suitcase)	**8.** (student)	**10.** (plant)
3. (page)	**5.** (shoe)	**7.** (horse)	**9.** (dog)	**11.** (window)

E. *<s> on Verbs.* Tell what each of the following kinds of people do.

1. What does a baker do?   A baker bakes cakes.
2. What does a pilot do?   A pilot flies planes.

3. What does a student do?	**6.** . . . a teacher?	**9.** . . . a mountain climber?
4. . . . a photographer?	**7.** . . . a baby?	**10.** . . . a mailman?
5. . . . an auto mechanic?	**8.** . . . a thief?	**11.** . . . a politician?

   12. (Make up your own question.)

F. Listen to the following sentences and circle the noun (singular or plural) that you hear (or write S or P).

1. She put the   (magazine / magazines)   away.

2. They came out with   (a new product / new products).

3. The   (Canadian / Canadians)   came to our party.

4. Our   (class is / classes are)   interesting.

5. Did you visit your   (sister / sisters)?

6. Please read the   (example / examples).

7. She broke the   (egg / eggs)   into a bowl.

8. Did you see the   (student / students)   in the cafeteria?

9. I need   (a match / matches).

10. My   (friend / friends)   visited me over the weekend.

11. Do you know which   (language / languages)   he speaks?

12. The   (animal is / animals are)   in that tree.

G. Listen to the following sentences and decide whether the subject is singular (S) or plural (P). In a few cases, the best clue for a singular subject is the <s> at the end of the verb.

1. The   (waitress works / waitresses work)   every weekend.

2. The   (boy studies / boys study)   hard.

3. The   (girl speaks / girls speak)   very quickly.

4. The   (student never comes / students never come)   to class.

5. The   (paragraph sounds / paragraphs sound)   funny.

6. The   (baseball game starts / baseball games start)   at 1:00.

7. My   (brother always telephones / brothers always telephone)   me.

8. (Does the cassette / Do the cassettes)   work very well?

9. The   (program wasn't / programs weren't)   on last night.

10. The   (teacher plays / teachers play)   volleyball on Sundays.

11. Your   (answer still doesn't / answers still don't)   help me.

12. The   (exercise was / exercises were)   difficult.

H. Make the following nouns plural and change the verbs to the third person singular present tense. Write /ɪz/ (extra syllable), /s/, or /z/ to show how the <s> or <es> ending should be pronounced.

1. success	8. experiment	15. science	22. arrange
2. word	9. year	16. vegetable	23. destroy
3. window	10. depart	17. conversation	24. country
4. service	11. arrive	18. minute	25. building
5. automobile	12. laugh	19. realize	26. page
6. crash	13. time	20. snowflake	27. type
7. eye	14. inch	21. mile	28. wristwatch

I. Choose a person you know well (mother, father, sister, roommate, etc.) and describe a typical day in this person's life to a partner. Be sure to *use <s> on the verb* in the third person singular present tense. Your partner should listen carefully and tell you (or write down) whenever you drop the final <s>. If you don't have a partner, tape-record yourself and play the recording back.

J. In your daily conversation in English, make an effort to use plurals and the third person singular <s> consistently. Although people will understand what you mean when you say *three dollar* or *he live* and probably will not correct you, it sounds uneducated and shows a strong accent.

K. *Reading for <s> Ending.* Write /ɪz/, /s/, or /z/ below the <(e)s> ending of each word to show how it is pronounced. Check your answers in pairs or groups. Then read and record the passage, linking wherever you can.

EXAMPLE: hous*es*   talk*s*   liv*es*
            /ɪz/   /s/   /z/

Laundry Time

Liz hates doing the laundry. She realizes that four weeks have passed since her last trip to the laundromat. There are piles of clothes in the closets, the sheets and towels are dirty, she's been wearing the same pair of blue jeans for nine days, and she doesn't have any clean socks or blouses left. She thinks about it while she watches one of her favorite TV shows. She wishes she didn't have to do such chores. Then she opens a book, turns the pages, and tries to study. The phone rings: one of Liz's friends reminds her about Sally's party tomorrow evening. She decides that it's now or never. She can't go to the party unless she washes one of her new dresses. She stuffs all her clothes into two laundry bags. She strips the bed and pulls the pillowcases off the pillows. She goes through the apartment, picking up everything in sight. Finally, she grabs some coat hangers, two boxes of detergent, and her keys, and closes the door behind her. She hopes she won't be too late. She arrives at the laundromat, carries in all her belongings, and searches for some empty machines. But they're all either in use or out of order. She sighs, picks up everything, and drives to the local video store to rent a couple of movies.

How is the <s> or <es> ending most commonly pronounced?

L. *Reading for <ed> and <s> Endings.* Record yourself reading the following passage to review the <ed> and <s> endings.

[Jesse /ˈdʒɛsi/ is a graduate student at the University of Michigan.]

Wonderland[2]

Jesse turned up one of the walks and went into a residence hall, walking quickly, as if he lived here, and once inside he paused to wait a few minutes. It was crowded here. Jesse had always felt oddly benevolent[3] toward the undergraduates at the university, though they had money and he was poor; he thought of them as children, they were so boisterous[4] and sure of themselves. They lived in rooms jammed[5] with junk, dirty clothes and towels flung[6] everywhere, sheets that went unchanged for weeks, they played poker[7] and drank happily and stupidly; they were children and could be blamed for nothing. Those who did not live in residence halls lived in palatial[8] fraternity houses—enormous houses where music blared[9] and curtains were blown outside windows. Jesse thought of these young people as jammed together warmly, perpetually.[10] They came alive in crowds. Their faces brightened in herds.[11] He envied[12] them but felt, in a way, protective of them: when he was a doctor he would be serving them.

---

[2]Joyce Carol Oates, *Wonderland* (New York: Vanguard Press, 1971), p. 213.
[3]benevolent /bə ˈnɛvəlɪnt/ = wishing to do good
[4]boisterous /ˈbɔɪstrəs/ = noisy and cheerful
[5]jam = to pack or crush tightly together
[6]flung = thrown (past tense of *fling*)
[7]poker = a card game played for money
[8]palatial /pə ˈleɪʃəl/ = large and luxurious, like a palace
[9]blare = to play loudly
[10]perpetually /pɚ ˈpɛtʃʊəli/ = always
[11]herd /hɚd/ = a group of animals
[12]envy /ˈɛnvi/ = to want something that someone else has

14.3 Consonant Groups

Adding <ed> or <s> to the end of a word can sometimes result in a very long sequence of consonants. In English, words can end in up to four consonants and begin with as many as three consonants so that it's possible to have seven consonants in a row in some sentences.

He glimpsed strangers.   /mpststr/

We exchanged scrapbooks.   /ndʒdskr/

Think of your own language. How many consonants can appear at the beginning of a word? At the end of a word? If your language only allows one consonant at the end of a word, you probably omit some final consonants in English or insert a vowel sound between them. If your language does not allow final voiced consonants such as /b, d, g, ð, v, z, ʒ, dʒ/, you may have a tendency to make them voiceless. These errors can result in poor rhythm and grammar. Long sequences of consonants can be difficult for native speakers too. There are several ways to make consonant groups easier to pronounce in fluent speech.

1. Link the final consonant to a following vowel.   Make the consonant that ends one word begin the next word. Remember to reduce pronouns and auxiliary verbs and drop /h/ in unstressed function words.

1. gets_up   /gɛt səp/
2. find_out   /faɪn daʊt/
3. told_her   /toʊl də-/
4. grabbed_it   /græb dɪt/
5. thanks_him   /θæŋk sɪm/
6. loves_it   /ləv zɪt/
7. most_of them   /moʊs təv ðəm/
8. first_of_all   /fə-s tə vɔl/
9. changed_his mind   /tʃeɪndʒ dɪz maɪnd/
10. picked_up_his date   /pɪk tə pɪz deɪt/
11. kept_her promise   /kɛp tə- prɑ mɪs/
12. words_are hard   /wə-d zə- hɑə-d/

2. Hold the final consonant and go right on to the following consonant.   Begin making the following consonant while holding the preceding consonant so that they connect smoothly to each other. If this is difficult for you, think of forming both consonants at the same time. If two of the same consonants follow one another, just make one long consonant. You should practice linking onto /ð/ because the word *the* frequently occurs after another consonant.

A. Same place of articulation
  1. a hard_day
  2. help_Bob
  3. the first_time
  4. we watched_television
  5. they served_dinner
  6. the birds_sing

B. Different place of articulation
  1. answered_correctly
  2. called_Bill
  3. crisp_toast
  4. walked_slowly
  5. works_fine
  6. saves_money
  7. learns_German
  8. storms_threaten

C. Linking onto /ð/
  1. since_then
  2. hits_them
  3. fails_the test
  4. returns_the book
  5. serves_the wine
  6. changes_the tires
  7. explained_that
  8. kept_them
  9. failed_the test
  10. returned_the book
  11. served_the wine
  12. changed_the tires

3. Pronounce final /t/ as a glottal stop when it is followed by a consonant. A glottal stop is made by closing the glottis (the space between the vocal folds) or holding your breath briefly as in the middle of the expression *uh oh.* You may substitute a glottal stop for /t/ at the end of a syllable before a consonant. (VIETNAMESE students should do this to prevent final /t/ from sounding like /s/.)

1. it was nice
2. it shrank
3. built the house
4. felt fine
5. can't remember

6. sent one
7. hurt the dog
8. short sleeves
9. doesn't think so
10. aren't closing

4. Omit one of the consonants, but not final grammatical <ed> or <s>. Groups of *three consonants* at the end of a word are also difficult for native speakers, so they sometimes *omit the middle consonant.* This is especially common in groups of voiceless consonants with a middle /t/ or /θ/.

ducts /dəkts/ → /dəks/ = ducks

acts /ækts/ → /æks/   = axe

guests /gɛsts/ → /gɛss/ (with a long final /s/)

In the last example, the final /s/ is longer than in the word *guess* /gɛs/. It is better to drop the middle consonant than to drop the final <s> or <ed> ending. There is still a difference between between singular *guest* /gɛst/ and plural *guests* /gɛss/, between *month* /mənθ/ and *months* /məns/. Say the following words, first trying to pronounce all the consonants, then dropping the middle consonant.

1. acts /ækts/ → /æks/
2. accepts /ək 'sɛpts/ → /ək 'sɛps/
3. asked /æskt/ → /æst/
4. lifts /lɪfts/ → /lɪfs/
5. consists /kən 'sɪsts/ → /kən 'sɪss/

6. tests /tɛsts/ → /tɛss/
7. months /mənθs/ → /məns/
8. fifths /fɪfθs/ → /fɪfs/
9. lengths /lɛŋθs/ → /lɛŋs/
10. depths /dɛpθs/ → /dɛps/

5. Slow down and pause after the word. Unfortunately, not all consonant groups can be made easier to pronounce. You can't drop any of the consonants in words like *wasps, marched, changed, girls,* or *world.* Sometimes you'll just have to *pause* after a difficult word. Or you can *lengthen* the end of the word, as if you're going to pause, without really pausing completely. However, you should not rush through or chop off a word that is difficult for you to pronounce; this destroys the rhythm and makes your English much more difficult to understand. If you're really having a problem with a particular word, *use a synonym* that is easier for you to pronounce!

EXERCISES

 A. Cross out any consonants that can be omitted according to rule 4 (p. 160).

1. I think he trusts me.
2. He asked a difficult question.
3. We went to the crafts fair.
4. It's three eighths of an inch too short.
5. She acts strangely.
6. The communists took over six months ago.

ADVANCED

 B. Record yourself reading the following sentences. Try to move smoothly between the consonants without omitting any consonants (except according to the rules above) or adding any sounds between them. Then play the tape back and check yourself.

1. She said thanks for the Christmas card.
2. The skirt and blouse matched each other perfectly.
3. We haven't had a chance to buy any gifts yet.
4. He asked for the test to be postponed until Friday.
5. They excused themselves and quickly left the room.
6. Those girls are not strong swimmers.
7. He resolved to quit smoking next spring.
8. He made several attempts to rearrange the desks.
9. She clasped her hands together and begged for forgiveness.
10. He likes fresh squeezed orange juice for breakfast.
11. The responsibility rests squarely on your shoulders.
12. Last year, I watched television nearly every night.
13. The wasps flew against the window.
14. He suggests that their next movie be filmed in Spain.
15. The world has changed tremendously in the past few months.

C. *Oral Presentation: Narration.* Prepare a short three-minute speech in which you tell a story about something that happened to you. Choose one of the following topics:

1. An important event that changed my life
2. A strange, frightening, or dangerous experience
3. A funny incident from my childhood
4. An automobile accident
5. An exciting or terrible trip

Make an outline of your speech with an introduction, a list of main events in time order, and a conclusion. Practice your speech aloud several times. Include details that will help your audience feel what you felt at that time. Work on pronouncing the past tense and plural endings correctly and linking them to other words in the same phrase.

D. *Review.* Add <ed> and <(e)s> to each of the following verbs and write down how the endings should be pronounced.

1. accept	**4.** watch	**7.** charge	**10.** tax	**13.** miss
2. plan	**5.** surprise	**8.** show	**11.** attend	**14.** try
3. save	**6.** stop	**9.** thank	**12.** appear	**15.** taste

E. *Dialogues for Consonant Groups.*

1. / kt, pt, st, nt, nd, bd, vd/

A: A man just rob<u>bed</u> a bank downtown. Have you hear<u>d</u> about it?

B: You mean the one where a man dres<u>sed</u> in a blue suit wal<u>ked</u> in and pas<u>sed</u> a note to the teller?

A: And she pic<u>ked</u> it up, loo<u>ked</u> around nervously, and step<u>ped</u> on the silent alarm.

B: Then she ope<u>ned</u> her drawer, pul<u>led</u> out some money, and drop<u>ped</u> it on the floor.

A: While she be<u>nt</u> over, the man threate<u>ned</u> her with a gun, but the police arri<u>ved</u> at that moment and grab<u>bed</u> him.

B: No, I don't know anything about it.

2. /zd/

A: I'm ama<u>zed</u>.

B: Well, I'm not surpri<u>sed</u> at all.

A: To think that someone so organi<u>zed</u> . . .

B: Hadn't reali<u>zed</u> it was your birthday.

3. /ts, ks, dz, vz, lz, nz/

A: It<u>'s</u> springtime.

B: The fiel<u>ds</u> are covered with flow<u>ers</u>.

A: The trees are full of fresh green lea<u>ves</u>.

B: The bir<u>ds</u> have returned from their winter trave<u>ls</u>.

A: The sun shi<u>nes</u> brightly overhead, and a gentle breeze blows through the trees.

B: It<u>'s</u> time to rela<u>x</u> under the blue skies.

A: It<u>'s</u> time to mow the lawn.

4. /ʃt, vd, ŋd/

A: You cru<u>shed</u> it!

B: That's impossible. When I arri<u>ved</u>, it was already sma<u>shed</u> to bits.

A: When you ru<u>shed</u> into the room, you ba<u>nged</u> the door open and pu<u>shed</u> it against the wall.

B: Then the door sma<u>shed</u> it, not me.

5. /sk, ks, pst, zd, dz, ŋz/

A: If you don't stop smoking, your lu<u>ngs</u> may become disea<u>sed</u>, and you ri<u>sk</u> getting heart atta<u>cks</u>.

B: A friend of mine recently colla<u>psed</u> on the street after suffering a heart attack.

A: You see? All I a<u>sk</u> is for you not to light up ne<u>xt</u> time.

B: I didn't a<u>sk</u> for your advice. Besi<u>des</u>, I haven't smo<u>ked</u> for si<u>x</u> years.

6. /st, sk, ks, fs, vz, dz, ŋz/

A: He's a fa<u>st</u> driver.

B: Yes, he dri<u>ves</u> quickly.

A: He's a bri<u>sk</u> walker.

B: Yes, he wal<u>ks</u> very briskly.

A: He's a har<u>d</u> worker.

B: Oh, he wor<u>ks</u> constantly.

A: He ta<u>kes</u> thi<u>ngs</u> seriously.

B: He lau<u>ghs</u> very little.

A: I can't stand him.

B: Neither can his ki<u>ds</u>.

7. /θs, sts, kts, skt/

A: I'm in the de<u>pths</u> of despair. For five mo<u>nths</u> we had a wonderful relationship, but now she a<u>cts</u> like a stranger.

B: Nothing la<u>sts</u> forever.

A: I went to such great le<u>ngths</u> to please her. It took me mo<u>nths</u> to build up the courage, but I finally a<u>sked</u> her to marry me.

B: What did she say?

A: Nothing la<u>sts</u> forever.

CHAPTER 15

Consonants in Detail

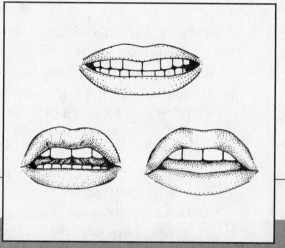

PREREADING QUESTIONS

Which figure shows /θ/ and /ð/, as in *thought, faith, then,* and *breathe*?
Which figure shows /s/ and /z/, as in *sought, face, Zen,* and *breeze*?
Which figure shows /t/ and /d/, as in *taught, fate, den,* and *breed*?
Do you pronounce all these words differently?

15.1 /s/ and /z/

/s/

Usual Spellings		Examples
<s>		see, smile, yes, us, this, its, hopes
<ss>		class, discuss, necessary
<c>	before <i, e, y>	city, recent, face, cycle
<sc>	before <i, e>	science, scenery, descend
<se>	after C	sense, course, false, collapse

Other Spellings		
<se>	after V	house, cease, loose, used to, precise, promise
<x> = /ks/		six, taxi, exercise, expect
Exceptions:		waltz, pretzel, pizza /ˈpitsə/

/**z**/

Usual Spellings		Examples
<z>		zoo, crazy, frozen, quiz, breeze
<zz>		buzz, fuzzy, blizzard
<s>	between Vs	easy, reason, disease, music
<se>	after V	these, cause, to lose, to use
<-s, -es> ending		plays, windows, tries, goes, does, dogs, comes, rides, girl's, washes, fixes, pleases, George's (see Sec. 14.2)

Other Spellings		Examples
<s>		is, was, has, his, as, always
<ism> = /ɪzəm/		communism, baptism
<x> = /gz/ before 'V		example, exist
Exceptions:		dessert, /dɪ'zɚt/, scissors, possess, dissolve, Xerox /'zirɑks/

PRACTICE 1

Both /s/ and /z/ are fricatives made by forcing air through a very narrow channel between the front of the tongue and the tooth ridge. The lips are spread. /s/ is *voiceless* with a *strong*, high-pitched hissing noise. /z/ is *voiced* with a *weaker* friction noise than /s/. In final position, /s/ is relatively long and is preceded by a short vowel; /z/ is short (and may become voiceless) and is preceded by a *long vowel*. Alternate /sszzsszz/, maintaining exactly the same articulation.

	1. /s/	**2.** /z/
Initial		
a.	I visited **Sue**.	I visited the **zoo**.
b.	They **sipped**[1] it up slowly.	They **zipped**[2] it up slowly.
c.	I said "**C**".	I said "**Z**".
d.	Was it **sewn** correctly?	Was it **zoned**[3] correctly?
Medial		
e.	They're **racing** horses.	They're **raising** horses.
f.	They're very **lacy**.[4]	They're very **lazy**.
g.	The **prices** are excellent.	The **prizes** are excellent.
h.	Is she **fussy**?[5]	Is she **fuzzy**?[6]
i.	That's not **recent** enough.	That's not **reason** enough.

(continued)

---

[1]sip = to drink (to sip hot coffee)

[2]zip = to pull up a zipper (to zip up a jacket)

[3]zone = to mark off an area for a particular kind of activity (a business zone)

[4]lacy = made of lace, a delicate, netlike cloth from fine thread (lacy curtains)

[5]fussy = too concerned with unimportant details (a fussy eater)

[6]fuzzy = unclear; covered with soft, short hair (fuzzy thinking, a fuzzy sweater)

PRACTICE 1 (continued)

	1. /s/	*2. /z/*

Final

	1. /s/	2. /z/
j.	What's the **price**?	What's the **prize**?
k.	It's a nice **place** to go to.	They're nice **plays** to go to.
l.	I'd like some **peace** for a change.	I'd like some **peas** for a change.
m.	His **niece** received some cuts in the crash.	His **knees** received some cuts in the crash.
n.	They **bus** people when they need to.	They **buzz** people when they need to.
o.	It **cost** him a lot of worry.	It **caused** him a lot of worry.
p.	There are some **lamps** in the room.	There are some **lambs** in the room.
q.	Do you have any **plants**?	Do you have any **plans**?
r.	I think they're **false**.	I think they're **falls**.
s.	Did you know he's **fierce**?[7]	Did you know his **fears**?

Nouns and Adjectives End in /s/	*Verbs End in /z/*
t. some **advice**	to **advise**
u. the **use**	to **use**
v. an **excuse**	to **excuse**
w. a **house**	to **house**
x. **close** (a close friend)	to **close**
y. **loose** (a loose jacket)	to **lose**

EXERCISES

A. Write /s/ or /z/ under the underlined letters to show the correct pronunciation.

1. The sun's going to rise at 6:00 A.M. tomorrow.
2. I'd like some peas and carrots.
3. He has brown eyes and a beautiful smile.
4. Do you like cheese and tomato sandwiches?
5. He's closing the windows.
6. Are you lazy? Yes, of course I am.
7. Did you lose these books?
8. The screw's loose; you should tighten it.
9. Did you use a pen or a pencil?
10. She used to sleep alot, but she doesn't anymore.
11. This exercise is too difficult. What's the use of trying.
12. You're late. What's your excuse?
13. Please excuse me for taking your science book.
14. Everyone was surprised by his music.

---

[7]fierce = strong, violent (a fierce wind, a fierce battle)

ADVANCED

B. Write /s/ or /z/ under the underlined letters to show how <se> is pronounced.

1. becau<u>se</u>   5. who<u>se</u>   9. noi<u>se</u>

2. choo<u>se</u>   6. purpo<u>se</u>   10. era<u>se</u>

3. relea<u>se</u>   7. mou<u>se</u>   11. tho<u>se</u>

4. cha<u>se</u>   8. revi<u>se</u>   12. ba<u>se</u>ball

SPANISH VIETNAMESE

C. <x> stands for *two* sounds: /ks/, or /gz/ before stressed vowels. Compare: *extreme* /ɪkˈstrim/ versus *a stream* /əˈstrim/; *next* /nɛkst/ versus *nest* /nɛst/; *six* /sɪks/ versus *sick* /sɪk/ and *sis* /sɪs/. Try dividing words like *excuse me* in different ways until you find a way that is good for you: /ɪk.ˈskyuz.mi/ or /ɪks.ˈkyuz.mi/. (If you still can't say this common word well, just say /ˈskyuzmi/!)

1. The e<u>x</u>am will start at e<u>x</u>actly si<u>x</u> o'clock.
2. It's an e<u>x</u>tremely good e<u>x</u>ample.
3. E<u>x</u>cuse me, but I'd like to e<u>x</u>change this sweater.
4. Were you e<u>x</u>cited about buying an e<u>x</u>pensive car?
5. I did all the e<u>x</u>ercises e<u>x</u>cept one.
6. Could you e<u>x</u>plain why you assigned e<u>x</u>tra homework?
7. They e<u>x</u>port many raw materials, for e<u>x</u>ample cotton, wood, and rice.
8. Do they e<u>x</u>pect the bomb to e<u>x</u>plode?
9. Ne<u>x</u>t time, get me a bo<u>x</u> of chocolate candy.
10. I'm going to rela<u>x</u> for si<u>x</u>ty minutes before I fi<u>x</u> dinner.
11. Preparing your income ta<u>x</u> is an unpleasant task.
12. Ma<u>x</u> had to ask for an a<u>x</u> to cut the wood.

SPANISH

D. Be careful not to add an extra vowel sound before words beginning with /sp, st, sk/. Make a long /s/ instead and link it to the preceding word.

KOREAN

Note that /p, t, k/ are unaspirated after /s/.

1. /sC/	*2.* /əsC/
1. It's a very big **state**.	It's a very big **estate**.[8]
2. Do you **steam**[9] them?	Do you **esteem**[10] them?
3. He did **study**.	He did **a study**.
4. It's **square**.	It's **a square**.
5. **School** is important.	**A school** is important.
6. Are you going to **skate**?	Are you going to **escape**?
7. He **screamed**.	He's **a scream**.[11]
8. This dinner is **special**.	This dinner is **a special**.[12]

---

[8]estate = a large piece of land with one house on it

[9]to steam = to cook food over boiling water

[10]to esteem = to value, respect, have a good opinion of

[11]to be a scream = (slang) to be very funny

[12]a special = an unusual offering, often with a lower price (a fried chicken special)

E. *Dialogues for* /sC, z/.

Be sure to pronounce <sn, sm, sl> with a *voiceless* /s/ at the beginning of words: *snow* = /snoʊ/, not [znoʊ]. However, <s> between vowels is *voiced*: *music* = /'myuzɪk/, not ['myusɪk].

Be sure your tongue and lips are in the position for /s/ when you make /z/: *zone* = /zoʊn/, not /dzoʊn/ or /ʒoʊn/.

1. /sC/ *smoke*

A: You shouldn't s̲moke in bed.

B: Well, I hate it when you s̲nore in your s̲leep.

A: I don't s̲nore. Occasionally I s̲neeze.

B: And you leave your s̲lippers lying around.

A: That's a rather s̲mall thing to complain about.

B: And you should s̲peak more s̲lowly. . . Why are you s̲miling? You s̲tarted it!

2. /z/ *music*

A: My cou̲s̲in Z̲uli'̲s̲ an excellent mus̲ician.

B: Really? What kind of mus̲ic doe̲s̲ he play?

A: He play̲s̲ all kind̲s̲ of mus̲ic—classical, jaz̲z̲, pop, eas̲y listening, new age. He'̲s̲
    also a compos̲er and recently won a thous̲and dollar priz̲e for hi̲s̲ compos̲ition,
    "Twilight Z̲one."

B: Wow! When'̲s̲ hi̲s̲ next concert?

A: He doe̲s̲n't give concerts. He only play̲s̲ for his friend̲s̲.

B: He must be craz̲y.

3. /z/ *zoo*

A: The z̲oology department is sponsoring a trip to the z̲oo.

B: Really? How did you find out about it?

A: My advi̲s̲or told me all about it last week; a̲s̲ a re̲s̲ult, I signed up.

B: Don't forget to take the z̲oom lens for your camera. You don't want to get too
    close to animal̲s̲ at the z̲oo. It can be haz̲ardous.

A: Who need̲s̲ a z̲oom lens? I love to sneak inside the protective z̲one and touch
    the animal̲s̲—especially the snakes and liz̲ard̲s̲.

15.2 /θ/ and /ð/

/θ/ — Voiceless <th>

	Usual Spelling	Examples
<th>	at the beginning of content words	think, thirsty, three
<th>	at the end of words	mouth, breath, health

/ð/ — Voiced <th>

	Usual Spellings	Examples
<th>	at the beginning of function words	the, they, this
<th>	between vowels	mother, leather
<the>	at the end of words	soothe, breathe

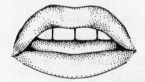 

/θ, ð/ *thought, then*   /t, d/ *taught, den*

FIGURE 15-1

PRACTICE 2

/θ/ is a voiceless fricative made by placing the *tip* of the tongue lightly against the *cutting edges of the upper front teeth* and blowing. Do not stick your tongue out of your mouth. When you look in a mirror, you should see just a little of the tongue between the teeth. (If you see too much of your tongue, slowly pull it in until just the tip touches the teeth.) The contact between the tongue and teeth must be *loose* enough to permit the stream of air to pass out. In comparison to /s/, the tongue is flat and lets a lot of air pass out.

	Initial /θ/	Medial /θ/	Final /θ/
1.	thank you	author	mouth
2.	thing	toothache	death
3.	thick	mathematics	breath
4.	thin	something	bath
5.	thought	birthday	truth
6.	Thursday	healthy	cloth
7.	thumb	wealthy	south
8.	third	filthy	health
9.	throw	northwest	month
10.	threw	southeast	fourth, fifth, etc.

(continued)

PRACTICE 2 (continued)

	1. /θ/	*2.* /t/
a.	It's **thin**.	It's **tin**.
b.	They want **thanks**.	They want **tanks**.
c.	He **thought** about the war.	He **taught** about the war.
d.	Those are good **themes**.	Those are good **teams**.
e.	Her **death** was terrible.	Her **debt** was terrible.
f.	He gave him a **bath**.	He gave him a **bat**.
g.	I saw **both**.	I saw a **boat**.
h.	What's his **faith**?	What's his **fate**?[1]
i.	They were **through**.	They were **true**.
j.	I've got a **three**.	I've got a **tree**.

	1. /θ/	*2.* /s/
k.	Where's your **thumb**?	Where's your **sum**?
l.	It's a lovely **thimble**.[2]	It's a lovely **symbol**.
m.	I never **thought** it.	I never **sought**[3] it.
n.	It's **unthinkable**.	It's **unsinkable**.
o.	It's very **mothy**.[4]	It's very **mossy**.[5]
p.	Her **mouth** is pretty.	Her **mouse** is pretty.
q.	They went over the **path**.	They went over the **pass**.[6]
r.	He has a strange **faith**.	He has a strange **face**.
s.	The **fourth** is near.	The **force** is near.
t.	He's the **tenth** child.	He's the **tense** child.

PRACTICE 3

/ð/ is made exactly like /θ/ except that it is voiced. Check in the mirror to make sure that you can *see just the tip of your tongue* between your teeth. Be sure to allow *air to continue flowing* between your tongue and teeth during /ð/. Alternate /θθðððθθðð/, maintaining exactly the same articulation.

Initial /ð/	*Medial* /ð/	*Final* /ð/
1. the	father	smooth
2. they	mother	soothe (=to calm)
3. their	brother	loathe (=to hate)
4. there	weather	breathe
5. then	together	clothe (=to put clothes on)
6. this	southern	bathe (=to take a bath)
7. that	northern	teethe (=to grow teeth)
8. these	clothing	
9. those	another	NOTE: /θ/ in the nouns:
10. though	although	breath bath
11. thus	either	cloth teeth

(continued)

PRACTICE 3 (continued)

1. /ð/	*2. /d/ or /t/*
a. **They** began early.	**Day** began early.
b. They want **those**.	They won't **doze**.[7]
c. **They've** talked about it.	**Dave** talked about it.
d. Did you see her **then**?	Did you see her **den**?[8]
e. He was **there** to do it.	He was **dared** to do it.
f. She found it with **the light**.	She found it with **delight**.
g. He threw the **leather** away.	He threw the **letter** away.
h. You'll see her **mother**.	You'll see her **mutter**.[9]
i. Is the **lather**[10] very good?	Is the **ladder** very good?
j. Don't **stop breathing**.	Don't **stop reading**.
k. He's a very **worthy**[11] person.	He's a very **wordy**[12] person.
l. How do rabbits **breathe**?	How do rabbits **breed**?[13]
m. We **loathe**[14] corn.	We **load** corn.
n. They **soothe** everyone.	They **sued**[15] everyone.

1. /ð/	*2. /z/*
a. **Theirs** is a big store.	**Zayre's** is a big store.
b. Do you know anything about **then**?	Do you know anything about **Zen**?[16]
c. Is it **clothing**?	Is it **closing**?
d. The child is **teething**.	The child is **teasing**.[17]
e. We must **clothe** all of them.	We must **close** all of them.
f. That's my **scythe**.[18]	That's my **size**.
g. He'll **soothe** many people.	He **sues** many people.
h. Do you like to **bathe**?	Do you like the **bays**?
i. Can you feel them **breathe**?	Can you feel the **breeze**?

---

[1]fate = a person's future, his fortune in life

[2]thimble = small cap put over a finger when you are sewing

[3]sought = past tense of 'to seek' (=look for)

[4]mothy = full of moths, small winged insects that fly into lights at night

[5]mossy = covered with moss, a soft, green plant that grows in dark, wet areas

[6]a pass = a narrow way through or over the mountains

[7]doze = to sleep lightly

[8]den = a hiding place, a play room

[9]mutter = to speak very unclearly

[10]lather = thick suds, as in shaving cream

[11]worthy = honorable, of value, worth a lot

[12]wordy = using too many words

[13]breed = to reproduce, make babies

[14]loathe = to hate

[15]sue = to take to court

[16]Zen = a kind of Buddhism, a religion

[17]tease = to make a joke, to annoy (to tease one's brother or sister)

[18]scythe = a large curved knife for cutting grass

EXERCISES

ADVANCED   **A.** The consonant group /θr/, as in the word *three* is difficult to pronounce. Your *tongue* should pull away from your teeth after you make /θ/, but it *should not hit the roof of the mouth.* Practice using the vowel /ɚ/ after /θ/ and then speeding it up: /θɚ·ɚ i/, /θɚ i/, /θri/. Another way is to begin with /ri/ and add /θ/ to the beginning: /ri/, /θri/. Practice the following phrases and sentences very slowly and try to feel whether or not your tongue is hitting the roof of your mouth.

1. three things
2. three thousand dollars
3. Thread the needle.
4. Throw them away.

5. I threw them away.
6. It got caught in my throat.
7. I'm through.
8. I got three free trees.

ADVANCED   **B.** Many non-native speakers pronounce initial /ð/ the same as /d/. Although this rarely causes serious misunderstandings, it does give you a definite accent and makes you sound uneducated. Advanced speakers should try to pronounce /ð/ correctly; remember that it is a *soft*, *weak* sound, not a stop like /d/. Try to relax when you say it. /ð/ often occurs in *unstressed* syllables (*the*, *them*, *another*); pronouncing it weakly will help you shorten and reduce these unstressed syllables. Your teacher will say *silently* one of the following words or phrases. Watch his or her lips and decide which one he or she is saying. Then say each pair yourself and feel the difference.

a. /ð/	*b.* /d/ *or* /t/
1. the light	delight
2. the test	detest (=hate)
3. the part	depart
4. the fence	defense
5. this cover	discover
6. to the side	to decide
7. mother	mutter
8. leather	letter
9. either	eater
10. together	to get her

C. Review linking *the* smoothly to words beginning with vowels.

1. the apples /ðɪˈʸæpəlz/
2. the end of a word
3. the other day
4. the unusual weather

5. the only thing
6. the airplane
7. the information
8. the evening air

D. /ð/ followed by /z/ is very weak. In normal conversational speech, /ð/ is omitted in the word *clothes* /kloʊðz/ → /kloʊːz/, which sounds the same as the verb *close*. If you have difficulty pronouncing /ðz/ in words like *breathes*, *soothes*, *loathes*, and *sunbathes*, omit /ð/; no one will notice in continuous speech.

E. /θ, f/. Some speakers mix up /θ/ with /f/. They sound similar, but the place of articulation is clearly different. Practice the following words and sentences both silently
and aloud, checking in the mirror to be sure that you see *the tongue* touching the
upper teeth for /θ/ (and the lips are out of the way), and *the lower lip* touching the
upper teeth for /f/.

1. He   (a. throws   b. froze)   it.
2. When did they   (a. thaw   b. fall)?
3. She wants   (a. three   b. free)   books.
4. Do you need   (a. thread   b. Fred)?
5. What happened to   (a. the roof   b. Ruth)?
6. Mr. Jones   (a. thought   b. fought   c. taught)   about women.
7. What does   (a. thin   b. fin   c. tin)   mean?
8. I understand   (a. his death   b. he's deaf   c. his debt).

 F. *Reading for* /θ, ð, z/. Underline the sounds /θ/, /ð/, and /z/ in this passage, and
write the phonetic symbol for each sound below it. Then record yourself reading it
aloud. Note: *with* and *without* may be pronounced with either /θ/ or /ð/. The first
sentence is done for you.

Today'<u>s</u> wea<u>th</u>er report i<u>s</u> brought to you by Ber<u>th</u>a'<u>s</u> Kitty Boutique,[19] where
     z   ð   z   θ z

you can get every<u>th</u>ing your cat ha<u>s</u> ever wanted and more.
               θ   z

There will be scattered showers this afternoon with a chance of

thunderstorms toward the evening. Highs will be in the seventies, with a light

breeze out of the north five to ten miles an hour, gusting to twenty miles an hour

in some southern locations. Skies will be clearing overnight, with lows in the

fifties. It will be sunny and warm tomorrow and Thursday, with temperatures

climbing up into the eighties both days. The weather outlook for the weekend is

quite good: you can expect sunny skies and very pleasant conditions right through

Sunday.

And if you're taking your cat with you this weekend, be sure to pick up your

kitty travel pack, for only thirteen ninety-five including tax, at Bertha's Kitty

Boutique. Don't leave home without it.

How many examples of /θ/ *did you find?* _____   *of* /ð/? _____   *of* /z/? _____

---

[19]The name 'Bertha's Kitty Boutique' is from Garrison Keillor's radio show, "Prairie Home
Companion."

G. *Dialogues for /θ, ð/.*

1. /θ/ *think*

A: When's Martha's birthday?

B: I think it's on Thursday.

A: Thursday, the thirteenth of the month?

B: I think so.

A: How old will she be then?

B: I think she'll be thirty-three.

A: Thirty-three? I thought she was older than that.

B: Well, she might be thirty-four.

A: Thanks. I don't think you know anything for sure.

2. /θ/ *both,* /t/ *boat,* /θr/ *through,* /tr/ *true*

A: We're through.

B: But it can't be true. I love you.

A: It must be fate. I have no faith in you anymore.

B: Give me another chance. Let's both get on a boat and sail away together.

A: I've thought about this for three months. We're truly through with each other.

B: But what have I done?

A: Nothing. That's the trouble.

3. /θ/ *thin,* /s/ *sincere*

A: He's thoughtful and sincere.

B: She's wealthy and sophisticated.

A: He's small and thin.

B: She's strong and healthy.

A: He's thorough and sympathetic.

B: She's sloppy and authoritarian.

A: He's from the North.

B: She's from the South.

A: You know what? They're getting married next month.

B: Something tells me it won't work.

4. /ð/ *this*

A: I'd like this one and that one.

B: How about some of these or some of those?

A: That's a good idea. I'll take some of those.

B: Which ones? These?

A: No, those over there.

B: How many of them?

A: Both of them.

B: Will that be all?

A: No, I think I'd like another one of these. That's right.

B: There you are. That'll be $3.50.

A: That's all?

5. /ð/ *then,* /d/ *den*

A: The mother, at the start of the day, wakes up and feeds her pups.

B: Then, she takes them from the den down to the lake to bathe them.

A: Then they go together with the daddy to find food in the meadow, although it's far away.

B: There they spend the day feeding and breathing the fresh air.

A: They don't mind if the weather is bad.

B: When dusk falls, they return to their den, ready for another day.

Then they go together with the daddy to find food in the meadow.

6. /ð/ *mother,* /t/ *mutter*

A: Don't mutter!

B: I'm not muttering, mother.

A: Yes you are. You mutter as bad as your brother.

B: No I don't. I speak loudly and smoothly.

A: There you go again. And another thing . . .

B: I wish you'd stop mothering me!

15.3 /ʃ/ and /tʃ/

/ʃ/

Usual Spellings		Examples
<sh>		ssh!, she, should, fashion, brush, wish
In unstressed endings:		
	<ti>	station, condition, partial, initial, ambitious, cautious, patient, negotiate, inertia
	<ci>	musician, suspicion, special, official, delicious, sufficient, appreciate, glacier
	<ssi>	permission, discussion, Russia

Other Spellings		Examples
<ch>	(from French)	Chicago, machine, brochure, mustache
<su>	(rare)	sugar, sure, assure, insurance
<ssu>	unstressed	pressure, tissue, issue
<si>	in <nsion, lsion>	dimension,[1] expansion, propulsion
<ce>	unstressed	ocean, curvaceous
<xu>, <xi> = /kʃ/		sexual, luxury, anxious, obnoxious

/tʃ/

Usual Spellings		Examples
<ch>		church, purchase, teacher, which, much
<tch>		kitchen, watch, scratch
In unstressed endings:		
	<tu>	nature, picture, statue, fortune, actual, century, situation, punctuate, congratulate

Other Spellings		
<ti>	after <s>	question, suggestion, Christian
<ce>	(from Italian)	cello, concerto
<te>	unstressed	amateur, righteous

---

[1]/ʃ/ after /n/ may also be pronounced /tʃ/: *dimension* /dɪˈmɛnʃən/ or /dɪˈmɛntʃən/, *ancient* /ˈeɪnʃənt/ or /ˈeɪntʃənt/.

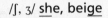
/ʃ, ʒ/ <u>sh</u>e, bei<u>ge</u>

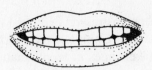
/s, z/ <u>s</u>ee, bay<u>s</u>

FIGURE 15-2

PRACTICE 4

/ʃ/ is a voiceless fricative made by pressing the front of the tongue toward the roof of the mouth a little *further back* than /s/ and rounding the lips slightly. The tongue should be more relaxed, and the hissing sound is lower pitched and softer than /s/. /tʃ/ is a voiceless affricate: make sure to *stop the air completely* before opening up into /ʃ/.

1. /ʃ/	2. /tʃ/
a. They're **sheep**.	They're **cheap**.
b. He **shows** nice pictures.	He **chose** nice pictures.
c. I counted ten **ships**.	I counted ten **chips**.[2]
d. He took my **share**.	He took my **chair**.
e. They're **washing** my car.	They're **watching** my car.
f. You should **cash** it.	You should **catch** it.
g. He put it in the **dish**.	He put it in the **ditch**.[3]
h. I'm going to **mash**[4] them.	I'm going to **match** them.
i. Your **Porsche**[5] is beautiful.	Your **porch**[6] is beautiful.
j. We've already **washed** it.	We've already **watched** it.

1. /ʃ/	2. /s/
k. I'll **shave** more.	I'll **save** more.
l. Who **showed** it?	Who **sewed** it?
m. I think they're **shoes**.	I think they're **Sue's**.
n. It was a **shock**.	It was a **sock**.
o. Did you find a new **sheet**?	Did you find a new **seat**?
p. Have they had many **clashes**?[7]	Have they had many **classes**?
q. His **leash**[8] is very long.	His **lease**[9] is very long.
r. It was caught in a **mesh**.[10]	It was caught in a **mess**.[11]
s. It was **crushed**.	It was **crust**.
t. They've **rushed** it.	They've **rusted**.

---

[2]chip = a small piece

[3]ditch = a long, narrow hole

[4]mash = to crush (potatoes)

[5]Porsche = a kind of sports car

[6]porch = terrace, patio

[7]clash = conflict, disagreement

[8]leash = a long strap to hold a dog

[9]lease = a contract to rent a place for a certain time period

[10]mesh = a net or screen

[11]mess = dirt or disorder

EXERCISES

A. /ʃ/ occurs in the unstressed endings <tial, cial, tion, cian, ssion, tious, cious, tient, cient, tiate, ciate>. Complete the following chart, adding the appropriate ending and noting the changes in pronunciation.

/s/ *or* /t/ *in the Noun*	/ʃ/ *in the Adjective*[12]
1. influence	influential
2. race	racial
3. president	_____
4. office	_____
5. benefit	_____
6. face	_____
7. finance	_____
8. commerce	_____
9. confidence	_____
10. _____	partial
11. _____	spatial

12. Think of three more examples of nouns ending in /ʃən/.

condition, physician, profession, _____

_____

13. Think of two more examples of adjectives ending in /ʃəs/.

spacious, suspicious, nutritious, _____

_____

B. /tʃ/ occurs in nouns ending in <ture> = /tʃɚ/. Can you think of two more examples?

culture, furniture, mixture, _____

_____

C. <ch> is the normal spelling for /tʃ/, but in a few words borrowed from French it is pronounced /ʃ/. Write /tʃ/ or /ʃ/ to show how the underlined letters are pronounced in the following words.

1. champagne	**6.** mustache	**11.** achieve
2. much	**7.** approach	**12.** purchase
3. parachute	**8.** brochure	**13.** Michigan
4. machine	**9.** chance	**14.** Massachusetts
5. peach	**10.** chef	**15.** Chicago

---

[12]After /n/, the sequence <ti> or <ci> may be pronounced either /ʃ/ or /tʃ/. The tongue stops the air going out the mouth during /n/; if there is a slight delay after the velum closes and before friction for /ʃ/ begins, this will result in /tʃ/.

ADVANCED

D. <ch> is also one of the spellings for /k/ in a few common words and in many technical words, including the following word roots: <chor>, <chlor>, <chron>, <psych>, <tech>. Write /tʃ/ or /k/ to show how the underlined letters are pronounced.

1. stoma<u>ch</u>a<u>ch</u>e
2. atta<u>ch</u>
3. monar<u>ch</u>
4. ar<u>ch</u>
5. e<u>ch</u>o
6. <u>ch</u>ore
7. <u>ch</u>ord
8. <u>ch</u>orus
9. ba<u>ch</u>elor
10. ar<u>ch</u>itect
11. or<u>ch</u>estra
12. or<u>ch</u>ard
13. arti<u>ch</u>oke
14. me<u>ch</u>anic
15. <u>ch</u>emist
16. <u>ch</u>aos

E. Write /s/, /z/, /ʃ/, /tʃ/, or /t/ to show how the underlined letters are pronounced in the following words.

1. artifi<u>c</u>ial
2. i<u>ss</u>ue
3. illne<u>ss</u>
4. for<u>t</u>unate
5. expre<u>ss</u>ion
6. holiday<u>s</u>
7. suspi<u>c</u>ious
8. pen<u>c</u>il
9. sugges<u>t</u>ion
10. adven<u>t</u>ure
11. bu<u>s</u>y
12. punc<u>t</u>ual
13. in<u>s</u>urance
14. <u>s</u>cenery
15. surpri<u>s</u>e
16. sta<u>t</u>ue
17. pa<u>t</u>ient
18. ac<u>t</u>or
19. apprecia<u>t</u>ion
20. si<u>t</u>uation
21. musi<u>c</u>ian
22. re<u>s</u>ult

F. Many students have difficulty pronouncing /tʃ/ before or after other consonants. Most of these cannot be simplified; however, the sequence /stʃ/ as in *question*, *gesture*, and *Christian* can be pronounced as /ʃtʃ/: /ˈkwɛstʃən/ → /ˈkwɛʃtʃən/.

1. I stre<u>tch</u>ed out on the cou<u>ch</u> and wa<u>tch</u>ed <u>t</u>elevision.
2. She scra<u>tch</u>ed him after he pun<u>ch</u>ed her.
3. Whi<u>ch</u> <u>ch</u>ild approa<u>ch</u>ed the table and rea<u>ch</u>ed for a cookie?
4. He didn't have mu<u>ch</u> <u>t</u>ime to complete his resear<u>ch</u> <u>p</u>roject.
5. Our Fren<u>ch</u> <u>t</u>eacher asked su<u>ch</u> difficult ques<u>t</u>ions that no one could answer them.
6. The army followed his sugges<u>t</u>ion and mar<u>ch</u>ed <u>th</u>rough the town that night.

15.4   /dʒ/ and /y/

/dʒ/

Usual Spellings		Examples
<j>, <dj>		judge, joke, major, enjoy, adjust
<g>	before <e, i, y>	George, manager, page, giant, religion, gym
<dge>		budget, edge, knowledge
<du>	unstressed	gradual, individual, educate, schedule, procedure

Other Spellings		Examples
<di>	(rare)	soldier, cordial
<gge>	(rare)	exaggerate
Exceptions:		margarine /ˈmɑɚ-dʒɚ-ɪn/, algae /ˈældʒi/)

/y/

Usual Spellings		Examples
<y>		you, year, beyond, lawyer[1]
<i>	between C and V	onion, convenient, million,[2] familiar
<u>, <ue> = /yu/		usually, university, computer, music, vacuum, cute, argue, human, fuel, value, continue

Other Spellings		Examples
<ew>, <eu>		few, Matthew, Europe, feud, therapeutic
Exception:		beautiful

/dʒ, tʃ/ jello, cello

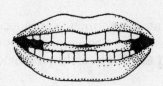
/y/ yellow

FIGURE 15-3

---

[1]Words like *lawyer, mayor, payer* may also be analyzed as /ˈlɔɪɚ/, /ˈmeɪɚ/, /ˈpeɪɚ/.

[2]/l/ may be weakened or omitted before /y/ in words like *million, brilliant, familiar, failure* (see p. 205).

PRACTICE 5

/dʒ/ is made exactly like /tʃ/ with the addition of voicing. Vowels before /dʒ/ are lengthened (sentences f-j). Be sure to *stop the air completely* as in /d/ before you open up and produce noticeable *fricative noise*. There is also a little lip rounding. /dʒ/ is pronounced further back in the mouth than /dz/ and further front than /y/. /y/ is a quickly pronounced /i/. There should be *no friction*.

1. /dʒ/	*2.* /tʃ/
a. I believe he's **joking**.	I believe he's **choking**.
b. The crowd **jeered**[3] them.	The crowd **cheered** them.
c. What happened to your **gin**[4]?	What happened to your **chin**?
d. She dropped her **jello**.	She dropped her **cello**.
e. They're **Jane's**.	They're **chains**.
f. Is that **badge** ready yet?	Is that **batch** ready yet?
g. **Marge** is fine with me.	**March** is fine with me.
h. Did you see her **lunge**?	Did you see her **lunch**?
i. It's a little **ridge**.	It's a little **rich**.
j. They're **surging**[5] now.	They're **searching** now.

1. /dʒ/	*2.* /y/
k. **Jello's** my favorite.	**Yellow's** my favorite.
l. Did he go to **jail**?	Did he go to **Yale**?
m. That's a good **joke**.	That's a good **yolk**.[6]
n. The **jam**[7] tasted good.	The **yam**[8] tasted good.
o. There's no **juice**.	There's no **use**.
p. He's a **major**, I think.	He's a **mayor**, I think.
q. Who's **paging**[9] him?	Who's **paying** him?

1. /dʒ/	*2.* /dz/
r. **Age** is a serious problem.	**AIDS** in a serious problem.
s. I don't see their **hedge**.[10]	I don't see their **heads**.
t. Do you have any **change**?	Do you have any **chains**?
u. Their **rage**[11] was destructive.	Their **raids**[12] were destructive.
v. I didn't know about the **siege**.[13]	I didn't know about the **seeds**.
w. They don't **budge**.[14]	They aren't **buds**.[15]
x. The **leakage**[16] can cause problems.	The **Lee kids** can cause problems.

---

[3]jeer = laugh at, mock

[4]gin = an alcoholic drink

[5]surge = move forward or upward like ocean waves

[6]yolk /youk/ = yellow part of an egg

[7]jam = jelly, marmalade

[8]yam = sweet, orange potato

[9]page = (verb) to call out a person's name

[10]hedge = row of trees or bushes

[11]rage = strong anger

[12]raid = attack

[13]siege = surrounding a town and letting nothing in

[14]budge = move

[15]bud = a flower before it opens

[16]leakage = result of having a leak, a small accidental hole that lets a liquid or gas pass out

EXERCISES

A. Many nouns end in <age> = /ɪdʒ/. Make nouns from the following words. Can you think of any other nouns that end in /ɪdʒ/?

   1. bag — *baggage*

   2. use — *usage*

   3. pack — _____

   4. carry — _____

   5. spoil — _____

   6. short — _____

   7. post — _____

   8. pass — _____

   9. marry — _____

   10. mile — _____

B. /dʒ/ is spelled <du> in unstressed syllables in words like *educate* /ˈɛdʒəkeɪt/. Write /dʒ/ or /d/ to show how <d> is pronounced in the following words.

1. sche<u>d</u>ule	**7.** <u>d</u>uty
2. a<u>d</u>ult	**8.** over<u>d</u>ue
3. indivi<u>d</u>ual	**9.** gra<u>d</u>ual
4. e<u>d</u>ucation	**10.** gra<u>d</u>uate
5. pro<u>d</u>uce	**11.** con<u>d</u>uctor
6. proce<u>d</u>ure	**12.** mo<u>d</u>ular[17]

CAMBODIAN
VIETNAMESE

C. Be careful not to drop /dʒ/ at the ends of words.

   1. It (a. ranged b. rained) over a large area.

   2. It's really quite (a. strange b. a strain) for her.

   3. He's a (a. marriage b. married) counselor.

   4. They (a. changed b. chained) the tires together.

   5. Is that a (a. language b. languid[18]) class?

---

[17]modular = made up of standard size parts or modules (modular furniture, space module)

[18]languid = slow, weak, and a little lazy

SPANISH JAPANESE

D. *Reading for unstressed* /dʒ/. Be sure to make /dʒ/ firmly and produce friction even in unstressed syllables: *energy* = /'ɛnɚ-dʒi/, not ['ɛnɚ-ʒi] or ['ɛnɚ-yi]. Use /tʃ/ and lengthen the preceding vowel if necessary. Record yourself reading the following passage.

There's a terrible war raging in that region. It originally started in two neighboring villages over religious differences, but it has gradually taken over the country. The situation is dangerous. Soldiers and refugees are gathering at the edge of the forest near the bridge that leads into the capital. Many were injured crossing the mountain range. There's a shortage of food and medical supplies. Major Johnson was in charge until he was injured; now Sargeant Rogers is managing the army. A special agent was just sent in to try to arrange a cease fire, but neither side will budge. Citizens in the capital are preparing for a long siege.

E. Insert /y/ before <u, ew, eu> word initially and after /p, b, f, v, m, θ, k, g, h/. Unstressed /yu/ often reduces to /yə/ as in *circulation* /sɚ-kyə'leɪʃən/ and *muscular* /'məskyələ-/.

1. Only a fool wouldn't put *fuel* in his car before leaving on vacation.
2. Who thought that *Hugh* would become president?
3. The air by the sea is *pure*, but in town it's poor.
4. The *cute* pigeon cooed softly.
5. They listened to *music* under the moon.
6. Have you seen our new *menu*?
7. *Huge* numbers of people *circulate* through the *museums* of *Europe*.
8. In the *future*, *computers* will *communicate regularly* with *humans*.

CHINESE KOREAN

F. Be careful with the sequences /yi/ and /yɪ/. The tongue is pushed further forward in /y/ than in /i/ or /ɪ/. Be sure to distinguish *ear* and *year*, *east* and *yeast*.[19] There are *three* syllables in *studying* /stə.di.ʸɪŋ/, *copying* /kɑ.pi.ʸɪŋ/, *marrying* /mæ.ri.ʸɪŋ/, etc.

1. One *year* ago, he lost his hearing in one ear.
2. Do they use a lot of *yeast* in the Far East?
3. I won't *yield;*[20] I'll never eat eel.
4. I began *studying* English a *year* ago.
5. Mother's always *worrying* about us *dirtying* up our room.
6. She's *marrying* the man she met on a *skiing* trip.

---

[19]yeast = the tiny organism that makes bread rise
[20]yield = give up

15.5 /ʒ/ and Review of /ʃ, tʃ, dʒ/

/ʒ/

Usual Spellings	Examples
<ge> (from French)	beige, garage, massage, rouge, prestige
In unstressed endings:	
<si>	vision, occasion, Asian, Indonesia
<su>	pleasure, measure, casual, usually
<zu>	azure, seizure
Exceptions:	regime /reɪˈʒim/, equation /ɪˈkweɪʒən/

PRACTICE 6

/ʒ/ is made exactly like /ʃ/, but it is voiced. It has soft, continuous, low-pitched friction. Don't stop the air as in /dʒ/. Round your lips a little and don't squeeze the tongue as much as in /z/. If you have trouble with this sound, begin by making /ʃ/ and lengthening the preceding vowel. Pronouncing /ʒ/ the same as /ʃ/ is not a serious mistake; sentences p–t are included only for comparison. /ʒ/ occurs only in medial and final position in English. Some Americans pronounce /ʒ/ at the end of a word as /dʒ/: garage /gəˈradʒ/.

	Medial			*Final*	
1.	measure	/ˈmɛʒɚ/	beige[1]	/beɪʒ/	
2.	leisure	/ˈliʒɚ/	garage	/gəˈrɑʒ/	
3.	pleasure	/ˈplɛʒɚ/	massage[2]	/məˈsɑʒ/	
4.	usual	/ˈyuʒʊəl/ or /ˈyuʒəl/	corsage[3]	/kɔɚˈsɑʒ/	
5.	occasionally	/əˈkeɪʒənəli/	mirage[4]	/mɪˈrɑʒ/	
6.	conclusion	/kənˈkluʒən/	camouflage[5]	/ˈkæməflɑʒ/	
7.	decision	/dɪˈsɪʒən/	espionage[6]	/ˈɛspɪənɑʒ/	
8.	Asia	/ˈeɪʒə/	rouge[7]	/ruʒ/	(continued)

---

[1]beige = the color of sand (light tan)

[2]massage = rub and press the body with hands

[3]corsage = flowers worn on a dress

[4]mirage = an illusion, the appearance of a non-existing thing

[5]camouflage = anything that hides something by making it look like its surroundings

[6]espionage = spying

[7]rouge = makeup that makes cheeks red

PRACTICE 6 (continued)

---

1. /ʒ/

a.   That's the Roman **version**.
b.   What's your **measure**?
c.   I'm upset by the **lesion**.[9]
d.   They're **Asian** refugees.
e.   She got a **massage**.
f.   We have the **pleasure**.
g.   Two **Asians** were sent there.
h.   **In the visual** arts they're important.

2. /dʒ/

That's the Roman **virgin**[8].
What's your **major**?
I'm upset by the **legion**.[10]
They're **aging** refugees.
She got a **message**.
We have the **pledger**.[11]
Two **agents** were sent there.
Individual arts are important.

---

1. /ʒ/

i.   Where's the **enclosure**?[12]
j.   The **seizure**[14] was terrible.
k.   The **rouge** didn't work.
l.   It looks like they're **beige**.
m.   The **pleasure**'s mine.
n.   That **regime**'s no good.
o.   It's a **casual** relationship.

2. /z/

Where's the **encloser**?[13]
The **Caesar**[15] was terrible.
The **ruse**[16] didn't work.
It looks like they're **bays**.[17]
The **plays are** mine.
That **reason**'s no good.
It's a **causal** relationship.

---

1. /ʒ/

p.   It was an **illusion**.
q.   The **delusion**[19] bothers me.
r.   Do you like **azure**?[21]
s.   A lot of **Asians** live in this city.
t.   The **pleasure** is great.

2. /ʃ/

It was an **Aleutian**.[18]
The **dilution**[20] bothers me.
Do you like **Asher**?
A lot of **Haitians** live in this city.
The **pressure** is great.

---

[8]virgin = pure, unmarried girl; pure (virgin olive oil, virgin forest)

[9]lesion = injury, wound

[10]legion = a large group of soldiers

[11]pledger = person who pledges or promises

[12]enclosure = fenced in (closed) area

[13]encloser = person who encloses something

[14]seizure = capture; epileptic fit

[15]Caesar /ˈsizɚ/= a king in ancient Rome

[16]ruse = trick, deception

[17]bay = large, partly enclosed area of water

[18]Aleutian = a native of the islands off Alaska

[19]delusion = deception, false belief

[20]dilution = weakening of a solution (noun form of dilute)

[21]azure = light blue (color of the sky)

EXERCISES

A. Practice the following sentences making sure that *voiced* air flows out *continuously* during /ʒ/.

1. The explo<u>s</u>ion was one of unu<u>s</u>ual force and completely wrecked the gara<u>ge</u>.
2. The re<u>gi</u>me announced the sei<u>z</u>ure of all private property.
3. The provi<u>s</u>ions that we took along on our excur<u>s</u>ion were inadequate.
4. He is a ca<u>s</u>ual acquaintance whom I meet occa<u>s</u>ionally.
5. Our trip to the Trea<u>s</u>ury building was very plea<u>s</u>urable.
6. The colli<u>s</u>ion was caused by the poor vi<u>s</u>ion of one of the drivers.
7. His deci<u>s</u>ion was to spend all his lei<u>s</u>ure time with his family.

B. Note the sound changes in the following related words. Fill in the blanks with the missing words.

	Verb — /d/	*Noun* — /ʒ/	*Adjective* — /s/
1.	explode	explosion	explosive
2.	conclude	conclusion	conclusive
3.	invade	_____	_____
4.	persuade	_____	_____
5.	_____	exclusion	_____
6.	_____	_____	decisive
7.	divide	_____	_____
8.	_____	collision	
9.	provide	_____	

	Verb — /z/	*Noun* — /ʒ/
10.	seize	seizure
11.	enclose	enclosure
12.	expose	_____
13.	compose	_____
14.	_____	pleasure

C. Compare words ending in <sion> = /ʒən/ in Exercise B above with words ending in <ssion> = /ʃən/. Fill in the blanks with the missing words.

	Verb — /t/ *or* /s/	*Noun* — /ʃ/	*Adjective* — /s/
1.	permit	permission	permissive
2.	express	_____	_____
3.	possess	_____	_____

	Verb — /t/ or /s/	*Noun — /ʃ/*
4.	admit	_____
5.	_____	discussion
6.	transmit	_____
7.	_____	confession
8.	_____	omission

D. Write /s/, /z/, /ʃ/, /ʒ/, /tʃ/, or /dʒ/ to show how the underlined words are pronounced.

1. pleasure	**6.** social	**11.** television
2. pleasant	**7.** peaceful	**12.** profession
3. pressure	**8.** suspicious	**13.** professor
4. picture	**9.** casually	**14.** garbage
5. occasionally	**10.** gradually	**15.** beige

E. Write down two examples of words containing each of the following sounds.

	Initial	*Medial or Final*
/s/	_____	_____
/z/	_____	_____
/ʃ/	_____	_____
/ʒ/	X X X	_____
/tʃ/	_____	_____
/dʒ/	_____	_____
/y/	_____	_____

F. Write the phonetic symbols for the underlined letters or syllables in the following words.

1. schedule /dʒəl/	**11.** superstitious	**21.** magic
2. relation	**12.** reason	**22.** insure
3. religious	**13.** future	**23.** damage
4. register	**14.** professional	**24.** decision
5. Irish	**15.** visual	**25.** measure
6. police	**16.** spatial	**26.** politician
7. unusual	**17.** surprise	**27.** situation
8. imagination	**18.** invasion	**28.** accusation
9. speech	**19.** especially	**29.** razor
10. refrigerator	**20.** education	**30.** horse

G. *Reading for* /ʃ, ʒ, tʃ, dʒ/. Underline the sounds /ʃ/, /ʒ/, /tʃ/, /dʒ/ and write the phonetic symbol for each sound below it. Then record yourself reading the passage.

The Department of Asian Languages and Literature is sponsoring a lecture
$$\underline{ʒ} \qquad \underline{dʒ} \qquad \underline{tʃ} \qquad \underline{tʃ}$$

by Professor George Wong entitled, "Changes in China during the Second Half of

this Century." Dr. Wong was an undergraduate at Yale College before receiving his

Ph.D. there in 1975. He will speak on some of the major issues that have shaped

China in recent years, including the Chinese Cultural Revolution, measures to deal

with the population explosion, reasons for dissatisfaction with the regime among

intellectuals, damage to the educational system caused by the student uprising, and

subsequent efforts to limit Western television news coverage. His speech will be

given in English. There will be a discussion period and a reception with

refreshments after the lecture. All interested persons are invited to attend this

special event.

H. *Oral Presentation: Reasons*. Choose one of the following topics for a three-minute speech.

1. Pretend you are running for political office. Tell us why you should be elected.

2. You have applied for a job. Tell your interviewer why you should be hired.

3. You are a salesperson trying to sell a product (such as a computer or car). Tell why we should buy it.

4. The political and economic conditions in your country are terrible. Explain why you want to leave your country and immigrate to the United States or Canada.

5. You are at a dinner for students and their advisors. Explain why you chose to study in this country.

6. Your own topic that you can support by causes or reasons.

Prepare an outline that includes an introduction, three major reasons, and a conclusion. Practice your speech aloud several times. Concentrate on pronouncing the consonants clearly, as well as improving your overall rhythm, linking, pausing, and non-verbal communication. If possible, have your speech videotaped.

I. *Dialogues for /ʃ, ʒ, tʃ, dʒ/.*

1. /ʃ/ *shore,* /s/ *sore*

A: I simply love the seashore, don't you?

B: No. There's too much sunshine and the sand is too hot.

A: But the sea breezes and waves crashing on the shore are so soothing.

B: I always get sunburned and sore.

A: You must like the social life on the beach at least.

B: I'd rather sit in a peaceful place in the shade.

A: Don't you even like to collect seashells or go swimming?

B: No.

A: I'm shocked at you. Your idea of fun is probably washing the dishes!

2. /ʃ/ *Sharon,* /tʃ/ *cherry*

A: One chicken sandwich, one fillet of fish, two cheeseburgers, two orders of French fries, and a chocolate shake. Was there anything else?

B: I think Sharon said she wanted a cherry coke.

A: And one cherry coke. Now let me see how much that comes to.

(A few minutes later)

B: Which one is mine?

A: Here it is. And here's yours Sharon. Now children, be patient and chew your food carefully. Remember what happened last time we had lunch at McDonalds.

B: Can we share the chocolate shake?

A: Sure. Do you want some ketchup? Watch out! You're going to choke!

B: Ach!

A: Not again!

Watch out! You're going to choke!

3. /dʒ/ *major,* /y/ *mayor*

A: George is a major in the army.

B: I thought he was the mayor of a large city.

A: He's been stationed in Europe for seven years.

B: That's strange. I thought he moved to Los Angeles just one year ago.

A: George graduated from Yale University and speaks five languages.

B: Are you sure we're talking about the same George?

4. /dʒ/ *pigeon,* /ʒ/ *vision*

A: Is that shirt orange or beige?

B: It's clearly orange. Your vision's no better than a pigeon's!

A: I've heard that pigeons have excellent vision.

B: Maybe so. I've never measured it, but they do usually manage to hit my windshield.

5. /ʒ/ *pleasure,* /z/ *president,* /dʒ/ *gentlemen*

Ladies and gentlemen, it's a genuine pleasure for me to be with you tonight. I would especially like to thank the president and treasurer of this great organization for giving me this marvelous occasion to speak to you in support of such a worthy cause. I'd like to begin with an unusual version of those famous words by John F. Kennedy:

Ask not what your congressman can do for you

Ask what you can do for your congressman.

And now, a generous donation would be most appreciated.

6. /tʃ/ + *Consonant: Which Channel*

A: Which channel do you watch the most?

B: I usually watch the sports channel. How about you? Which channel is your favorite?

A: I don't watch much television. There are too many commercials.

B: I change channels whenever a commercial comes on.

A: That's a useless gesture. Each channel has commercials on at the same time.

B: You can always watch PBS, the educational channel.

7. /dʒ/ + *Consonant: Orange Juice*

A: Please give me a large orange juice. No, change that, a small orange juice.

B: Yes sir. Here you are. That'll be $4.60.

A: $4.60! You've overcharged me. That's way too much for a small orange juice.

B: I can't change prices. A large orange juice costs $6.00.

15.6 Final /dz/ and /ts/ ADVANCED

PRACTICE 7 CHINESE KOREAN JAPANESE
CAMBODIAN   VIETNAMESE

When you pronounce the sequence /dz/ or /ts/ at the end of a word, be sure that you *stop the air completely* for a short time before opening up for the fricative /z/ or /s/. /ts/ is easier to pronounce than /dz/, so begin by substituting /ts/ for /dz/ and lengthening the preceding vowel. Link when ever possible: *he needs it* /hi nid zɪt/; *she rides it* /ʃi raɪd zɪt/.

	1. /ts/	*2.* /s/
a.	The **rates** kept getting worse.	The **race** kept getting worse.
b.	They don't have any **rights** in that country.	They don't have any **rice** in that country.
c.	He lost his **plates**.	He lost his **place**.
d.	Did you hear the **hits**?	Did you hear the **hiss**?
e.	Did the **lights** bother you?	Did the **lice**[1] bother you?
f.	I want a **pizza** pie.	I want a **piece of** pie.
g.	The **courts** convinced us.	The **course** convinced us.

	1. /dz/	*2.* /z/
h.	The **roads** were dirty.	The **rows** were dirty.
i.	Did he watch the **nudes** on TV?	Did he watch the **news** on TV?
j.	Something's wrong with the **sides**.	Something's wrong with the **size**.
k.	Her **needs** are unusual.	Her **knees** are unusual.
l.	Some **trades** were made there.	Some **trays** were made there.
m.	Did you hear the **words**?	Did you hear the **whirs**?[2]
n.	It's **worlds** apart.	It **whirls**[3] apart.

	1. /ts/	*2.* /s/	*3.* /tʃ/
o.	eights	ace	"H"
p.	mats	mass	match
q.	hits	hiss	hitch[4]
r.	pizzas	pieces	peaches

	1. /dz/	*2.* /z/	*3.* /dʒ/
s.	aids	A's	age
t.	raids	raise/rays	rage
u.	buds	buzz	budge
v.	seeds	seize/sees/seas	siege

[1]lice = tiny insects that lay eggs in people's hair
[2]whir = sound of wings moving quickly
[3]whirl = to turn around and around quickly, spin
[4]hitch = to attach using a rope or chain; to travel in a stranger's car (hitchhike)

EXERCISE

 A. Record yourself reading the following sentences. Be sure to pronounce the italicized words differently.

1. There are no *plates* at my *place*.
2. There've been some *nice nights* recently.
3. In this *course*, you learn about the *courts*.
4. I'd like a *piece* of *pizza*.
5. There were *sighs* on all *sides*.
6. She *needs* bandages on her *knees*.
7. Doing homework *aids* you in getting *A's* in your courses.
8. *Rows* of trees lined the *roads*.
9. *Liz* bought a dozen *lids* for canning vegetables.
10. The *news* was all about the *nudes* shown on TV.
11. The *bees* landed on her shiny *beads*.
12. They go for bike *rides* after sun*rise*.

 B. Record yourself reading the following sentences. Pronounce the ends of the italicized words strongly so that there is a clear difference between them.

1. Those *cats* are hard to *catch*.
2. *Each* of us *eats* in the cafeteria.
3. It was so cold that the *coach* wore two *coats*.
4. Can you *match* the color of those *mats*?
5. The *Ritz* Hotel has *rich* customers.
6. The *peaches* were better than the *pizzas*.
7. Their *heads* were hidden behind the *hedge*.
8. They were in a *rage* about the police *raids*.
9. They're going to *change* those gold *chains*.
10. It often *rains* in that mountain *range*.

15.7 /f, v, w/

Sound	Spelling Patterns	Examples
/f/	\<f\>, \<ff\>	four, free, leaf, prefer, traffic, off
	\<ph\>	pharmacy, telephone, sphere, photograph
	\<gh\> (common words)	laugh, cough, enough, rough, tough
/v/	\<v\>	very, view, seven, solve, arrive
	Exception:	of /əv/

Sound	Spelling Patterns	Examples
/w/	\<w\>	was, wood, away, twenty, sweet
	\<wh\>	why, when, where
	\<u\> after \<q, g, s\>	quiet, squeeze, language, persuade
	Exceptions:	one, once, choir /kwaɪɚ/, marijuana /mærəˈwɑnə/

PRACTICE 8

/f/ and /v/ are both fricatives in which the *inside of the lower lip* moves up and touches the *upper teeth*. The *air flows out continuously* and makes a noise. /f/ is voiceless; /v/ is voiced. Make sure that the upper lip is up and out of the way and that you don't round your lips. You should clearly see your two front teeth in a mirror. Also be sure that you *squeeze* the lip and teeth together and force air to flow out of the mouth the whole time. First practice /v/ and /f/, concentrating on forming /v/ exactly like /f/. Vowels are lengthened before final /v/.

<table>
<tr><td colspan="2">1. /v/</td><td colspan="2">2. /f/</td></tr>
<tr><td>a.</td><td>I'd like a view.</td><td colspan="2">I'd like a few.</td></tr>
<tr><td>b.</td><td>A van would be nice to have.</td><td colspan="2">A fan would be nice to have.</td></tr>
<tr><td>c.</td><td>She thinks it's a vine.</td><td colspan="2">She thinks it's fine.</td></tr>
<tr><td>d.</td><td>The service was pretty good.</td><td colspan="2">The surface was pretty good.</td></tr>
<tr><td>e.</td><td>Did he ever succeed?</td><td colspan="2">Did the effort succeed?</td></tr>
<tr><td>f.</td><td>I got a dollar of gas.</td><td colspan="2">I got a dollar off gas.</td></tr>
<tr><td>g.</td><td>They lived over there.</td><td colspan="2">They lift over there.</td></tr>
<tr><td>h.</td><td>It's alive. /əˈlaɪv/</td><td colspan="2">It's a life.</td></tr>
</table>

	Verbs Ending in /v/	*Nouns and Adjectives Ending in* /f/
i.	They want to **leave**.	They want a **leaf**.
j.	We've had to **save** time.	We've had a **safe** time.
k.	Do you need to **prove** it?	Do you need **proof** of it?
l.	I want to **have** an apple.	I want a **half** an apple. /hæf/
m.	Do you know they **believe** in God?	Do you know their **belief** in God?

FIGURE 15-4   /f, v/ f̲ine, v̲ine   /p, b/ p̲ine, b̲ind   /w/ w̲ine

PRACTICE 9

/b/ is a voiced *stop* in which both lips come tightly together, as in /p/, and *stop the flow of air completely*. Be sure to make a difference between /v/ and /b/ in *all positions*—initial, medial, and final. Use your mirror to check yourself.

1. /v/	*2.* /b/
a. She made a **vest** of it.	She made the **best** of it.
b. They've all gone **voting**.	They've all gone **boating**.
c. Did he make a **vow**[1] to her?	Did he make a **bow** to her?
d. He lifted the cotton **veil**.[2]	He lifted the cotton **bale**.[3]
e. She's got to **have it**.	She's got a **habit**.
f. They're wonderful **marvels**.[4]	They're wonderful **marbles**.[5]
g. Is it **covered**?	Is it a **cupboard**?[6]
h. He's a **Slav**.[7]	He's a **slob**.[8]
i. The **curve** is very dangerous.	The **curb** is very dangerous.
j. How many **calves** were in the road?	How many **cabs** were in the road?
k. He **curved** it.	He **curbed** it.

PRACTICE 10

> CHINESE PERSIAN CAMBODIAN

/w/ is a voiced approximant, which is simply a quick pronunciation of the vowel /u/. The sides of *both lips* come together and the lips are even more tightly rounded than in the vowel /u/. Alternate /v - w/ and check in your mirror.

1. /v/	*2.* /w/
a. That's a nice **vine**.	That's a nice **wine**.
b. I think it's **verse**.[9]	I think it's **worse**.
c. The **veil** was enormous.	The **whale** was enormous.
d. What happened to the **veal**?[10]	What happened to the **wheel**?
e. He's still a **vet**.[11]	He's still **wet**.
f. The cow stopped **moving**.	The cow stopped **mooing**.[12]
g. He's a **rover**.[13]	He's a **rower**.
h. They're **driving** there.	They're **drawing** there.
i. Do you want to **travel**?	Do you want a **trowel**?[14]

---

[1]vow = promise (wedding vows)

[2]veil = a thin piece of cloth that covers a woman's face (a wedding veil)

[3]bale = a large, tied-up package of cotton, hay, etc.

[4]marvel = wonder, marvelous thing

[5]marble = small, round stone that children play with

[6]cupboard = small closet in the kitchen for storing plates, food, etc.

[7]Slav = person who speaks a Slavic language (Czech, Polish, Russian, etc.)

[8]slob = a very messy or sloppy person; not neat and clean

[9]verse = a line of words in a poem

[10]veal = meat from a young cow

[11]vet = short for veterinarian (an animal doctor) or veteran (a person who fought in a war)

[12]moo = the sound that a cow makes

[13]rover = a person who wanders around with no clear purpose

[14]trowel = a garden tool, like a large spoon, for digging up plants

EXERCISES

A. Watch as your teacher *silently* says one word from each group. Decide which word it is. Then pick a word to say silently yourself and have members of the class decide which word it is.

	1. /b/	*2.* /v/	*3.* /w/
a.	be	"v"	we
b.	bet	vet	wet
c.	bow /baʊ/	vow	wow
d.	boat	vote	won't
e.	a bale	a veil	a whale
f.	berry	very	where he
g.	the best	the vest	the west
h.	cupboard	covered	coward
i.	rubber	rover	rower
j.	curb	curve	
k.	robe	rove	

B. Answer the following questions in the negative using the plural ending in /vz/ of these italicized nouns ending in /f/.

1. Would you like a *loaf* of bread?   No, I'd like two <u>loaves</u> of bread.
   No, I don't want any <u>loaves</u>.

2. Does a cat have only one *life*?
3. Did you see a *calf* in the field?
4. Did you buy a new *scarf*?
5. Does he have one *wife*?
6. Did you use a *knife* to cut it?
7. Did she pick up a *leaf*?
8. Did one *thief* rob the bank?
9. Did you hang up one *shelf*?
10. Did you lose one *glove*?

C. Answer the following questions using the past tense /vd/.

1. How much money did you *save* last summer?   I <u>saved</u> five hundred dollars.
2. When did you *move* here?
3. How long did you *believe* in Santa Claus?
4. When did you *arrive* in the United States?
5. Who did you *wave* good-bye to?
6. How long have you *lived* in _____ ?
7. How many people *survived* the war in _____ ?
8. How many women/men have you *loved*?
9. How many of your goals have you *achieved*?
10. How much has your English *improved* recently?

| BENGALI
CHINESE
JAPANESE
KOREAN |

D. Don't omit /w/ before /u/ and /ʊ/ (<u>w</u>oman, <u>w</u>ould, <u>w</u>ounded). /w/ has very *tight lip rounding*, more than in the vowels. /ʊ/ has very little lip rounding; try saying /wə/ for /wʊ/ at first. Do not insert a glottal stop at the beginning of these words. For additional practice, review Dialogue 8 in Sec. 5.2 (p. 59).

| VIETNAMESE |

Don't substitute /gʊ/ for /wʊ/. Although the back of the tongue goes up during /w/, it should not touch the roof of the mouth and block the air.

1. A <u>w</u>ood stove <u>w</u>ouldn't heat this room very <u>w</u>ell.
2. <u>W</u>e <u>w</u>ould have <u>w</u>aited for <u>o</u>ne more <u>w</u>oman.
3. <u>O</u>ne thousand soldiers <u>w</u>ere <u>w</u>ounded in the <u>w</u>ar.
4. That <u>w</u>oman <u>w</u>ould like to buy some <u>w</u>ool for a sweater.
5. Candidates try to woo[15] voters by telling <u>w</u>hat they <u>w</u>ould do for them.
6. <u>W</u>e need some good <u>w</u>ood for our fireplace.

| VIETNAMESE
KOREAN |

E. /f/ and /p/ are both voiceless, but /p/ *stops the air completely.* Be careful to make a difference in final as well as initial position.

1. /p/	*2.* /f/
a. Did you **peel** it?	Did you **feel** it?
b. It was a wonderful **pear**.	It was a wonderful **fair**.
c. Is he going to **supper**?	Is he going to **suffer**?
d. Don't take that **leap**.[16]	Don't take that **leaf**.
e. It's the **cheap** thing to do.	It's the **chief** thing to do.
f. What happened to my **cups**?	What happened to my **cuffs**?
g. How many **laps** were there?	How many **laughs** were there?
h. He **leapt** quickly.	He **left** quickly.
i. She **sipped it** slowly.	She **sifted**[17] slowly.

| KOREAN |

F. Don't omit /w/ after consonants: *question, quiet, quick, quality, language, linguistics, twelve.* Practice Dialogue 6 (p. 198).

---

[15]woo = to try to win success

[16]leap = jump forward

[17]sift = to separate large from small pieces (to sift flour before making a cake)

G. *Dialogues for* /v, b, w/.

1. /v/ *very,* /b/ *berry*

A: Which fla<u>v</u>or would you like—straw<u>b</u>erry or <u>v</u>anilla?

B: Straw<u>b</u>erry's my fa<u>v</u>orite, but may<u>b</u>e I'<u>v</u>e <u>b</u>een too conser<u>v</u>ative.

A: People who lo<u>v</u>e ad<u>v</u>enture ha<u>v</u>e <u>b</u>een ordering a<u>v</u>ocado sher<u>b</u>ert.

B: It sounds mar<u>v</u>elous. Gi<u>v</u>e me a <u>b</u>ig cone of a<u>v</u>ocado sher<u>b</u>ert. If it's <u>v</u>ery good,
   it may <u>b</u>ecome a ha<u>b</u>it!

A: Oh, I'm <u>v</u>ery sorry, but we'<u>v</u>e run out of it. How a<u>b</u>out a cone of <u>b</u>anana <u>b</u>lue-
   <u>b</u>erry crunch?

Which flavor would you like—
strawberry or vanilla?

2. /v/ *have (reduced to* /əv/)*,* /vd/ *saved*

A: We should ha<u>v</u>e sa<u>v</u>ed more money last year.

B: Yes, we could ha<u>v</u>e sa<u>v</u>ed enough for a <u>v</u>acation in the <u>V</u>irgin Islands.

A: Well, we might ha<u>v</u>e sa<u>v</u>ed more if you hadn't spent so much on your expen-
   si<u>v</u>e hobbies.

B: We still would ha<u>v</u>e had enough to tra<u>v</u>el if you hadn't been in<u>v</u>ol<u>v</u>ed in an
   automobile accident!

3. /v/ *move,* /vz/ *themselves*

A: The Ree<u>v</u>es ne<u>v</u>er ask for help. They do e<u>v</u>erything by themsel<u>v</u>es.

B: They're <u>v</u>ery selfish. They li<u>v</u>e only for themsel<u>v</u>es.

A: Would you like us to help you mo<u>v</u>e those hea<u>v</u>y shel<u>v</u>es?

B: No, we'd rather do it by oursel<u>v</u>es.

4. /v/ *very,* /w/ *well*

A: I haven't been feeling <u>v</u>ery <u>w</u>ell recently. I couldn't even go to <u>w</u>ork <u>W</u>ednesday.

B: <u>W</u>hat's wrong?

A: I ha<u>v</u>e a sore throat and ha<u>v</u>e lost my <u>v</u>oice.

B: <u>W</u>hy don't you take <u>o</u>ne of these e<u>v</u>ery fi<u>v</u>e hours. I'm sure you <u>w</u>ill feel better
   by the <u>w</u>eekend.

A: Thank you doctor. I knew you <u>w</u>ould gi<u>v</u>e me something to make me <u>w</u>ell
   again. I <u>w</u>ill dedicate my next <u>v</u>iolin concerto /kən'tʃɛɚ·toʊ/ to you.

5. /v/ *five*, /w/ *we*

A: We had a wonderful vacation out West.

B: How long were you away?

A: We went away for five weeks.

B: How was the weather?

A: Well, it was very windy and rainy when we first arrived, but then it improved, and the last twelve days were perfectly marvelous.

B: What did you do while you were there?

A: We went to all the national parks. There we took walks in undeveloped areas, saw a variety of wildlife, and learned about the environment.

B: Did you visit any native Indian villages?

A: Yes, we drove to several villages within a few miles of Santa Fe. They were definitely worth it. I wish we had been able to visit some of the well-known caves.

B: Oh well, you have to save some activities for your next vacation.

6. /kw/ *question*, /gw/ *language*

A: Have you ever played twenty questions?

B: I'm not quite sure. Is it a language game?

A: Sort of. It uses language. You try to guess the word I'm thinking of by asking up to twenty yes–no questions.

B: I quit already. I don't even know what a yes–no question is.

15.8 /h/

Usual Spellings	Examples
<h>	how, hand, heavy, behind, alcohol
<wh> (in a few words)	who, whom, whose, whole, whore
<h> is *silent* in	hour, honest, honor, herb, heir,
	exhaust, exhibit, ghost, rhythm
in unstressed syllables	Graham, Buckingham Palace, Amherst
in unstressed non-initial	
function words	he, him, his, her, have, has, had

PRACTICE 11   FRENCH GREEK

To make /h/, the glottis (space between the vocal folds) must be *open*, as in breathing. The vocal folds are not vibrating: it's a voiceless sound. The tongue is in the position for the following vowel, and there should be *no friction or scraping noise between the tongue* and the back of the roof of the mouth. Try saying words beginning with /h/ after taking a deep breath. Then let the air come out slowly and softly, and begin sounding the vowel. /h/ is a very *relaxed* sound. Breathe in and out a few times; then try /ha/, /ha/, /aha/, *hot, hat, who, hoe, a hat, a hoe, a hero.*

Be sure to *link* words beginning with vowels to the preceding word. Do not begin these words with a glottal stop (closing the glottis). Americans only use a glottal stop before a stressed vowel to show strong emphasis: "It's 'excellent!"

	1. h	2. 0
a.	I **hate** it.	I **ate** it.
b.	Are you **hungry**?	Are you **angry**?
c.	**Haiti** would be fine.	**Eighty** would be fine.
d.	His **heart** isn't very good.	His **art** isn't very good.
e.	She's **heating** her supper.	She's **eating** her supper.
f.	Don't go too near the **hedge**.	Don't go too near the **edge**.
g.	He needs more **hair**.	He needs more **air**.
h.	They **harmed** the soldier.	They **armed** the soldier.

EXERCISES

A. Cross out <h> in the following words whenever it is *not* pronounced.

1. horrible
2. rehearse
3. humid
4. handsome
5. dishonest
6. rhyme
7. neighborhood
8. half an hour
9. history
10. exhibition

11. alcoholic
12. ghost
13. honorable
14. perhaps
15. heir
16. inherit
17. behave
18. hotel
19. vehicle
20. whose

B. Cross out <h> when it is not pronounced in the following verbs and pronouns in connected speech, and practice the sentences (review Sec. 8.2).

1. I just had to do it!
2. The boys have eaten dinner already.
3. The doctor has spoken to you, hasn't he?
4. He's coming soon, isn't he?
5. I saw her in the supermarket.
6. Do you know his wife?
7. His mother should have taken him to a psychologist.

C. Circle the correct article (use *an* when <h> is silent). Then practice reading the sentences and make sure to *link* the article to the following word.

1. It's (a/an) humid, hot, and hazy day.
2. I'll see you in (a/an) half (a/an) hour.
3. She had (a/an) horrible accident and is in the hospital.
4. It's (a/an) honor to receive this award.
5. She's (a/an) honest housewife.
6. They gave us (a/an) humorous account of their trip to Haiti.
7. (A/An) heiress is a woman who has inherited a lot of money.
8. They happen to be staying at (a/an) hotel downtown.
9. Professor Hamilton is writing (a/an) history book.
10. (A/An) hungry man is (a/an) angry man.

JAPANESE   **D.** Japanese students sometimes have difficulty pronouncing /h/ correctly before /u/ or /ʊ/, as in *who* and *hook*. The lips are *rounded* during /hu/ and slightly rounded during /hʊ/, but they should *not touch* each other or the teeth. *No friction noise* should be produced *at the lips* during /h/.

1. *Who'd* like some food?
2. Don't put your foot on that *hook*!
3. I don't know *whose* food this is.
4. A *hoof* is the foot of an animal like a horse.
5. *Who* knew him during his child*hood*?
6. Herbert *Hoover* was the thirty-first president of the United States.

E. *Dialogue for* /h/.

A: Have you heard about Henry?
B: No, I haven't. What happened?
A: He inherited a huge fortune from his aunt Harriet.
B: Honestly? It's hard to believe. I thought he hated her.
A: Fortunately for him, he didn't have the heart to tell her.

15.9 /r/ and /l/

Sound	Spelling Patterns	Examples
/r/	\<r>, \<rr>	red, try, string, zero, carry, arrive
	\<wr>	wrong, write, wrap, wrist
	\<rh> (academic words)	rhythm, rhyme, rhapsody, diarrhea
/l/	\<l>, \<ll>	like, splash, relate, ability, fool, told, yellow, ball

FIGURE 15-5 /r/ right   /l/ light   /pr/ pray   /pl/ play

SYLLABLE INITIAL /r/ and /l/

/r/ is a quick version of the vowel /ɚ/. The tip of the tongue points to, but *never touches*, the roof of the mouth. Air flows over the *center* of the tongue; the sides of the tongue are raised (you can feel them against the back upper teeth). The lips are slightly rounded (push the corners of the lips in a little).

/l/ is a lateral. The tip of the tongue *touches the tooth ridge*, and air goes out the *sides* of the tongue (the sides of the tongue are lowered). The lips are *not rounded*. The back of the tongue takes the shape of the following vowel. When you release /l/ into the following vowel, the tongue tip should drop down quickly.

PRACTICE 12 | CHINESE JAPANESE |

1. /r/	2. /l/
a. She bought a **red** pencil.	She bought a **lead** pencil.
b. That's a big **rock**.	That's a big **lock**.
c. He's **reading** them.	He's **leading** them.
d. There's a **rake**[1] behind his house.	There's a **lake** behind his house.
e. Is it **right** now?	Is it **light** now?
f. It's a **dairy** truck.	It's a **daily** truck.
g. Have you **corrected** the papers?	Have you **collected** the papers?
h. He's a dangerous **pirate**.	He's a dangerous **pilot**.
i. Are you **sorry**?	Are you **Sally**?
j. Will they **arrive**?	Were they **alive**?

[1]rake = tool for collecting leaves

/r/, /l/ AND MEDIAL /t/, /d/

In English /r/, the tongue tip does *not* hit the tooth ridge, although it does in many other languages. In medial /t/ or /d/, which is pronounced as a voiced flap in North American English (see Sec. 13.4), the tongue *very briefly hits* the tooth ridge by a flicking action and briefly stops the flow of air. There is *no lip rounding*, and the air goes over the *center* as soon as the tongue comes away from the tooth ridge.

PRACTICE 13 | SPANISH JAPANESE |

	1. /r/	*2.* /d/ *or* /t/	*3.* /l/
a.	Her **berry** is large.	Her **Betty** is large.	Her **belly** is large.
b.	They were **fearing** another child.	They were **feeding** another child.	They were **feeling** another child.
c.	What happened to the **barrel**?	What happened to the **battle**?	
d.	I want a **parrot**.²	I want to **pat it**.	I want a **palette**.³
e.	It wasn't **marrow**.⁴	It wasn't a **meadow**.⁵	It wasn't **mellow**.⁶
f.	Are they **hiring** anybody?	Are they **hiding** anybody?	
g.	I saw **Carol** on the road.	I saw **cattle** on the road.	

/r/ AND /l/ IN INITIAL CONSONANT GROUPS

In *initial consonant groups*, be sure to make /r/ or /l/ *long enough* to be clearly heard. Remember that /r/ and /l/ begin *voiceless* after the voiceless stops /p, t, k/ (Practice 2, pp.136–137). Begin to make /r/ and /l/ during the stop so that your tongue is in position as soon as you release it. For more practice, do Exercises A and B (p. 206).

TO DO

If you don't make /r/ or /l/ long enough, it may sound like you have omitted them. Practice [gɚɚɚoʊ] to get to *grow*; [glll‿oʊ] to get to *glow*, lengthening the /r/ or /l/ at first. This is also a good technique for making the difficult groups /θr/ and /ʃr/: *three* [θɚɚɚi] → [θɚ·ri] → /θri/; *shrimp* [ʃɚɚɚɪmp] → [ʃɚrɪmp] → /ʃrɪmp/. The tongue slowly slides down but *should not go back up and hit the tooth ridge* during /r/. Another method is to begin with /r/ and /l/ and then add the preceding consonants: *low → glow, light → flight; right → bright.*

---

²parrot = a colorful, tropical bird

³palette = the board an artist mixes his colors on

⁴marrow = substance inside of a bone

⁵meadow = a large open grassy area

⁶mellow = soft and smooth

PRACTICE 14

Practice the following sentence pairs.

1. /Cr/	*2.* /Cl/
a. The children often **pray** there.	The children often **play** there.
b. It was a terrible **crime**.	It was a terrible **climb**.
c. The animals are **breeding**.[7]	The animals are **bleeding**.
d. Are they going to **fry** them?	Are they going to **fly** them?
e. A huge **crowd** gathered.	A huge **cloud** gathered.
f. It's **growing** brighter.	It's **glowing**[8] brighter.
g. I had an awful **fright**.[9]	I had an awful **flight**.
h. The **grass** is still wet.	The **glass** is still wet.

/r/, /l/, AND /w/

/w/ is a quick version of the vowel /u/. It has much *tighter lip rounding* than /r/ and the tongue tip is *down*. Remember /l/ has *no lip rounding*.

PRACTICE 15 | CHINESE JAPANESE |

Practice the following sentence pairs.

1. /r/	*2.* /w/
a. It's a large **ring**.	It's a large **wing**.
b. They **run** every race.	They **won** every race.
c. It's all **right**.	It's all **white**.
d. Please don't **rake** them.	Please don't **wake** them.
e. Where's the **rest**room?	Where's the **west** room?
f. I think it's **rain**.	I think it's **Wayne**.
g. They're going to **roar**[10] now.	They're going to **war** now.
h. His toy duck **cracked**.	His toy duck **quacked**.[11]

1. /Cl/	*2.* /Cw/
i. She's **sleeping** downstairs.	She's **sweeping**[12] downstairs.
j. They **slept** a lot yesterday.	They **swept** a lot yesterday.
k. The **sleet**[13] was very heavy.	The **sweet** was very heavy.
l. It looked **clear** to me.	It looked **queer** to me.
m. She's used to **Clairol**.[14]	She used to **quarrel**.

---

[7]breed = give birth to baby animals
[8]glow = shine brightly
[9]fright = frightening experience
[10]roar = make a loud noise

[11]quack = the sound a duck makes
[12]sweep = to clean using a broom
[13]sleet = freezing rain
[14]Clairol = a brand name for several kinds of hair products

FINAL <r> AND <l>

<r> at the end of a word or before a consonant is pronounced the same as the vowel /ɚ/ in *her* or *better* (Sec. 4.6). Be sure to make it *long* enough, especially after the front vowels and diphthongs. Think of words like *fear*, *fair*, and *fire* as taking up the time of two syllables. Make sure that the tongue tip does not go up and hit the roof of the mouth when another consonant follows, as in *cord*, *court*, and *course*.

<l> at the end of a word or before a consonant has a special pronunciation called *dark l*. Like initial /l/, the tongue tip touches the tooth ridge and the air goes out the sides; however, the *back of the tongue* is also *bunched up* and *pushed back* as in the vowel /oʊ/, but with no lip-rounding. At the end of a word after a consonant, *dark l* often forms an unstressed syllable by itself which may be written as /əl/ or [l̩]. It is spelled <le, al, el, il, yl, ol, ul>, as in *whistle*, *medal*, *model*, *pencil*, *vinyl*, *symbol*, and *careful*. The word *table*, /ˈteɪbəl/ or [ˈtʰeɪbl̩], has two syllables; in the second syllable, the consonant /b/ is released directly into *dark l* without any intervening vowel (even though it is written as /əl/). In the sequence /təl/ or /dəl/ (*little*, *middle*), just the sides of the tongue go down and the tip of the tongue stays on the tooth ridge.

TO DO

Make a long /oʊ/, then slowly raise the tongue tip to the tooth ridge for /l/ *without moving the back of the tongue*. Alternate /ool-loolloolḷ/, then try *hole*, *bowl*, *coal*, and *cold*. Now try /olll/; hold the long /l/ sound, and slowly unround the lips. Try *hull*, *gull*, *dull*, *skull*; *subtle* /ˈsətəl/, *shuttle*, *little*, *legal*, *travel*, and *final*. Finally, try going into *dark l* after other vowels, and be sure to make it *long* enough. You should feel the tongue shooting back strongly in *feel*, *fail*, *file*, and *foil*; the movement is less obvious in *fill*, *fell*, *shall*, and *furl*. The back of the tongue is already in position in *doll*, *fall*, *fold*, *full*, *fool*, and *foul*, but remember to unround the lips during /l/. Another way to get at this sound is to make a long /l/ holding the tip of the tongue firmly to the back of the teeth and at the same time try to say the vowel /ʊ/.

PRACTICE 16

Be sure to make /ɚ/ and /l/ long enough and link them smoothly to the following words.

1. V + /ɚ/	*2. V + /l/*
a. Do you **fear** it?	Do you **feel** it?
b. It was a **boring** match.	It was a **bowling** match.
c. It was at the end of the **war**.	It was at the end of the **wall**.
d. He takes care of the **poor**.	He takes care of the **pool**.
e. Good **tires** are expensive.	Good **tiles**[15] are expensive.
f. My dog **hears** very well.	My dog **heels**[16] very well.
g. He gave me a **cord**.	He gave me a **cold**.
h. They've already **fired** them.	They've already **filed** them.

(continued)

---

[15]tiles = small squares of porcelain (on bathroom walls)
[16]heels = follows right behind

PRACTICE 16 (continued)

1. /ɚ/	2. /əl/ = [l̩]
i. Do you think it's **over**?	Do you think it's **oval**?
j. The **tower** is over there.	The **towel** is over there.
k. The **shutter**[17] needs to be fixed.	The **shuttle**[18] needs to be fixed.
l. They were **inserted** later.	They were **insulted** later.
m. I think they're **litter** bugs.[19]	I think they're **little** bugs.
n. What's the **finer** thing to do?	What's the **final** thing to do?
o. They finished the **batter**.[20]	They finished the **battle**.
p. It was **murder**, I'm sure.	It was **Myrtle**, I'm sure.

WEAKENING FINAL /l/

<l> *is not pronounced* in many words after the vowel /ɔ/ and before a consonant (*talk, walk, chalk, although, always, all the*). It is also silent in *should, could, would, folk, yolk, calm, palm, half, calf, Lincoln* /ˈlɪŋkən/, and *colonel* /ˈkɚnəl/. Americans often replace final /l/ by *an unrounded back vowel*. The back of the tongue moves toward the position of /ʊ/, but the tip of the tongue stays down. Thus the words *belt* [bɛʊtʔ], *wild* [waɪʊd], *he'll (go)* [hɪʊ], *apple (pie)* [ˈæpʊ], *fail* [feɪʊ], and *failure* [ˈfeɪʊyɚ], appear to have no /l/, but they still sound different from *bet, wide, he (go)*, and *Fay*. A non-native speaker may likewise use a back unrounded vowel somewhere between [o] and [u] for final /l/, but /l/ should not be dropped completely or pronounced too quickly. When final /l/ is *followed by a vowel* in the same phrase, it is again pronounced as /l/ and must be *linked* to the vowel: *he'll‿ask, apple‿is, fail‿it*. The combination of /ɚ/ plus /l/ at the end of a word is very long; think of it as taking up the time of two syllables—*girl* [gɚ.əl].

PRACTICE 17

1. V	2. V + /l/	3. V + /ɚ/	4. /ɚ/ + /l/	5. /ɚ/
a. pay	pail/pale	pear/pair	pearl /pɚl/	
b. he	heel/he'll	hear/here	hurl[21] /hɚl/	
c. bow	bowl	bore	Berle	
d. feed	field	feared	furled	
e. code[22]	cold	cord	curled	
f. wide	wild	wired[23]		
g. odor	older	order		
h. ties	tiles	tires		
i. walk /wɔk/	wall /wɔl/	war /wɔɚ/	whirl[24] /wɚl/	work /wɚk/
j.	walled /wɔld/	ward /wɔɚd/	world /wɚld/	word /wɚd/
k.	gull[25] /gəl/		girl /gɚl/	

---

[17]shutter = part of a camera that opens and closes quickly
[18]shuttle = something that goes back and forth (space shuttle)
[19]litter bugs = people who throw trash (litter) everywhere
[20]batter = uncooked mixture for a cake or cookies
[21]hurl = to throw strongly

[22]code = a system of letters, symbols, or laws
[23]wire = to put electrical wires in
[24]whirl = turn around quickly
[25]gull = a seabird, seagull

FINAL /ɚ/, /əl/ AND /oʊ/ | ADVANCED |

/oʊ/ is a diphthong: the lips gradually become more and more rounded, but /əl/ has no lip rounding.

PRACTICE 18

Compare the following words.

	1. /ɚ/	2. /əl/	3. /oʊ/
a.	shutter	shuttle	shadow
b.	mutter[26]	model	motto[27]
c.	litter	little	Lido[28]
d.	met_her	metal	meadow
e.	need_her	needle	neato![29]

EXERCISES

CHINESE (especially CANTONESE)

A. Be careful not to drop /l/ or /r/ after a consonant. Read the sentences with each of the three words, being sure to make them different; then read any one sentence and have your partner tell you which word he or she heard.

1. Can we   (a. pray   b. play   c. pay)   over here?
2. I had a terrible   (a. fright   b. flight   c. fight)   yesterday.
3. We need more   (a. grass   b. glass   c. gas).
4. Did you see the   (a. crowd   b. cloud   c. cow)?
5. Don't make that   (a. breed   b. bleed   c. bead).
6. They're   (a. growing   b. glowing   c. going) all the time.
7. I think he was   (a. present   b. pleasant   c. a peasant).
8. The   (a. crash   b. clash   c. cash)   didn't last long.

CHINESE

B. Record yourself reading the following sentences. Then listen to check that the italicized words are pronounced differently.

1. The winning *prize* consisted of three *pies*.
2. The *fat* bird was nesting on the *flat* sand.
3. She found some *bread* in his *bed*.
4. *Please* give me some more *peas*.
5. A *bunch* of us had *brunch* together.
6. He took the *black* coffee *back* and added cream.
7. We ran over the *frog* in the dense *fog*.
8. The dog's *bone* has *blown* away.
9. It's not *free*; you have to pay a small *fee*.
10. His eyes became *bright* when he took his first *bite*.

---

[26]mutter = talk to yourself in a low voice
[27]motto = slogan or saying
[28]Lido = an Italian beach (near Venice)
[29]neato = slang for "neat"

11. The *flier* was burned in the *fire*.

12. Everyone *sped* away as the fire *spread*.

13. He *crawled* out and *called* for help.

 C. Mixing up initial /l/ and /n/ can make it very difficult for people to understand you. Practice the words and record yourself reading the sentences.

1. n	*2. l*	*3. r*	*4. w*
a. need	lead	read	weed
b. knock	lock	rock	wok
c. night	light	right	white
d. Ned	led	red	wed
e. no	low	row	
f. connect	collect	correct	
g. number	lumber		

1. There's not a lot of time left.

2. This university has a lot of minorities.

3. No one knows my problems with this lesson.

4. You must not forget to lock the door before you leave.

5. Do you like natural food?

6. A cat has nine lives.

7. An enormous number of people waited in a noisy line.

8. Please turn on the night light.

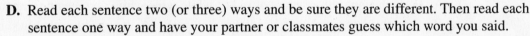 **D.** Read each sentence two (or three) ways and be sure they are different. Then read each sentence one way and have your partner or classmates guess which word you said.

1. Did you make a   (a. bet   b. belt)?

2. (a. I come   b. I'll come)   home at 5:00.

3. She   (a. walks   b. works)   four hours a day.

4. The horse needs a good   (a. feed   b. field).

5. I think   (a. he plays it   b. he'll place it)   in his room.

6. Are you   (a. walking   b. working)   there?

7. The   (a. word   b. world)   is very big.

8. I saw a beautiful   (a. gull   b. girl)   on the beach.

9. Do you wanna   (a. pay   b. pail   c. pear)   ?

10. What a terrible   (a. bow   b. bowl   c. bore)!

11. The   (a. wall   b. war   c. ward)   was very long.

12. Do you   (a. feed   b. feel   c. fear)   it?

13. Do you have a   (a. code   b. cold   c. cord)?

14. We need some new   (a. ties   b. tiles   c. tires)   right away.

15. (a. We closed   b. We'll close   c. We're closed)   Saturday.

16. It's really   (a. wide   b. wild   c. wired).

17. Did you see the   (a. meadow   b. metal)?

18. They left   (a. the Lido   b. a little   c. the litter).

19. The   (a. shadow's   b. shuttle's   c. shutter's)   getting bigger.

20. Where's the   (a. battle   b. batter   c. barrel)?

ADVANCED

E. *Reading for <l> and <r>.* Record yourself reading the following paragraph aloud. Then play it back and check your pronunciation of /l, r, əl, ɚ, v/.

The space shuttle Challenger is due to lift off the launch pad at seven thirty tomorrow morning. The weather report is favorable and so far no problems have developed, so everyone is hopeful that the flight won't be cancelled. On board will be some unusual passengers—a polar bear, several rabbits, a squirrel, and some fruit flies in a bottle. Scientists plan to measure the effects of weightlessness on these experimental animals. This flight is scheduled to circle the earth longer than any previous shuttle flight. Reporters, television crews, and tourists are expected to begin gathering as early as four-thirty A.M. to be able to observe this historic event. They'll all be ready to snap their shutters at the first glimpse of the shuttle.

 F. *Dialogues for /l, r, əl, ɚ/.*

1. /l/ *like,* /r/ *rice*

A: Would you like our roast lamb with rice?
B: I'm sorry. Too many calories. Do you have anything lighter?
A: We have a delicious soup made with fresh clams.
B: I'm very sorry. I'm allergic to clams.
A: Well, a lovely green salad with our special house dressing shouldn't cause you any problems.
B: I'm really sorry. Too much sodium.
A: Perhaps you'd like a glass of red or white wine while you read our menu.
B: I'm terribly sorry. I only drink mineral water. By the way, I probably should tell you: I'm on a low sugar, low fat, low sodium, low cholesterol diet.

2. /Cl/ *blue, glass*

A: I'm looking for a blue glass bottle.
B: I have a lovely black hand-blown bottle that glows in the dark.
A: But I want a blue one. Besides, that one is broken.
B: It isn't broken. The flaws in the glass show that it's hand blown.
A: Then why is your hand bleeding?

3. /Cr/ *three, fried, shrimp*

A: That was strange. Did you see what happened at the next table?
B: Yeah. The woman complained that the fried shrimp she'd ordered weren't fresh.
A: The waiter just shrugged[30] his shoulders and threw them on the floor.
B: She shrieked[31] and threatened to sue the restaurant.
A: The shrewd[32] manager solved the problem by giving them coupons for three free dinners.
B: The woman was thrilled![33]

---

[30]shrug = to raise both shoulders (= I don't care)
[31]shriek = to cry out

[32]shrewd = clever, smart
[33]thrill = to excite

4. /əl/ little, /ɚ/ letter

A: I just received a le<u>tt</u>er from my li<u>ttle</u> broth<u>er</u>. His li<u>ttle</u> poo<u>dle</u>[34] is i<u>ll</u> and in the anim<u>al</u> hospit<u>al</u>.

B: How did he fa<u>ll</u> i<u>ll</u>?

A: He fe<u>ll</u> in a pu<u>ddle</u> of wat<u>er</u> and caught a bad co<u>ld</u>. That was a week ago, and he sti<u>ll</u> hasn't gotten bett<u>er</u>.

B: That's too bad. Peo<u>ple</u> have to be careful with miniat<u>ure</u> poo<u>dles</u>. Your broth<u>er</u> must fee<u>l</u> terri<u>ble</u>.

A: Yeah. The hospit<u>al</u> bi<u>ll</u> is ov<u>er</u> a hundred doll<u>ars</u> a day.

---

[34]poodle = a kind of dog that has curly hair and barks a lot

His li<u>ttle</u> poo<u>dle</u> fe<u>ll</u> in a pu<u>ddle</u> of wat<u>er</u>.

15.10 Final /m/, /n/, /ŋ/

Sound	Spelling Patterns	Examples
/m/	<m>, <mm>	me, smart, crumble, summer, time, farm
	<mb> word finally[1]	comb, bomb, climb, crumb, dumb, plumber
	<mn> word finally[1]	autumn, condemn, column
	<gm> word finally	diaphragm, paradigm
/n/	<n>, <nn>	no, snow, sunny, ignore, son, alone, barn
	<kn> word initially	knife, knew, knee
	<pn> word initially	pneumonia, pneumatic
	<gn> initial or final	gnat, sign, foreign, campaign
/ŋ/	<n> before /g/ or /k/	angle, thank, uncle, larynx, stronger, finger
	<ng> word finally[1]	sing, singing, singer, strong, strongly
	<ngue> word finally	tongue

When you make the nasals /m, n, ŋ/, the air comes out of the nose instead of the mouth. In /m/, *both lips* come together to stop the air from coming out of the mouth. In /n/, the *tip of the tongue* touches the *tooth ridge* and stops the air. In /ŋ/, the *back of the tongue* touches the soft palate (the back part of the roof of the mouth) and stops the air there. Be

---

[1]And when followed by verb suffixes <ing, s, ed>, noun suffixes <s, er>, or the adverb suffix <ly>.

sure to make a difference between these three sounds at the end of a word. These nasals are all *long* at the end of a word. Don't chop them off with a glottal stop. *Link* them to following vowels.

In informal speech, the ending <ing> is often pronounced as /ɪn/, /ən/, or just [n̩]. In songs or novels, this is written as <in'>: "he's goin' home," "they're ridin' away," "nothin' doin'." The common word *something* is often pronunced as ['səmʔm̩] in fast speech. In stressed syllables, however, the difference between /m, n, ŋ/ is maintained.

TO DO

Looking in your mirror, make /p, b, m/, /t, d, n/, /k, g, ŋ/ silently and observe that each group looks exactly the same. Observe yourself both silently and aloud making /m/, /n/, and /ŋ/ and try to feel the difference between them. Say *mom* /mɑm/, *none* /nən/, and *gang* /gæŋ/ and make sure that the tongue is in exactly the same position at the beginning and the end of each word. Then observe yourself as you say *some*, *sun*, and *sung* very slowly. If you have trouble, think of making initial nasals: /m/ in *some* is the same as in *summer* and *some more*; /n/ in *sun* is the same as /n/ in *sunny* and *sun never*.

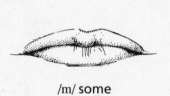

/m/ so<u>m</u>e

/n/ so<u>n</u>   /ŋ/ su<u>ng</u>

FIGURE 15-6

PRACTICE 19

Check in the mirror if necessary to make sure that you are pronouncing the words correctly.

1. /m/	*2.* /n/	*3.* /ŋ/
a. They don't need to **simmer**.[2]	They don't need a **sinner**.[3]	They don't need a **singer**.
b. I have **some** at home.	I have a **son** at home.	I have **sung** at home.
c. It's **them** I know.	It's **thin** I know.	It's a **thing** I know.
d. They have **rum**.	They have **run**.	They have **rung**.
e. He's our **Kim**.	He's our **kin**.[4]	He's our **king**.
f. It's really **dumb**.	It's really **done**.	It's really **dung**.[5]
g. The **clams** were big.	The **clans**[6] were big.	The **clangs**[7] were big.
h. —	It's now our **lawn**.	It's an hour **long**.
i. —	They **banned**[8] it.	They **banged** it.

---

[2]simmer = to boil very gently

[3]sinner = person who sins, does something against God's laws

[4]kin = relative, member of your family

[5]dung = waste from animals, manure (cow dung)

[6]clan = a group of families (the Scottish clans)

[7]clang = loud ringing noise, as from a bell

[8]ban = to make something against the law (to ban smoking)

PRACTICE 20

When final /m/, /n/, or /ŋ/ are followed by a voiceless consonant, they are shorter and cut off sharply. Do not pronounce <g> in final <ng>.

1. Long /ŋ/, /n/, /m/	*2. Short* /ŋk/, /nt/, /mp/
a. Are they going to **sing** fast?	Are they going to **sink** fast?
b. They've already **sung**.	They've already **sunk**.
c. I've got a **thing** about it.[9]	I've got to **think** about it.
d. I don't like loud **bangs**.	I don't like loud **banks**.
e. The **ring** was important to her.	The **rink**[10] was important to her.
f. Do you need a **ten**?	Do you need a **tent**?
g. What happened to your **plans**?	What happened to your **plants**?
h. The little **lamb** got lost.	The little **lamp** got lost.

SILENT LETTERS ADVANCED

When the verb suffixes <ing, ed, s> or noun suffixes <s, er> are added to words that end in silent letters, they remain silent. However, when other endings that begin with a vowel are added, these letters are pronounced because they begin a new syllable. In some accents (notably on Long Island), <g> in final <ng> is regularly pronounced.

<g, b, n> Are Silent	*<g, b, n> Are Pronounced*
sing, singing, singer	single, singular, finger (there is no "fing")
hang, hanging, hanger	hunger, anger
strong, strongly	stronger, strongest
sign, signing, signer	signal, signature, significant
design, designed, designer	designate
resign, resigning	resignation
benign, malign	malignant
bomb, bombed, bombing, bomber	bombard
crumb, crumbs	crumble
thumb, thumbnail	thimble
plumb, plumbing, plumber	lumber, slumber
autumn	autumnal
condemn, condemning	condemnation
solemn, solemnly	solemnity, solemnize

<c, t, p, s> Are Silent		*<c, t, p, s> Are Pronounced*	
muscle	/ˈməsəl/	muscular	/ˈməskyələ˞/
debut	/deɪˈbyu/	debutante	/ˈdɛbyʊtɑnt/
corps	/kɔə˞/	corporation	/kɔə˞pəˈreɪʃən/
bourgeois	/bʊə˞ˈʒwɑ/	bourgeoisie	/bʊə˞ʒwɑˈzi/

---

[9]have a thing about = to have a strong feeling about, to be obsessed by

[10]rink = a man-made surface for ice skating or roller skating (skating rink)

EXERCISES

A. Your teacher will say one word from each group *silently*. Which word is it?

1. /m/   *2.* /n/   *3.* /ŋ/

1. some   son   sung
2. Kim   kin   king
3. dumb   done   dung
4. clam   clan   clang
5. rum   run   rung
6. Pam   pan   pang[11]
7. them   thin   thing
8. ram[12] ran   rang

B. Cross out <g> whenever it is silent.

1. belong   4. hungry   7. tongue   10. bilingual
2. belongings   5. anger   8. triangle   11. young
3. singular   6. coat hanger   9. language   12. younger

C. *Dialogues for final* /m, n, ŋ/.

Pronounce <-ing> as /ɪŋ/ not /ɪn/.

Don't drop or shorten /n, m/ after the diphthongs /aɪ/ and /aʊ/.

1. /n/ *lawn,* /ŋ/ *long*

A: How long will it take to mow my lawn?
B: Your lawn? Not long.
A: Well then. How long? When will you be done?
B: It should only take one hour. Your lawn is not very long.

2. /m/ *come,* /n/ *one*

A: Some of them are coming.
B: You're wrong. Only one of them is coming.
A: It won't be any fun if they don't all come.
B: Maybe none of them will come.

3. /n/ *run,* /ŋ/ *rung*

A: Run and answer the phone. It's rung at least ten times.
B: Why don't you run. I ran the last time it rang, and it was a wrong number.
A: It's a sin for it to ring and ring.
B: If you run, it'll help you get thin.
A: What kind of a thing is that to say. I'd rather get an answering machine.

---

[11]pang = a sudden feeling of pain
[12]ram = a male sheep; to hit hard

4. /n/ *town,* /m/ *time*

A: I heard a loud sound coming from around behind the house.

B: Now is the time that Dad comes home from downtown. It must be him.

A: We can find out if we climb up the stairs and look down.

B: You're such a clown all the time. We can just call out his name.

15.11   Fast Speech Rules

When people speak their native language quickly and informally, their pronunciation changes. This is often considered to be "sloppy" or "lazy" speech and is corrected by some teachers. Most of the following fast speech rules are just further applications across word boundaries of what goes on within some words already. You might be making some of these reductions already without knowing it. Try out each rule and compare it to what you usually say. Using fast speech rules can make some sequences of consonants easier to pronounce. You may decide not to speak this way, but you should be aware of these reductions in order to understand native speakers.

1. SIMPLIFICATION OF CONSONANT GROUPS

We already learned that some groups of three consonants at the ends of words can be simplified by omitting the middle consonant ($C_1C_2C_3 \rightarrow C_1C_3$): accepts /ək'sɛpts/ → /ək'sɛps/; months /mənθs/ → /məns/; tests /tɛsts/ → /tɛss/ (Sec. 14.3). In words like *handsome, sandwich, raspberry,* and *government,* the middle consonant has been lost.

In fast speech, final /t/ and /d/ are often very reduced or omitted in groups of three (or more) consonants across word boundaries. This is especially common in words whose base form ends in /d/ or /t/ (irregular verbs and words like *first, next*), but sometimes even the <ed> ending can be dropped. This should *not* be done when the following word begins with a vowel, to which the consonant can be linked. (You will sound uneducated if you omit the consonant before a vowel, since this is done in non-standard English.)

Ct + C → CC; Cd + C → CC		*Link Before Vowels*	
1. lef*t* there → /'lɛf'θɛɚ/		left_it	/'lɛftɪt/
2. tol*d* Bob → /'toʊl'bab/		told_him	/'toʊldɪm/
3. kep*t* quiet → /'kɛp'kwaɪt/		kept_away	/'kɛptə'weɪ/
4. film*ed* that movie → /'fɪlmðæt/		filmed_it	/'fɪlmdɪt/
5. firs*t* thing → /'fɚs'θɪŋ/		first_hour	/'fɚst'aʊɚ/
6. milk*ed* the cow → /'mɪlkðə/		milked_it	/'mɪlktɪt/
7. slep*t* late → /'slɛp'leɪt/		slept_a lot	/'slɛptə'lat/
8. spen*d* money[1] → /'spɛn'məni/		spend_it	/'spɛndɪt/
9. wors*t* joke → /'wɚs'dʒoʊk/		worst_apple	/'wɚst'æpəl/
10. nex*t* man → /'nɛks'mæn/		next_event	/'nɛkstɪ'vɛnt/

---

[1]When /t/ follows /n/, as in *spent money,* it is pronounced as a glottal stop instead of being omitted.

2. OMISSION OF /t/ AFTER /n/

In fast speech, /t/ is often omitted after /n/ in unstressed syllables of common words and place names. This is especially common in Canada and the Mid West.

winter = winner   painting = paining   planter = planner = plan her

The underlined <t> in the following words is frequently omitted. Can you think of any other words like these?

1. twen*t*y   4. advan*t*age   7. Toron*t*o
2. plen*t*y   5. gigan*t*ic   8. San*t*a Fe
3. coun*t*y   6. quan*t*ity   9. wan*t*ed

Many people omit /t/ across word boundaries in these very common words:

10. I wan*t* to do it.   /wɑntə/ → /ˈwɑnə/   (informally written as "wanna")
11. I'm going *t*o do it.   /ɡoʊɪŋtə/ → /ˈɡənə/   ("gonna")
12. I don'*t* know.   /doʊnt noʊ/ → /dʊ ˈnoʊ/   ("dunno")

3. PALATALIZATION ACROSS WORD BOUNDARIES

Palatalization occurs when /s/, /z/, /t/, or /d/ combines with a following /i/ or /y/ to produce /ʃ/, /ʒ/, /tʃ/, or /dʒ/. This has already happened within words such as *discussion*, *confusion*, *suggestion*, and *gradual* (compared to *discuss*, *confuse*, *suggest*, and *grade*). In fast speech, palatalization occurs across word boundaries within phrases, particularly with auxiliary verbs and the common words *you* and *your*. Thus, *miss you* rhymes with *issue*; *sees your* sounds the same as *seizure*; *ate your* rhymes with *nature*; *made your* sounds the same as *major*. Can you think of any other examples?

1. /s + y/ → ʃ   miss you   /ˈmɪs yu/ → [ˈmɪʃu] → [ˈmɪʃə]
2.   bless you   /ˈblɛs yu/ → [ˈblɛʃu]
3. /z + y/ → ʒ   sees your (friend)   /ˈsiz yɚ/ → [ˈsiʒɚ]
4.   loves you   /ˈləvz yu/ → [ˈləvʒu] → [ˈləvʒə]
5. /t + y/ → tʃ   ate your (dinner)   /ˈeɪt yɚ/ → [ˈeɪtʃɚ]
6.   bet you ($10)   /ˈbɛt yu/ → [ˈbɛtʃə]
7. /ts + y/ → tʃ   pats your (back)   /ˈpæts yɚ/ → [ˈpætʃɚ]
8.   last year   /ˈlæst'yiɚ/ → [læs'tʃiɚ]
9.   didn't you (try)   /ˈdɪdənt yu/ → [ˈdɪdn̩tʃə]
10.   don't you, won't you, aren't you, can't you . . .
11. /d + y/ → dʒ   made your (bed)   /ˈmeɪd yɚ/ → [ˈmeɪdʒɚ]
12. /dz + y/ → dʒ   reads your (mind)   /ˈridz yɚ/ → [ˈridʒɚ]
13.   did you (do it)   /ˈdɪd yu/ → [ˈdɪdʒə]
14.   would you, should you . . .

In addition, /s/ and /z/ combine with a following /ʃ/ to become a long /ʃː/.

15. /s + ʃ/ → ʃː   a nice shop   /ˈnaɪs ˈʃɑp/ → [ˈnaɪʃʃɑp]
16. /z + ʃ/ → ʃː   please show (me)   /ˈpliz ˈʃoʊ/ → [ˈpliʃʃoʊ]

4. FURTHER REDUCTION OF FUNCTION WORDS

In normal English, unstressed function words have weak or reduced forms (Sec. 8.2). Many auxiliary verbs have standardized contractions in which the reduced vowel is omitted, leaving the final consonant: <'s, 'm, 're, 've, 'd, 'll>. In fast speech, the auxiliary *do* can also be very reduced, although it is never written as a contraction. What does ['dʒiʔˈdʒɛtʔ] "jeet jet?" mean?

1.	do	/du/ → də → d	What <u>do</u> you want?	[wədyəˈwənʔ]
2.	does	/dəz → dz → z	When <u>does</u> it start?	[wɛnzɪʔˈstartʔ]
3.	did	/dɪd/ → d	Where <u>did</u> he go?	[wɛɚ-diˈgoʊ]
4.		→ dʒ	What <u>did</u> you say?	[wədʒəˈseɪ]
5.		→ tʃ	<u>Did</u> she visit them?	[tʃiˈvɪzɪɾm̩]
6.	you	/yu/ → yə → dʒə or tʃə	Did <u>you</u> do it?	[dʒəˈduɪt]
7.	your	/yuɚ/ → yɚ → dʒɚ or tʃɚ	Lost <u>your</u> book?	[ˈlɔʃtʃɚˈbʊk]
8.	him	/hɪm/ → ɪm → m̩	Take <u>him</u> away.	[ˈteɪkm̩əˈweɪ]
9.	them	/ðɛm/ → ðəm → əm → m̩	Take <u>them</u> away.	[ˈteɪkm̩əˈweɪ]
10.	their	/ðɛɚ/ → ðɚ	They lost <u>their</u> dog.	[ðeɪˈlɔsðɚˈdɔg]
11.	than	/ðən/ → n̩	less <u>than</u> five	[lɛsn̩ˈfaɪv]
12.	of	/əv/ → ə	cup <u>of</u> coffee	[ˈkəpəˈkɔfi]
13.	have	/əv/ → ə	would <u>have</u> gone	[wʊdəˈgɔn]

15.12 Review of Consonants: Place of Articulation

Read across each row in Tables 15-1 and 15-2 and check that each consonant is clearly different from the others.

Table 15-1
/θ, ð, s, z, ʃ, ʒ, tʃ, dʒ, ts, dz/

Group 1. *VOICELESS*

	1 /s/	2 /ʃ/	3 /tʃ/	4 /ts/	5 /t/	6 /θ/
a.	sin	shin	chin	—	tin	thin
b.	Sue	shoe	chew	—	too	through
c.	massing	mashing	matching	—	—	nothing
d.	pieces	precious	peaches	pizzas	pitas[1]	Bertha's
e.	mass	mash	match	mats	mat	math
f.	a lease	a leash	a leech[2]	elites	elite[3]	Leith[4]

(continued)

---

[1]pita = flat, round bread (pita pocket)
[2]leech = a small, wormlike animal that sucks blood
[3]elite = upper-class group of people
[4]Leith = place name in Scotland

Table 15-1
(continued)

Group 2. VOICED

1 /z/	2 /ʒ/	3 /dʒ/	4 /dz/	5 /d/	6 /ð/
g. Zen	—	gin	—	din[5]	then
h. zoo	—	Jew	—	do	though
i. amaze_her	measure	major	maids_are	made_her	mother
j. reason	regime	region	reads_and	reading	breathing
k. bays	beige	page	braids[6]	paid	bathe
l. sees	seizure	siege	seeds	seed	seethe[7]

Table 15-2
/p, b, w, f, v, h, r, l, m, n, ŋ/

Group 1. VOICED

1 /b/	2 /v/	3 /w/	4 /r/	5 /l/	6 /y/
a. bale	veil	whale	rail	Lael	Yale
b. bent	vent	went	rent	lent	yen[9]
c. cupboard	covered	coward	mirror	Miller	million
d. habit	have_it	away	pirate	pilot	beyond
e. slob	Slav	—	tire	tile	—
f. curbed	curved	—	cord	cold	—
g.			butter	bottle	

Group 2. VOICELESS

1 /p/	2 /f/	3 /h/	4 0
h. pail	fail	hail	ail
i. put	foot	hook	oops[10]
j. the pear	the fair	the hair	the air
k. supper	suffer	rehash[11]	react
l. lap	laugh	—	—
m. sipped	sift	—	—

(continued)

---

[5]din = low, continuous noise

[6]braid = to twist strands of hair under and over each other

[7]seethe = to be very angry

[9]yen = a strong desire; Japanese unit of money

[10]oops = exclamation said when one has made a mistake

[11]rehash = (slang) to repeat the same ideas again

**Table 15-2
(continued)**

Group 3. NASALS

	1 /m/	2 /n/	3 /ŋ/
n.	mail	nail	—
o.	moon	noon	—
p.	simmer	sinner	singer
q.	ram	ran	rang
r.	some	sun	sung
s.	bottom	button	putting

EXERCISES

A. Write in the symbol /θ, ð, s, z, ʃ, ʒ, tʃ, dʒ/ for the underlined letters.

1. He's an influential politician in South Carolina.

2. She usually wears a beige jacket to class.

3. I'd rather not go bathing in the sea in this season.

4. Her decision to major in religion surprised everyone.

5. He gradually made a fortune producing commercials for television.

6. His financial situation has actually improved.

7. Fish is both delicious and nutritious.

8. There are many advantages to a college education.

9. We had a pleasurable vacation in the Virgin Islands.

10. Take a deep breath, and then breathe out thoroughly.

11. The statue showed an Asian soldier in a strange posture.

12. Every individual should purchase insurance.

13. He lost consciousness in the collision.

14. There's rising social pressure to do something about the drug issue.

15. Although I like math, I think I'll take an easier course.

B. Circle the letter of the word you hear (Secs. 15.1–15.6).

1. I saw her   (a. then   b. den).
2. (a. They   b. Day)   will be coming soon.
3. Where's the   (a. leather   b. letter)?
4. We need to   (a. clothe   b. close)   them.
5. Are those   (a. threes   b. trees)?
6. You need a   (a. bath   b. bat).
7. She   (a. thought   b. taught   c. sought)   a lot.
8. She's   (a. thinking   b. sinking)   quickly.
9. Is that his   (a. mouth   b. mouse)?
10. Give me my   (a. chair   b. share).
11. Three   (a. chips   b. ships)   is enough.
12. You should   (a. watch   b. wash)   it carefully.
13. He's sitting on my   (a. porch   b. Porsche)!
14. His   (a. lease   b. leash)   is too short.
15. Did you find the   (a. seat   b. sheet)?
16. That's a good   (a. yoke   b. joke).
17. Are they   (a. Asian   b. aging)?
18. I don't know about the   (a. version   b. Virgin).
19. I think they're   (a. beige   b. bays).
20. The   (a. range   b. rains)   caused problems.

C. Circle the letter of the word you hear (Secs. 15.7–15.10).

1. I think it's the   (a. vest   b. best   c. west).
2. He's a   (a. slob   b. Slav).
3. The accident was on the   (a. curve   b. curb).
4. Two   (a. calves   b. cabs)   were in the road.
5. She's got   (a. to have it   b. a habit).
6. It's a   (a. marvel   b. marble).
7. We really   (a. hate   b. ate)   them.
8. Yes, it's   (a. right   b. light   c. white).
9. She hasn't   (a. corrected   b. collected)   our homework.
10. The   (a. barrel   b. battle)   isn't finished.
11. Will they   (a. breed   b. bleed)?
12. They don't like the new   (a. war   b. wall).
13. I never   (a. fear   b. feel   c. feed)   them.
14. They left   (a. the litter   b. a little).
15. It's a wonderful   (a. shutter   b. shuttle   c. shadow).
16. He's our   (a. kin   b. king   c. Kim).
17. He   (a. sins   b. sings)   a lot.
18. When did they   (a. ban   b. bang   c. bank)   it?
19. Did you say   (a. thin   b. thing   c. think)?
20. They have   (a. a son   b. sung   c. sunk)   already.

CHAPTER 16

Intonation

PREREADING QUESTIONS

You meet your friend and say, "How are you doing?"
> On what syllable does the highest pitch occur in your question?
> Does your voice rise or fall at the end?

Your friend replies, "I'm fine. How are you doing?"
> Do your question and your friend's question have the same intonation pattern?

16.1 Intonation and Sentence Stress

Intonation is the **melody** of speech, the **changes in the pitch of the voice** over time. Intonation is fundamentally different from the other aspects of speech that we have talked about. Consonants, vowels, and stress have no meaning apart from the words they belong to. Intonation, on the other hand, can convey meaning directly. Besides being closely connected to grammar and words, it can express a speaker's emotions (anger, surprise), relationship to the listener (polite, superior), and attitude toward what he or she is saying (serious, joking). Most people use and respond to the intonation patterns of their native language without being aware of what they are doing. Intonation patterns are difficult to isolate and master in another language. First, you must learn to become conscious of the rises and falls of the voice and to be able to hear and recognize highs and lows, falls and rises, apart from the syllables on which they occur. Then you can put together these tunes on words and phrases to make the intonation patterns of English.

TO DO

Repeat each of the following pitch patterns several times on the vowel /ɑ/. Put your hand on your larynx to feel it moving up and down. Pitch patterns are shown between two lines that represent the top and the bottom of the speaker's range. **Lines** indicate **stressed syllables**, and small **dots** represent **unstressed syllables**. High and low are *relative* to your own pitch range. What is high and low for a man won't be the same as for a woman. Do these exercises in your *natural* speaking voice; don't sing or make excessively high or low tones.

Basic

Jumps: High-low, high-low . . .   Low-high . . .   Mid-mid . . .

Glides: Fall (high to low)   Rise (low to high)   Level (no change)

Advanced

Jumps: High-mid-low   Low-mid-high   Mid-high-low   High-low-mid

Glides: High fall   Low rise   Rise-fall   Fall-rise

Low fall   High rise

PRACTICE 1

Say each word three different ways. Then listen to your teacher or classmate say just one word in each group. Which pitch pattern did you hear?

	1. Fall (High-Low)	2. Rise (Low-High)	3. Level (No Change)[1]
Jumps:			
a.	Uh oh.	Uh oh?	Uh oh . . .
b.	Monday.	Monday?	Monday . . .
c.	Fifty.	Fifty?	Fifty . . .
d.	Coming.	Coming?	Coming . . .
e.	Later.	Later?	Later . . .

(continued)

---

[1]"Level" may actually be very slightly falling. It is included for comparison and should sound a little unnatural before a pause. Think of a sentence that is interrupted in the middle.

PRACTICE 1 (continued)

	1. Fall (High-Low)	2. Rise (Low-High)	3. Level (No Change)
Glides:	＼	／	＝
f.	Oh.	Oh?	Oh . . .
g.	Here.	Here?	Here . . .
h.	Where.	Where?	Where . . .
i.	What.	What?	What . . .
j.	Yes.	Yes?	Yes . . .

PRACTICE 2

Now listen for the pitch *beginning on the stressed syllable* to the end of the word or phrase. Listen carefully to the *end* of the word or phrase: falls end low; rises end high. Syllables before the stressed syllable are mid or low.

	1. Fall	2. Rise	3. Level
a.	An 'apple.	An 'apple?	An 'apple . . .
b.	To'morrow.	To'morrow?	To'morrow . . .
c.	Im'possible.	Im'possible?	Im'possible . . .
d.	In the 'morning.	In the 'morning?	In the 'morning . . .
e.	A'nother one.	A'nother one?	A'nother one . . .
f.	'Now.	'Now?	'Now . . .
g.	Hel'lo.	Hel'lo?	Hel'lo . . .
h.	On the 'phone.	On the 'phone?	On the 'phone . . .
i.	In your 'book.	In your 'book?	In your 'book . . .
j.	I'll be 'seeing you.	I'll be 'seeing you?	I'll be 'seeing you . . .
k.	'Fortunately.	'Fortunately?	'Fortunately . . .
l.	The re'frigerator.	The re'frigerator?	The re'frigerator . . .

INTONATION GROUPS

From the practice exercises, you can see that an intonation pattern in English can extend over one syllable or many syllables and that the same word can be said with different intonation patterns. The span of speech over which an intonation pattern extends is called an **intonation group**. It must include at least one stressed syllable. An intonation group is the same as a pause group or a potential pause group as discussed in Sec. 8.4. It represents a way of dividing up spoken language into units of information similar to the way punctuation is used in written language. Depending on the number of phrases and clauses and the speaker's rate of speech, a sentence may be made up of one or several intonation groups. Sometimes we don't actually pause completely at the end of an intonation group within a sentence; but we slow down, change the pitch of our voice, and lengthen the final syllables as if we were going to pause. Thus, the following example consists of two intonation groups even if there is no actual pause after the word *Monday*. The end of intonation groups will be marked by | except at the end of sentences, where it is obvious.

On 'MONday,| I'm 'playing 'TENnis.

Within each intonation group in English, the speaker must make two choices:

1. Where does the major fall or rise in pitch occur? That is, what is the location of sentence stress?
2. Which tune or pitch pattern will be used? That is, will there be a fall or rise at the end of the intonation group?

NEUTRAL LOCATION OF SENTENCE STRESS

Every intonation group contains one major change in pitch (a fall or rise), which begins on a stressed syllable. This combination of stress and pitch change is called **sentence stress**.[2] Normally, sentence stress occurs on the *last stressed syllable* of an intonation group. Since stress normally occurs only on content words, we can say that in English, *sentence stress normally occurs on the last content word before a pause* or potential pause. Note how the sentence stress moves to the last content word in the following examples. The syllable with sentence stress on it is in **boldface** print. Sentence stress with falling pitch:

1. It's '**RAN**dy.
2. 'Randy's '**GO**ing.
3. 'Randy's 'going to '**WORK**.
4. 'Randy's 'going to 'work '**NIGHTS**.
5. 'Randy's 'going to 'work the '**NIGHT** shift.[3]
6. I 'think it's '**IN**teresting.
7. I 'think it's an 'interesting i '**DE**a.

Sentence stress with rising pitch:

8. Do you 'think it's '**IN**teresting?
9. Do you 'think it's an 'interesting '**I**dea?

Sentence stress is extremely important in English. One word must clearly stand out over the others in an intonation group. A common mistake by non-native speakers is either to put a major pitch change on every stressed syllable or to have no one word with a major pitch change. Having one clear sentence stress helps the listener to figure out which words belong together in clauses and phrases and where the end of an intonation group is. A second common mistake is putting sentence stress in the wrong place. In this case, sentence stress may fall on a word that should be unstressed, such as a pronoun; or sentence stress may fall too early, on the first word instead of the last word. These errors confuse the listener, who is expecting *one sentence stress on the last stressed syllable*. If this does not happen, your listener will think that you mean something else. Moving sentence stress to other syllables and what that means will be discussed in Sec. 16.3.

---

[2]Sentence stress is also called primary stress, accent, the tonic, or the nucleus of a tone group (intonation group).

[3]*Night shift* is a compound noun.

Exception. Because of the structure of English, the last content word in an intonation group is usually a noun or verb. When the last content word is an adverb, especially an adverb of time, the preceding content word often receives sentence stress instead of the adverb. In these cases, the adverb appears to be a minor addition to the sentence. *What* is happening (the fact) is more important than *when* it's happening (the time).

10. I 'have to go 'back to '**school** to'morrow.
11. There was a 'major 'earthquake in '**Chi**le 'yesterday.
12. 'Where shall we '**eat** to'night?

EXERCISE

A. Mark in the stress and underline the syllable that normally receives sentence stress.

1. I'd like to see a movie.
2. It starts at eight o'clock.
3. He's a very handsome man.
4. I don't have time to help you.
5. You shouldn't give up.
6. What time do you plan to leave?
7. I think I'll leave after dinner.
8. I have to get there as soon as possible.
9. You'd better give them to me.
10. When will you be finished doing your homework?
11. Where can I buy a good wool sweater?
12. I'd like a glass of orange juice.

16.2 Neutral Pitch Patterns

Most intonation groups begin on a low to mid pitch and jump up a little to mid or between mid and high on the first stressed syllable. Following syllables are about mid pitch and gradually fall until the syllable with sentence stress. From the sentence stress to the end of the intonation group is the most important part of an intonation pattern in English. At that point, there is either a major fall or a major rise in pitch. The basic kinds of falls and rises used in normal, polite speech in American English are as follows.

FALL (HIGH TO LOW)

Jump up to high at the beginning of the syllable with sentence stress, and then let the pitch *fall rapidly* until it reaches *low at the end* of the intonation group. It's not necessary to jump up very high, but the stressed syllable must begin higher than the previous unstressed syllable, and the intonation pattern must end very low. This pattern is harder to do on short one-syllable words like *sit* or *look* because you have a very short time to fall from high to low.

The fall is normally used at the end of *factual statements* and *commands* and at the end of *information questions*, questions that begin with a question word like *who, what, when, where, how, how many*, etc. In reading aloud, it is used before periods (.), colons (:) and semicolons (;). The fall indicates finality, completeness, and certainty. It clearly shows that you are at the end of something, that you are confident, that you mean what you say, and that you are being polite to your listener.

Following Unstressed Syllables	*No Following Unstressed Syllables*
Jump up and jump down	*Jump up and glide down*

1. I'm 'going to 'Boston.

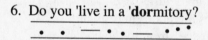

    I'm 'going to New 'York.

2. I'm 'leaving to'morrow.
3. 'Please 'open the 'window.
4. 'When are you 'going?
5. 'Who will you be 'visiting?

    I'm 'leaving 'soon.
    'Please 'close the 'door.
    'When can you 'go?
    How 'long will you be a'way?

Four kinds of mistakes are typically made by non-native speakers. One is simply falling without jumping up first; this makes you sound uninterested, unfriendly, or superior to your listener. It also makes it difficult for the listener to determine where the sentence stress is. Be careful not to begin the intonation group too high; save your highest pitch for the end of the intonation group. Another mistake is falling only to mid; this makes you sound unsure of yourself or unfinished, and it might be confused with the low rise. A third mistake is rising on the stressed syllable instead of jumping up to it; this makes you sound overly enthusiastic or not serious. Finally, some students rise instead of fall on information questions. This has another meaning which will be discussed in Sec. 16.4.

RISE (LOW TO HIGH)

Begin the syllable with sentence stress at low or mid and *rise sharply to high* at the end of the intonation group. The sentence stressed syllable may begin even lower than preceding unstressed syllables. When it is the last syllable in the intonation group, there is a long rise on it. When unstressed syllables follow the sentence stressed syllable, each one is a little higher than the preceding syllable. Although high in pitch, these syllables should be softer and shorter than the stressed syllable, and there should be no rise on them.

6. Do you 'live in a 'dormitory?

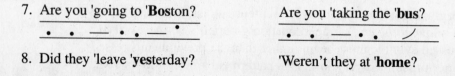

The rise is normally used on *yes–no questions*. These are questions that begin with an auxiliary verb such as *are, was, do, did, have, can*, etc., and must be answered with *yes* or *no*. You are sincerely asking the listener to tell you if something is true or not. You do not know the answer and ask the listener to complete your idea.

7. Are you 'going to 'Boston?

    Are you 'taking the 'bus?

8. Did they 'leave 'yesterday?

    'Weren't they at 'home?

Non-native speakers usually do well on the rise. The main mistake is that high unstressed syllables following the sentence stress can sound like they are stressed if they are too strong or rising (see Example 6).

LOW-RISE (LOW TO MID)

Begin low to mid and *rise slightly to about mid* or between mid and high at the end of the intonation group. The low-rise is similar to the rise, but it doesn't end as high.

The low-rise is used for all words but the last in a *series* and for any *mid-sentence pause*, such as the end of an introductory phrase, a dependent clause, or a long subject. It is often used before a comma (in reading) or before coordinating conjunctions such as *and* and *or*. The low-rise indicates that you are not finished speaking, that you plan to continue after pausing, or that what you are saying is incomplete or dependent on something else. A common sentence pattern is a low-rise followed by a fall. In conversation, the low-rise is used on words like *yes* or *uh huh* to show that you are listening and to encourage the speaker to continue talking.

9. I'm 'going to '**Bos**ton,| New '**York**,| and '**Wa**shington.

10. I'm 'driving to '**Bos**ton,| and 'then I'm 'flying to New '**York**.
11. When I 'get to '**Bos**ton,| I'll '**call** you.
12. In a few '**mi**nutes,| 'class will be '**over**.
13. The 'President of the U'nited '**States**| is a'bout to 'give a '**speech**.
14. **Well**,| I'll **think** about it.
15. **Yes** . . .| **Yes** . . .| Uh **huh** . . .| (I'm listening)

The low-rise is also used in *direct address*, when you are talking politely to someone and use their name. Using a fall to address someone shows that the person speaking is of higher rank than the listener. The low-rise is also used in adding parenthetical remarks such as *he said*, *she asked*, and *you know*. In these cases, start very low and rise only a little to mid or low-mid.

16. '**Mrs**. '**Fos**ter,| I'd 'like you to 'meet my '**room**mate.

17. 'How are you '**fee**ling,| 'Mr. '**Jones**?
18. She'd 'like to '**come**,| she '**said**,| but she '**can't**.

FALL-RISE (HIGH TO LOW TO MID)

Jump up to high or mid on the syllable with sentence stress, *fall to low*, and then *rise to mid* at the end of the intonation group. The fall-rise is a combination of a fall followed by a low-rise.

The fall-rise is similar in meaning to the low-rise and can be used in most of the same situations. Like the low-rise, it indicates incompleteness and can be used before any *mid-sentence pause* when the speaker intends to continue or connect his or her ideas to following information. Thus, it's often used before commas and coordinating conjunctions (especially *but*). It is more common than the low-rise on *introductory adverbs* and *transitions* (*unfortunately*, *sometimes*, *usually*, *therefore*, *however*, *consequently*, *on the other hand*, etc.) and at the end of *longer phrases* and *clauses*. Sometimes we don't know how we're going to finish a sentence when we begin it. This pattern allows you to jump up on the stressed syllable, fall, and then add a rising tail if you decide to pause but want to continue your sentence. When there is no pause, it's not always clear whether we have one intonation group, a fall-rise, or two short intonation groups, a fall followed by a low rise, as is possible in Examples 17, 18, and 22. In conversation, the fall-rise on a single word like *yes* or *well* implies that you have some reservations.

19. Un'**for**tunately,| he 'dropped out of '**col**lege.

20. After I 'heard the 'news on the '**te**levision,| I was 'very up'**set**.
21. I'd 'like to 'take a 'trip to Ha'**wa**ii,| but I 'can't af'**ford** it.
22. 'Good '**mor**ning, 'Mrs. 'Johnson.
23. '**Well**,| it's **pos**sible. . .| (but I'm against it)

The fall-rise may also be used in *polite* statements and information questions. A rising tail is added to a fall to make it sound a little nicer and softer. It is often used by receptionists on the telephone.

24. Hel'**lo**. Who '**is** it? (answering the phone politely)

25. 'Dr. 'Jones is '**bu**sy right '**now**. (but he'll be available later)
26. '**No** 'thank you. (politely refusing more food at a party)

The main mistake made by non-native speakers on the low-rise or fall-rise is to simply fall. This makes it sound as if you are at the end of a sentence when you aren't. Your listener might have difficulty knowing which clauses and phrases belong together in the same sentence. You also might be interrupted. Falling instead of rising in direct address might insult the person you are talking to. Sometimes native speakers, as well as non-native speakers, end every sentence with a rise. This makes them sound uncertain, as if they are always checking with their audience and asking for approval. It also makes it unclear where sentences end.

Summary of Neutral Intonation Patterns

Overall Pitch Pattern		*Function*
1. Fall		Statements, commands, information questions
2. Rise		Yes–no questions
3. Low-rise		Mid-sentence pause (after short phrase/clause), series, direct address, parenthetical remarks
4. Fall-rise		Mid-sentence pause (after long phrase/clause), polite statements and information questions

EXERCISES

 A. *Fall (Jumps):* Jump up to high at the beginning of the sentence stressed syllable, and then jump down to low on following unstressed syllables.

1. I'm 'happy.
2. She's a 'wonderful 'tea**cher.
3. I'll be 'happy to 'see you.
4. It's 'terrible.
5. I'd 'like a 'ham**burger.
6. She'll be 'glad to 'speak to you.
7. He 'spent his va'cation in 'southern 'Italy.
8. 'Milk and 'eggs 'need to be re'frigerated.
9. 'Where are you 'going?
10. 'When can I 'see you?
11. What 'time is it?
12. 'Why did she 'want to 'talk to you?
13. How 'long have you 'lived in A'merica?
14. 'How can I 'get the 'operator?
15. 'What's the 'cost of a 'new 'air conditioner?

 B. *Fall (Glides):* Jump up to high at the beginning of the sentence stressed syllable and then quickly glide down to a very low pitch by the end of the same syllable. Lengthen the final syllable if necessary so that the fall can be heard clearly.

1. I'm 'fine.
2. 'Let me 'see.
3. 'Please go 'home.
4. It's a 'beautiful 'day.
5. We 'don't have e'nough 'time.
6. 'Don't 'throw those 'papers a'way.
7. I 'need 'something to 'eat.
8. I'd 'like some to'mato 'soup.
9. 'When do you 'leave for 'school?
10. What 'time does the 'class be'gin?
11. 'Where can I 'buy a 'new 'car?
12. How 'long will you 'be in 'class?
13. 'What do you 'usually 'have for 'lunch?
14. We'll be 'ready to 'go at 'five o''clock.
15. 'When can you 'pick me 'up?

C. *Rise (Jumps):* Keep at about the same pitch or a little higher on the sentence stressed syllable, then jump up to high on following unstressed syllables. The last unstressed syllable is the highest.

1. Are you 'happy?
2. Can I 'help you?
3. Can you 'lend me some 'money?
4. Will you 'see her to'morrow?
5. Did she 'talk to you?
6. Have you 'ever 'visited 'northern 'Germany?
7. Did you 'see it on 'television?
8. Do you 'own a 'sewing machine?

 D. *Rise (Glides):* Begin the sentence stressed syllable at the same pitch or a little higher and then glide up sharply during that syllable and end high. Stretch out the final syllable if necessary.

1. Can you 'see?
2. Do you 'have the 'time?
3. Has the 'test be'gun?
4. Are you 'glad?
5. Can I 'help?
6. Is he 'going to 'France?
7. Would you 'like some des'sert?
8. Are you 'sure you can 'pick me 'up?
9. Did he 'turn it 'off?
10. Will 'classes be'gin at the 'end of the 'week?

E. *Low-rise or Fall-rise.* Begin low and end mid; or jump up to high, fall to low, and rise again slightly. The important thing is to end relatively high, but not as high as in Exercises C or D.

1. 'After the 'movie,| 'let's go 'out for a 'cup of 'coffee.

2. Be'fore you be'gin,| be 'sure to 'read the di'rections.
3. In a few 'minutes,| the 'president will ar'rive.
4. 'After a 'while,| 'television gets 'boring.
5. At the 'end of this 'week,| you'll be 'able to 'take a va'cation.
6. Un'fortunately,| I 'have a 'very 'bad 'cold.
7. When you 'go to the 'store,| 'please 'get me a 'quart of 'milk,| a 'dozen 'eggs,| and a 'loaf of 'French 'bread.|
8. 'Greece,| 'Italy,| and 'Spain| be'long to the 'Common 'Market.
9. 'Which do you pre'fer:| 'oranges,| 'apples,| or ba'nanas?
10. She 'speaks 'English,| 'French,| 'German,| and I'talian.
11. 'Winters in New 'England| 'tend to be 'very 'cold.
12. 'Please 'open the 'window,| 'Michael.

13. 'Dr. 'Lester,| I'd 'like you to 'meet my '**room**mate.
14. 'Good '**morning**,| '**Mary**.
15. 'Good '**night**,| '**John**.| 'Sleep '**well**.

F. Divide the class into small groups and have students introduce class members to each other. Use the low rise on the names of people you are talking to. For example: "**John**, this is my friend Bill." "Hi, **Bill**. Nice to meet you." "**Sha**ron, I'd like you to meet my roommate Joan." "Hi, **Joan**. I'm glad to meet you."

G. Divide the class into groups or pairs. Ask and answer the following questions with a series of at least *three* items.

1. What are your favorite **veg**etables?
   Carrots,| onions,| and **cel**ery.
2. What are your favorite colors?
3. What are your favorite sports?
4. What countries have you visited?
5. Where do students in your class come from?
6. What other classes are you taking now?
7. What do you have in your pocket or purse?

H. The following sentences are not marked. Underline the syllables that will receive *sentence stress*. Then draw an arrow down for *fall* or an arrow up for *rise* under each one to indicate the general pitch pattern.

1. Waiter: Good evening, Mr. Thompson. Are you ready to order?
2. Mr. Thompson: No, not yet. I need a little more time to look at the menu.
3. W: Would you like to order a cocktail?[4]
4. T: No thank you. I'll probably order some wine later.
5. W: Fine. I'll be back in a few minutes.
   (a few minutes later)
6. W: Have you decided?
7. T: Yes. I'll have a tossed salad, the New York strip steak, and a baked potato.
8. W: How would you like the steak?
9. T: Medium rare.
10. W: What kind of dressing would you like on your salad?
11. T: What kind do you have?
12. W: French, Italian, blue cheese, or vinegar and oil.
13. T: I'll have vinegar and oil.
14. W: And would you like anything to drink?
15. T: Yes. A glass of red wine.

ADVANCED

I. Compare the fall and rise to the basic intonation patterns in your native language. Translate the following sentences loosely into your own language. Say them aloud to the class as naturally as possible (or hum them). Is the pitch pattern similar to English? How does it differ?

1. How are you doing?
2. Where are you going?
3. I'm leaving tomorrow.
4. I'm taking the bus.
5. Are you taking the bus?
6. Do you live in a dormitory?

---
[4]cocktail = an alcoholic drink before dinner

16.3 Moving Sentence Stress

The "rules" given in the last section are only general guidelines. In fact, sentence stress can fall on any word in a sentence, and any intonation pattern can be used on any kind of sentence. It all depends on what the speaker means. Intonation can change the meaning of a sentence just as much as words can. Intonation is like gesture; you can shake your head or you can say *no*. A speaker can use intonation instead of saying in words "this is the most important part of this sentence," "I don't really mean what I'm saying," "I'm surprised to hear that," or "I'm superior to you." This is done by making changes to the neutral, expected intonation patterns.

In neutral intonation patterns, those given in Secs. 16.1 and 16.2, you mean exactly what the words and grammar say. You are not adding any other information and are not emphasizing any particular part of the sentence. However, you can *add a new meaning* that is not in the grammar or words *by changing the intonation* only. You can either change the location of sentence stress, or you can change the particular pitch pattern.

Sentence stress, the major fall or rise, normally falls on the last stressed syllable before a pause. However, *sentence stress can be moved to any word in the sentence that you want to call attention to* or emphasize for any reason. It can even be moved onto a word that is usually unstressed.

In a *fall*, as in statements and information questions, jump up to high on the word you want to emphasize, then immediately fall and say the rest of the sentence on a low pitch. The syllable with sentence stress is often lengthened. When the word to be emphasized is the same word that would normally receive sentence stress (the last content word), it is very high in pitch.

PRACTICE 3

Listen to your teacher or classmate and identify which sentence you hear.

A. 1. George is moving to Toronto next **month**.   (not some other time)
    2. George is moving to Toronto **next** month.   (not some other month)
    3. George is moving to To**ron**to next month.   (neutral; not some other city)
    4. George is **mov**ing to Toronto next month.   (not just going there)
    5. George **is** moving to Toronto next month.   (he really is)
    6. **George** is moving to Toronto next month.   (not someone else)

B. 1. When did you finish your **home**work?   (neutral; not your laundry)
    2. When did you **fin**ish your homework?   (not begin it)
    3. When did **you** finish your homework?   (not someone else)
    4. **When** did you finish your homework?   (what time exactly)

In the *rise*, begin on a mid pitch, jump down on the syllable with sentence stress, and then rise immediately and keep rising steadily on all following syllables. You must listen very carefully to hear where the rise begins. The syllable with sentence stress will also be lengthened and louder.

PRACTICE 4

Listen to your teacher or classmate and identify which sentence you hear.

1. Did they visit London on their way to **Paris**?   (neutral; not Rome)
2. Did they visit London on their way **to** Paris?   (not from Paris)
3. Did they visit London on their **way** to Paris?   (as part of the trip)
4. Did they visit **Lon**don on their way to Paris?   (not another city)
5. Did they **vi**sit London on their way to Paris?   (really see it)
6. Did **they** visit London on their way to Paris?   (not someone else)

SENTENCE STRESS FOR FOCUS

Sentence stress is moved in order to focus on a particular word in the sentence. When sentence stress is in its normal position, on the last content word, no particular word or part of the sentence stands out. We may want to emphasize a word simply to make it stronger. The same meaning could also be shown by adding a word like *very* or *really* and changing the word order. But because word order in English is fairly fixed, we can't always do this.

1. I had a **horrible** time at the beach. (= My vacation was really **horrible**.)

2. She just **loves** mystery stories.
3. This is the **best** book I've ever read.

SENTENCE STRESS ON NEW INFORMATION

Sentence stress is also moved to separate new information from old information. Old information is what the speaker assumes the listener already knows, either because it was just mentioned in a previous sentence or because it is part of the physical situation. Sentence stress will fall on the new information. If the old information is repeated, it will not receive sentence stress. In the following examples, the same meaning can also be expressed by using auxiliaries, omitting the old information, reordering the sentence, or using pronouns.

4. A: Who borrowed my **era**ser?
   B: **I** borrowed it. (= I did.)
   > *I* is new information, not known by A;
   > *borrowed it* is old information.
5. A: I bought a new **car**.
   B: What **kind** of car did you buy? (= What kind?)
6. Teacher: This is a **difficult** test.   (= This test is difficult.)
   > The teacher has the test in her hands,
   > so it's known or old information.
7. I think that **all** handguns should be outlawed. (= All of them.)
   > In a discussion, laws against some types
   > of guns were just mentioned.

SENTENCE STRESS FOR CONTRAST

Sentence stress can also be moved to show contrast between two words or between a word and its possible opposite. Often sentence stress will fall on both words that are being compared.

8. She **likes** married life,| but her husband **hates** it.
9. **I** wasn't accepted at Harvard,| but my **bro**ther was.
10. Should I buy a **white** dress or a **pink** one?
11. Don't get up**set**. I just **bor**rowed your book. (I didn't steal it)
12. I'm going to Ja**pan** on my next vacation. (not somewhere else)
13. **This** time we're going to be careful. (the last time we weren't)

SENTENCE STRESS TO INSIST OR DENY

Finally, sentence stress can be moved to insist that something is true or to deny something the listener thinks is true. You are correcting what the listener has said or implied, so you need to emphasize that part of the sentence. Sentence stress may even fall on words that are not usually stressed, such as auxiliary verbs or prepositions.

14. A: Did you like the **par**ty? (A assumes B went to the party)
    B: I didn't **go** to the party. (B corrects A, denies that he went)
15. A: I'm really worried about my **grade**. (A thinks he might fail)
    B: You **should**n't be. You're **not** going to fail. (B insists that A isn't going to fail)
16. A: You look **ter**rible. You should see a **doc**tor.
    B: I've already **been** to the doctor. (B corrects A)
17. A: You don't understand the as**sign**ment| because you weren't in **class**.
    B: I **was** in class. (B denies that he was absent)
18. A: (in a discussion, A implies that B doesn't like the new law)
    B: As a matter of **fact**,| I voted **for** the new law. (not against it)

In all these cases, *sentence stress is used on words that have particular importance to the speaker*. Non-native speakers usually don't have much difficulty using sentence stress in this way. Other languages often do something similar. The main problem that non-native speakers have in English is putting sentence stress in its *normal* position. Whenever you move sentence stress, it means something special. Be sure you move sentence stress only when you mean it. (Review Practice 1 in Sec. 9.1 for function words with and without sentence stress.)

EXERCISES

 A. Say each sentence and move the sentence stress in order to express the meanings in parentheses. (See Practices 3 and 4, pp. 230 and 231, for examples.)

1. Betty's going to work tomorrow.
   a. (Betty, not someone else)
   b. (she's definitely planning on it)
   c. (work, not sleep or relax; also normal)
   d. (tomorrow, not today)

2. I have to wash the dishes.
   a. (not the clothes; also normal)
   b. (not dry them)
   c. (it's really necessary)
   d. (not somebody else)

3. Will your brother ski in the Winter
   Olympics?
   a. (not the Summer Olympics)
   b. (not your sister)
   c. (not ice skate)
   d. (not someone else's brother)

4. The new law raises taxes.
   a. (What does the law do to taxes?)
   b. (What does it raise? Also normal)
   c. (What raises taxes?)
   d. (Which law raises taxes?)

B. Make information questions like those in Ex. A (4) above for each of the following
answers.

1. a. My wife bought a red **sports**car.
   b. My wife bought a **red** sportscar.
   c. My wife **bought** a red sportscar.
   d. My **wife** bought a red sportscar.
   e. **My** wife bought a red sportscar.

2. a. I borrowed five hundred dollars from **Tom**.
   b. I borrowed five hundred **do**llars from Tom.
   c. I borrowed **five** hundred dollars from Tom.
   d. **I** borrowed five hundred dollars from Tom.

C. Writers often use italics to indicate sentence stress on words that would not normally be stressed or on words that are especially emphasized. Read the following
passage[1] and pay attention to the location of sentence stress.

*[Billy, an Earthling, is talking to a "Tralfamadorian," a being from outer space.
He suggests that other planets are in danger from the Earth.]*

"We know how the Universe ends—" said the guide, "and Earth has nothing
to do with it, except that *it* gets wiped out, too."

"How—how *does* the Universe end?" said Billy.

"We blow it up, experimenting with new fuels for our flying saucers. A
Tralfamadorian test pilot presses a starter button, and the whole Universe
disappears." So it goes.

"If you know this," said Billy, "isn't there some way you can prevent it?
Can't you keep the pilot from *pressing* the button?"

"He has *always* pressed it, and he always *will*. We *always* let him and we
always *will* let him. The moment is *structured* that way."

D. Mark the stresses and pauses in the following paragraph.[2] Use the context to figure
out which words should receive sentence stress and underline them. Then practice
reading the paragraph aloud.

As a child I learned three things well: how to be quiet, what not to say, and
how to look at things without touching them. When I think of that house I think of
objects and silences. The silences were almost visible; I pictured them as gray,
hanging in the air like smoke. I learned to listen for what wasn't being said,
because it was usually more important than what was. My grandmother was the
best at silences. According to her, it was bad manners to ask direct questions.

[1]Kurt Vonnegut, *Slaughterhouse Five* (New York: Bantam
Doubleday Dell Publishing Group, Inc., 1968), pp. 116–117.

[2]Margaret Atwood, *Bodily Harm* (New York:
Simon & Schuster, 1982), pp. 53–54.

16.4 Changing the Pitch Pattern

The other way that we can a vary a neutral intonation pattern is by changing the pitch used on a particular kind of sentence. We can change it completely, such as using a rise in place of a fall. Or we can change it a little, such as by making a fall into a low fall.

RISE ON STATEMENTS

A rise is normally used on yes–no questions. It asks the listener whether or not something is true. In informal English, a rise can change a statement into a question with no change in word order. It adds the meaning: "Really? I didn't know that. I'm surprised. Is that what you said? Did I understand you?" It may also mean, "I can't believe it."

1. You're buying a **house**? Is **that** what you said?

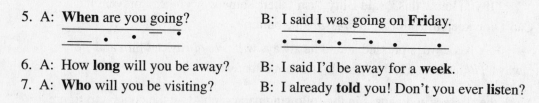

2. They left **yes**terday? I thought they left three **days** ago.
3. They weren't at **home** last night? But they're **u**sually at home then.
4. They just got **ma**rried? But they've only **known** each other| for three **weeks**.

RISE ON INFORMATION QUESTIONS (ECHO QUESTIONS)

Information questions normally ask for particular types of information and are said with a fall. If you rise sharply on them, it adds the meaning, "Please repeat what you just said. I didn't hear you well and I'm checking to see if I understand you correctly. Is this what you said?" These are called *echo questions* because they ask the listener to repeat something that he or she just said, to repeat information that the speaker should know. The answer will usually be a repetition of the previous sentence. Sometimes the listener will get angry at having to repeat himself or herself. Usually, sentence stress also moves to the question word in echo questions.

5. A: **When** are you going?   B: I said I was going on **Fri**day.

6. A: How **long** will you be away?   B: I said I'd be away for a **week**.
7. A: **Who** will you be visiting?   B: I already **told** you! Don't you ever **listen**?

Non-native speakers often get asked echo questions when people don't understand them. It's best to try to repeat what you said in a different way or very slowly.

LOW FALL

In normal polite speech there is a jump up or *step up* at the beginning of the sentence stressed syllable before the fall in statements and information questions. If the fall begins at the same level or below the preceding syllables, the speaker appears to be *uninterested*, not excited, distant, or not very involved (Example 8). The low fall may show boredom, unfriendliness, or even anger, especially on an information question (Example 9). It is used on strong commands by people of superior rank to people of inferior rank (Example 10). A low fall on a question can show impatience and turn it into a command (Example 11).

8. I'm tired of **stu**dying.
   _\. — \. — \. \._

9. Where are you **go**ing.
10. Close the **door**.
11. Well, are you **co**ming. (father to child who is very slow)

Since we normally expect people to be friendly and to treat us with equality, a non-native speaker risks insulting people by using the low fall. People may think you are unfriendly, acting superior, or being impolite, particularly if you also cut off the end of your sentences abruptly.

RISE-FALL

In the normal fall, the beginning of the sentence stressed syllable is high, and the voice immediately begins falling. In the rise-fall pattern, the pitch on the stressed syllable is begun mid to high but keeps rising to high or extra high and then falls later (it *glides up on* rather than *jumping up to* the stressed syllable). This is accompanied by lengthening the stressed syllable and pronouncing it louder than usual. The rise-fall can show that the speaker is really *impressed*, strongly affected emotionally, or surprised, and is often used for exclamations.

12. That's **won**derful!
    _—   ⌣   \. \._

13. How **aw**ful!
14. What a per**for**mance!

However, the rise-fall can also be used to *protest*, *challenge*, *disapprove* of, *disagree* with strongly, or *complain* about something someone has said or done. It's often used in family arguments.

15. (A: I couldn't do the homework.)
    B: But it's **ea**sy. You **ought** to be able to do it. (B scolds A)
    _\. \. — \.   \. ⟋   \. \. — \. \. — \._

16. He stayed there for **hours**! (= he stayed there much too long)
17. Oh **no**! **Now** what do we do?
18. I didn't do anything **wrong**! (Why are you shouting at me?)

The rise-fall can also be used when the speaker is being *ironic or sarcastic*, when he or she means exactly the opposite of what he or she is saying. Humor results from the fact that the intonation pattern doesn't go at all with the words.

19. That's a **bri**lliant idea! (= that's a really stupid idea)
    _— \. ⌣ \. \. —\._

20. I just **love** my math class! (= in fact, I hate it)

Although the rise-fall can make a speaker sound really interested and enthusiastic, it can very easily sound insincere or negative. Non-native speakers should avoid using the rise-fall unless they are very certain they are using it properly.

MID LEVEL

A mid level or slightly falling pitch is normally used on unstressed syllables and stressed syllables in the middle of an intonation group before the sentence stress. It therefore indicates *non-finality*. If it occurs before a pause, it shows hesitation, as if the speaker hasn't decided how to finish the sentence or how to relate what has been said to what will follow. A fall that does not go all the way down may also be heard as level pitch by the listener. Non-native speakers will sound very indecisive, hesitant, and unsure of themselves if they don't use a clear rise or fall at the end of intonation groups. In our culture, non-finality is perceived as a weakness in men.

EXERCISES

   A. Try saying each of the following sentences first as a statement (with a fall) and then as a question (with a rise). Then just say it one way and have the class guess which one you meant.

    1. He's a very good tennis player.
    2. Monday is a holiday.
    3. We're having a test next week.
    4. They bought a new car.
    5. They just had a baby.
    6. His sister's a famous dancer.
    7. He's related to the President.
    8. He jogs five miles a day.
    9. They got divorced.
  10. She's pregnant.

   B. Say each of the following questions both as a normal information question (with a fall) and as an echo question (with a rise). Then say just one of them and have a classmate answer the information question with the information requested or the echo question with "I said . . ." or "I already told you."

    1. What's your name?
       (Fall) *Carlos.*
       (Rise) *I said it was Carlos.*   OR   *I already told you.*
    2. Where do you live?
    3. What's your telephone number?
    4. What's your social security number?
    5. Where did you take your vacation?
    6. How do you like your steak? (rare, medium, well-done, etc.)
    7. How much does it cost?
    8. When are you leaving?
    9. How many children do they have?
  10. How long have you been here?

C. Read the following selection[1] with appropriate intonation.

[Ruth is talking to Cody and his teenage son, Luke, who have just returned from a hunting trip.]

Late Sunday, when they returned, Ruth came out to the driveway. . . .

"It's bad news," she said. "I'm sorry."

"What happened?"

"Your mother's passed away."

"Grandma *died*?" asked Luke, as if correcting her.

Ruth kissed Luke's cheek. . . .

"She died in her sleep, early yesterday," Ruth said. . . .

[on the way to the funeral, driving through the suburbs of Baltimore]

"When I was a boy, this was country," Cody said to Luke.

"You told me."

"Baltimore was nothing but a little harbor town."

There was no answer. Cody searched for Luke in the rearview mirror. "Hey," he said. "You want to drive the rest of the way?"

"No, that's all right."

"Really. You want to?"

"Let him be," Ruth whispered.

"What?"

"He's upset."

"What about?"

"Your mother, Cody. You know he always felt close to her."

D. Say the same sentence with different intonation patterns to express each of the meanings indicated.

   1. You're a terrific tennis player. [*tennis player* is a compound noun]
     a. Neutral.
     b. Disbelief. (Really? I'm surprised to hear that.)
     c. Enthusiastic or sarcastic. (Just terrific!)
     d. Bored or uninterested. (So what. I don't care.)

   2. What are you doing?
     a. Neutral.
     b. Disapproving. (You shouldn't be doing that.)
     c. Echo question. (Please repeat what you just said.)
     d. I'm asking about you. (I just told you what we were doing.)

   3. We've really enjoyed this course.
     a. Neutral.
     b. Not some other course.
     c. Bored or uninterested.
     d. Very enthusiastic. (Really and truly.)

---

[1]Anne Tyler, *Dinner at the Homesick Restaurant* (New York: Knopf, 1982), pp. 279 and 281.

E. *Oral Presentation: Explanation.* We are often called upon to explain an idea to someone who is not familiar with it or to demonstrate our knowledge in a particular area. Choose a topic that would probably not be very familiar to your audience and explain or teach about this topic in a three to five minute speech. Here are some suggestions:

1. a problem, theory, idea, or mechanism in your field of study
2. some aspect of a hobby or special interest of yours
3. some special customs or traditions in your country
4. a current problem in your country or an important period in your country's history

Limit your topic to just a few main points, and select only the most important or interesting details to discuss. Make an organized outline, and practice your speech aloud several times. Use good rhythm and intonation, moving sentence stress to focus on new or important information.

16.5 Choice Questions and Tag Questions   ADVANCED

These questions can be asked with either a final rise or final fall depending on the meaning intended by the speaker.

CHOICE QUESTIONS

Choice Questions are questions that begin with an auxiliary verb and ask the listener about two or more choices connected by the word *or*. When the listener is asked to choose only *one* of the choices, it ends in a *fall*, like an information question, which also asks for just one bit of information. Example 1, with a rise on *tea* and a fall on *coffee* means, "Which one do you want?" The listener is expected to answer by giving one of the choices. This is the most typical kind of choice question. However, Example 2, with a *rise* on *coffee*, means, "Do you want anything to drink?" This question ends the same way as a normal yes–no question, and the listener is expected to answer *yes* or *no*.

1. A: Would you like **tea**l or **co**ffee? (Which one? - ends with a fall)

    •   •   —   ⌣   •   —   •

   B: **Coffee**, please. (or **Tea**, please.)

2. A: Would you like tea or **co**ffee? (Anything? - ends with a rise)

    •   •   —   —   •—   •

   B: **No**, thank you. (or Yes, I **would**.)

TAG QUESTIONS

Tag Questions are questions that begin like a statement, but finish with an auxiliary verb and a pronoun. The first part ends with a fall, but the end can either fall or rise depending on how certain the speaker is. In Examples 3 and 4, A is reasonably sure that he or she is correct. He *strongly expects agreement*, so *ends with a fall*. It's not really a question, so it has the same intonation as a statement. In Examples 5 and 6, A still expects agreement (otherwise he or she would use a normal yes–no question) but is *not so sure* about the answer. A is really asking so *ends with a rise*, more like a yes–no question. The rise may also show that the speaker is very concerned or hopeful. The fall is more demanding and allows little disagreement; the rise is more doubtful and allows B much more possibility to disagree.

3. A: You under**stand**,| **don't** you?

   B: **Yes**, of **course**.
   A: That's what I **thought**.

4. A: You didn't have any **prob**lems,| **did** you?

   B: **No**, I **did**n't.
   A: **Good**. That's what I **thought**.

5. A: You under**stand**,| **don't** you?

   B: **Well**, as a matter of fact, I **don't**.
   A: **Oh**. Well let me ex**plain** it again.

6. A: You didn't have any **prob**lems,| **did** you?

   B: **Well**, I just had a **few**.
   A: I'm sorry to **hear** that.

In actual conversation, tag questions can be confusing even for native speakers. Often they are not answered directly.

EXERCISES

 A. Ask each of the questions two ways, first with a fall at the end (more usual), and then with a rise. Another student will answer the questions appropriately. Then try it only one way and have another student answer. Continue the exercise with some of your own choice questions.

1. Do you like to swim or sunbathe?
   (Fall at end) *I like to swim.*   OR   *I like to sunbathe.*
   (Rise at end) *Yes, I like both.*   OR   *No, I don't.*
2. Would you like to go to a movie or a concert tonight?
3. Would you like to have the test on Thursday or on Friday?
4. Would you like French, blue cheese, or Italian dressing?
5. Do you prefer American cars or Japanese cars?
6. Did you go camping or hiking on your vacation?
7. Is Mt. Washington in Maine or New Hampshire?
8. Would you like a CD player or a VCR for your birthday?

B. Ask each tag question both ways, with either a fall or a rise at the end. Then say just one of them and have the class decide if you were *confident* (fall) or *unsure* (rise). Then make up some of your own tag questions. Another student will agree with you if you fall, but will disagree with you if you rise.

1. You didn't win the lottery, did you?
   (Fall) *Confident.*
   (Rise) *Unsure.*
2. This town isn't dangerous, is it?
3. There weren't any airplanes 100 years ago, were there?
4. Children are required to go to school, aren't they?
5. I shouldn't eat a lot of sweets, should I?
6. You haven't been to Thailand, have you?
7. You're doing well in this course, aren't you?
8. The banks will be closed on Monday, won't they?

16.6 Dialogues for Intonation

1. Would you like to see a movie?

A: Would you like to see a movie?

B: I'd love to. What kind of movie were you thinking of?

A: There's a great horror film playing at the mall.

B: I don't like horror films.

A: How about a Woody Allen film?

B: I've seen them all.

A: There's a really neat Western that's playing right down the street.

B: I hate Westerns.

A: I just read about an interesting foreign film coming to the Pleasant Street Theater.

B: I don't understand foreign films.

A: Well, what do you like? I thought you wanted to see a movie.

B: Are there any cartoons playing? I just love Walt Disney.

2. May I help you?

A: May I help you?

B: Yes. I'm looking for something to give my best friend for his birthday.

A: What's your price range? Are you looking for something cheap or something special?

B: Something special, of course.

A: We have some imported ties on sale this week. They come in shades of blue, green, red, or purple. Each is a unique design, and they only cost $125.

B: No, I don't think so.

A: Well, would you be interested in a cashmere sweater or some fine leather gloves?

B: No, I don't think either would be appropriate. You see, my friend is a dog.

A: What did you say? Your friend is a dog?

B: Yes. You know, man's best friend.

3. How's my accent?

A: Come in, Peter. How are you?

B: Fine. Mrs. Sweet, I'd like to ask you an important question. You'll answer it honestly, won't you?

A: Well I'll try.

B: How's my accent?

A: What do *you* think?

B: I've studied hard in your course, but I don't know.

A: I think you've made a lot of improvement.

B: Improvement? But do I sound like an American?

A: Not exactly. But you will some day. There's still the question of those final consonants. And then there's your grammar and your vocabulary. . . . And of course your sentence structure could be improved . . . and sometimes . . . .

For Further Reading

Abercrombie, David, *Elements of General Phonetics*. Edinburgh: Edinburgh University Press, 1967. A detailed introduction to articulatory phonetics.

Catford, J. C., *A Practical Introduction to Phonetics*. Oxford: Oxford University Press, 1988. Basic phonetic principles underlying all languages, introduced with introspective experiments (like the TO DO sections of this book).

Fry, Dennis. *Homo loquens: Man as a talking animal*. Cambridge: Cambridge University Press, 1977. The process of speech from an articulatory, acoustic, and psychological point of view.

Hornby, A. S., Dolores Harris, and William A. Stewart, eds. *Oxford Student's Dictionary of American English*. Oxford and New York: Oxford University Press, 1983. A paperback dictionary for ESL students.

Kenyon, John Samuel, *American Pronunciation* (10th ed.). Ann Arbor, Michigan: George Wahr Publishing Co., 1977. The phonetics of American English with exercises, historical comments, notes on British English, and a definition of the phoneme.

Kreidler, Charles W., *The Pronunciation of English: A Course Book in Phonology*. Oxford and New York: Basil Blackwell, 1989. Modern phonological theory applied to English, with exercises and an answer key.

Kurath, Hans, *A Phonology and Prosody of Modern English*. Ann Arbor: University of Michigan Press, 1964. A good reference for spelling, history, and regional variation of the English consonants and vowels.

Ladefoged, Peter, *A Course in Phonetics*. New York: Harcourt Brace Jovanovich, 1975. An introduction to phonetics, including acoustics and feature analysis, with exercises and examples from English.

Longman Dictionary of American English: A Dictionary for Learners of English. White Plains, New York: Longman Inc., 1983. A paperback dictionary for ESL students.

Glossary

affricate a sound made up of a stop plus a fricative made at the same place: /tʃ, dʒ/ in *charge*

approximant a sound in which the articulators approach each other but create no friction: the vowel-like consonants /r, l, w,y/.

articulate /ɑɚ 'tɪkyləleɪt/ to make a sound

articulators speech organs, such as the tongue, teeth, and lips, that approach each other to make a sound

aspiration a period of voicelessness, like /h/ or breath, after a stop is released and before the following vowel begins: [pʰ, tʰ, kʰ] in *pie*, *time*, *come*

back vowel a vowel formed by pushing the body of the tongue back: /u, oʊ, ɔ, ɑ/

central vowel a vowel in which the tongue is neither pushed forward nor back: /ə, ɚ, ɪ, ʊ/

closed syllable a syllable that ends in one or more consonants (*it, made, walks, laughed*)

consonant a sound that is pronounced with a vowel to make a syllable: /p t k b d g f θ s ʃ tʃ h v ð z ʒ dʒ l r y w m n ŋ/

diphthong /'dɪfθɔŋ/ a vowel in which the quality changes from one sound to another: /aɪ, aʊ, ɔɪ, eɪ, oʊ/

fricative a sound in which the articulators come very close together so that friction or noise is produced: /f, v, θ, ð, s, z, ʃ, ʒ, h/

friction a noisy hissing or hushing sound created when air is forced through a very narrow channel

front vowel a vowel in which the body of the tongue is pushed forward: /i, eɪ, ɛ, æ/

glottal stop a sharp silence produced by closing the vocal folds, as in the middle of the word *uh oh*, or when getting ready to lift a heavy object:—[ʔ]—it is often used in place of medial or final /t/ in *button* or *it was*

glottis /'glɑtɪs/ the space between the vocal folds; the glottis is open when you are breathing and closed completely when you hold your breath or make a glottal stop

hard palate /'pælɪt/ the smooth, hard top of the inside of the mouth

high vowel a vowel in which the body of the tongue is bunched and pushed up toward the roof of the mouth: /i, u, ɚ/

intonation the changes in pitch over a stretch of speech; the melody or tune

larynx /'lærɪŋks/ the "voice box" or part of the throat in which the vocal folds are located; it is protected by the "Adam's apple," a bony structure that sticks out of a man's neck, and can move up and down

lateral a sound in which air flows out around the sides of the tongue: /l/

linking joining syllables together smoothly by releasing the final consonant of one syllable directly into the next syllable or by blending two vowels together

low vowel a vowel in which the tongue is lowered and the mouth is open: /æ, ɑ/

mid vowel a vowel that is neither high nor low: /eɪ, ɛ, ə, oʊ, ɔ/

nasal consonant a consonant in which the soft palate is lowered so that air flows out of the nose, not the mouth: /m, n, ŋ/

open syllable a syllable that ends with a vowel (*me*, *throw*, *tie*)

palatalization the combining of /s, z, t, d/ with /i/ or /y/ to produce /ʃ, ʒ, tʃ, dʒ/, e.g., *bless you* /blɛs yu/ → /ˈblɛʃu/

pause group a group of words not separated from each other by any pause

pitch the degree of highness or lowness of a voiced sound

pure vowel a vowel in which the quality stays about the same from the beginning to the end: /ɪ, ɛ, æ, ə, ɚ, ɑ, ɔ, ʊ/

reduced vowel an unstressed vowel that has become central in quality like /ɪ, ə, ʊ, ɚ/

reduction the change to a more central quality of a vowel when it becomes unstressed: *family* /ˈfæmli/ versus *familiar* /fə ˈmɪlyɚ/

rhythm /ˈrɪðəm/ the time pattern of speech; the pattern of successive long and short, stressed and unstressed syllables in English; the beat

sentence stress the major change in pitch in a pause group; it occurs on a stressed syllable

soft palate the soft muscle at the back of the roof of the mouth; it can move down to allow air to enter the nose or it can move up to stop air from entering the nose

sound the smallest unit that can make a difference in meaning (/k/ in *came* versus /g/ in *game*; /oʊ/ in *so* versus /i/ in *see*); in English spelling, a sound may be represented by one letter, more than one letter, or less than one letter: in *used* <u> = /yu/, <se> = /z/, <d> = /d/

stop a sound in which the articulators come together tightly to stop the flow of air out of the mouth: /p, b, t, d, k, g/, [ʔ]

stress the extra loudness, length, and clarity that makes one syllable stand out over the others in a

word; the accent; the place where the beat falls in a sequence of syllables

stressed syllable a syllable that sounds louder, has clearer vowels, begins with stronger consonants, and may be longer than other syllables in a word or phrase; changes in pitch often occur on stressed syllables

strong form the dictionary pronunciation of a function word, with clear vowels and consonants: *to* /tu/, *at* /æt/, *him* /hɪm/

syllable the smallest unit that can be pronounced alone; syllables are made up of vowels and consonants; a word in English can be made up of one syllable (*no*, *off*, *meet*, *streams*) or many syllables (*introduction* = *in.tro.duc.tion*)

tap a voiced consonant that often replaces unstressed /t/ or /d/ in words like *butter* or *lady*, a fast /d/—[ɾ]—the tip of the tongue lightly and briefly hits or "taps" the roof of the mouth

tooth ridge the rough, bumpy part of the mouth just behind the upper teeth

transcription the spelling of a word using the phonetic alphabet to show its pronunciation

unstressed syllable a syllable that tends to be weaker, shorter, and more reduced than a stressed syllable in a word or phrase; major pitch changes do not begin on unstressed syllables

velum /ˈviləm/ the soft palate, the muscle at the back of the roof of the mouth

vocal folds /ˈvoʊkəl ˈfoʊldz/ or "vocal cords" two thin muscles, arranged like shelves that stretch across the larynx; they can be open to let air through (as in breathing), they can be closed, or they can vibrate (alternately close and open) to produce voicing

voiced in a voiced sound, the vocal folds are vibrating and producing a sound: /b d g w v ð z ʒ dʒ y l r m n ŋ/ and all vowels

voiceless in a voiceless sound, the vocal folds are not vibrating: /p t k f θ s ʃ tʃ h/

vowel a sound that can stand alone to make a syllable: /i ɪ eɪ ɛ æ ɑ ə ɔ oʊ ʊ u ɚ aɪ aʊ ɔɪ/

weak form the unstressed, reduced pronunciation of function words, which normally occurs when they are linked together with other words in a phrase: *to* /tə/, *at* /ət/, *him* /ɪm/

Index

< > are used around letters of the English alphabet. / / are used around phonetic symbols. Figures are denoted by *f*; dialogues are denoted by *d*; footnotes are denoted by *n*. Boldface denotes pages containing spelling patterns and most explanations of phonetic symbols.